MW01193311

Cemetery Birding

THE TEXAS EXPERIENCE

Books made possible by
Sarah '84 and Mark '77 Philpy

Snowy Egret at dawn

Cemetery Birding

An Unexpected Guide to Discovering Birds in Texas

Jennifer L. Bristol

TEXAS A&M UNIVERSITY PRESS | COLLEGE STATION

∞ This paper meets the requirements of ANSI/NISO Z39.48–1992
(Permanence of Paper).
Binding materials have been chosen for durability.
Manufactured in China through Martin Book Management

Library of Congress Cataloging-in-Publication Data

Names: Bristol, Jennifer L., 1971– author.
Title: Cemetery birding : an unexpected guide to discovering birds in Texas
    / Jennifer L. Bristol.
Other titles: Texas experience (Texas A & M University. Press)
Description: First edition. | College Station : Texas A&M University Press,
    [2023] | Series: The Texas experience | Includes bibliographical
    references and index.
Identifiers: LCCN 2023003015 | ISBN 9781648431449 | ISBN 9781648431456
    (ebook)
Subjects: LCSH: Birding sites—Texas—Guidebooks. | Bird
    watching—Texas—Guidebooks. | Cemeteries—Recreational
    use—Texas—Guidebooks. | BISAC: NATURE / Birdwatching Guides | NATURE /
    Animals / Birds | LCGFT: Guidebooks.
Classification: LCC QL684.T4 .B747 2023 | DDC
    598.072/34764—dc23/eng/20230126
LC record available at https://lccn.loc.gov/2023003015

Photos by the author unless otherwise noted.
Maps by James M. Fenelon unless otherwise noted.

*In memory of
my grandparents, Martha and Walter Scott,
and Lottie Bristol*

Male Indigo Bunting in spring migration

Contents

Preface

Orange-crowned Warbler, Harlingen City Cemetery

I began researching and writing *Cemetery Birding: An Unexpected Guide to Discovering Birdsin Texas* in the fall of 2019. I was anxiously awaiting the publication of my first book, *Parking Lot Birding: A Fun Guide to Discovering Birds in Texas*, and was ready to dive into my next project. At the time, I was also conducting interviews and doing research for another book about women in conservation in Texas. Everything was going pretty smoothly until March 2020. That is when the world was hit by the COVID-19 global pandemic.

I don't sit still easily, not even in the comfort of my tranquil home, especially not during the spring migration. During the first few months of the lockdown, gas prices hit an all-time low. I decided to take advantage of the low gas prices and no traffic to venture out to as many cemeteries as I could. I would pack a lunch and a backpack with my camera, binoculars, masks, gloves, disinfectant, and other essentials and head out before dawn. It was an experience I will never forget. I drove in one day, with my mother, all the way from Austin to Laredo and saw only a handful of semi-trucks or other cars on Interstate 35. It was surreal. We birded all day at the cemeteries in Laredo, traveled back by way of Freer and Three Rivers, and got home in time for dinner. It's amazing how much of the state I could explore when traffic was not an issue. The reduction of traffic noise also allowed me to better hear the birds, which I really enjoyed.

I will note that it was a stressful time in those early days as no one really knew how the deadly virus was transmitted or how many people were infected. Every person and indoor space seemed dangerous, especially when I was traveling with my mother, whose age made her vulnerable. As COVID progressed and the state opened back up, I traveled only on occasion. Once the spread really went wild in the summer of 2020, I decided to play it safe and stayed home more often. That summer my dear grandmother, Martha H. Scott, took a turn for the worse and passed away in July at the age of 101. She was born in a global pandemic in 1918 and died in one. She lived an amazing life. However, because of the lockdown, we were unable to support her during her final month, nor were we able to celebrate her with a proper memorial service. The toll was heavy on my family. I took my mother out for a West Texas adventure to see the hummingbirds and escape into the wonders of nature after so many emotionally difficult months. It was a magical trip, and each new cemetery seemed better than the last, with migrating birds and interesting discoveries.

COVID-19 touched all aspects of my life while writing this book. However, I had a profound epiphany while reading the historical marker at the Old La Grange Cemetery. The marker told the tale of the yellow fever outbreak and how hard the city was hit by waves of disease. The facts it reported were indeed sad and even gruesome. However, it somehow comforted me to know that the community persevered and thrived. That fact eased my mind, as I understood that this pandemic would also pass. It made me reflect on the fact that since the year I was born, 1971, my generation has survived the Vietnam, Iraq, and Afghanistan wars; AIDS epidemic; opioid epidemic; and now COVID-19. Despite these major causes of death, the population continues to rise, and we humans carry on, even in the face of pollution-driven climate change. It was a sobering thought but comforting nonetheless given the challenges we were experiencing.

During February 2021, Texas endured one of the worst winter storms to hit the state in decades. I stood on my back deck watching the birds mob my feeder, and I had another epiphany. Humanity was collectively feeling the stress and fear created by such profound and widespread loss. The fear was compounded by the uncertainty of the entire situation. As I considered that fact, I felt an intense empathy for the birds whose populations have been dwindling for decades. Each year they navigate the perils of extreme weather, habitat loss, and disease, to name but a few of their challenges. The thought made me want to double down on my efforts to conserve spaces for wildlife. In the grips of the winter storm and the pandemic, things felt grim. And yet, I still found comfort and tranquility at the cemeteries I visited and the nature I found there. By the following winter it was apparent that the Cedar Waxwing population had taken a major hit during winter storm Uri. Prior to the storm I had flocks of up to one hundred Cedar Waxwings feeding in the trees in my yard. The following year, I saw six of them from January to April 2022.

By the beginning of 2023 there were approximately 672,170,355 reported cases world wide and more than 6.8 million deaths, with over one million of those deaths occuring in the United States. Some countries refused to report their cases or deaths, and I doubt we will ever know the full global impact of the virus. I certainly came across many grieving families while at the cemeteries, and I always gave them the space and respect they deserved. Some people buried in the summer of 2020 still did not have their headstones in 2022—another reminder of the depth of the impact.

While researching the book, I explored over 250 cemeteries across the state, looking for the perfect nexus of habitat and history. When I was able, I visited a cemetery more than once if it seemed worthy of putting in the book. I would do bird counts and make notes on each visit about the habitat, wildlife, and who was buried at that location. Some cemeteries already had records on eBird and had fairly frequent visitors, which made it easy to get a feel for the birds that inhabited that site and surrounding habitat. I am always grateful to those who take the time to accurately record on eBird what they see. I am also profoundly grateful to have been able to do the research for this book in such an interesting period in America's history and our collective human experience.

Galveston Cemetery with wildflowers in bloom

Acknowledgments

I want to first say thank you to my husband, Thomas Nilles, for his love and support as I endeavored to write this book. I am grateful that we share the love of birds, photography, and outdoor exploration, as he makes every trip fun. Thomas and my mother, Valarie Bristol, visited several of the locations in this book with me and are both excellent birders. I also want to acknowledge the birding clubs that take field trips and conduct bird counts at the cemeteries in their communities. I was thrilled when the City of Austin Parks Department and Travis Audubon wanted to cohost bird walks with me as a guide at the Austin cemeteries. I am grateful for all the municipalities and cemetery associations that manage the cemeteries for the dual purpose of a park and burial grounds. While on this journey, I also met "the cemetery birder" herself, Danielle Belleny. Thanks to an introduction by a mutual friend, Romey Swanson, we teamed up for a fun day geeking out on birds and cemeteries. Since I did the research for this book during the COVID-19 pandemic, I was solo for the most part, which made having a cemetery bird buddy even more special. Along those same lines, I am thankful for Heaven Lindsey and Lisa Tanner for editing the manuscript. Lisa gets a double scoop of thanks for editing and discussing the direction of the book on our weekend horseback rides with Sophia Krajewski. During the early days of COVID, birding, riding horses, and walking the dog were about the only safe activities to fill the day. The laughter and encouragement Lisa and Sophia provided were invaluable. I also want to acknowledge my good friend and fellow writer James M. Fenelon. The writing process can be a little lonely, so having a friend to share the ins and outs of writing, publishing, and marketing is amazing and much appreciated. Multitalented, he also created the maps included in the book. I want to say thanks to author Bill Harvey, who took my call one afternoon to talk about cemeteries and our shared love of birds. Chatting with him was like finding a long-lost friend. Everyone who enjoys the Great Texas Wildlife Trails, World Birding Centers, and Great Texas Birding Classic owes a debt of gratitude to Madge Lindsey, Ted Eubanks, Shelly Plante, Andrew Sansom, and everyone at Texas Parks and Wildlife Department who continues to support nature tourism. I could not have completed this book without the support of all the wonderful people at Texas A&M University Press.

Male Bay-breasted Warbler in spring migration

Introduction

Male Vermilion Flycatcher on headstone in Del Rio

I have always been fascinated by cemeteries. Part of that love developed because there was a small graveyard across the street from the Eanes elementary school I attended as a young child. The graveyard was overgrown and ripe for conjuring ghost stories in my developing creative brain. The other part of the attraction came from my mother, Valarie Bristol, and my grandfather, Walter Scott; both loved all things history and never shied away from an afternoon stroll through a cemetery. On long family road trips, we would stop at a cemetery to take a walk and to allow my grandfather to have a smoke on his pipe. In hindsight, I realize the adults might have also been searching for a place for me to run off some of my boundless energy and give them an opportunity to enjoy a peaceful moment and a conversation that didn't involve responding to my incessant inquiries. Either way, the fascination has lasted. My parents' and grandparents' love for all things Texas also stuck with me.

I eventually got my BA in history from Texas State University (then known as Southwest Texas University) with the idea that I would someday be a high school history teacher. I never ended up teaching in a formal setting; instead, I devoted my career and volunteer time to conservation, informal education, and helping others build their connection and understanding of nature. Birds did not capture my attention until later in life. Even as a resource manager at Bastrop State Park, I was not always aware of the avian life around me. In 2014, I was recovering from a back injury caused from being bucked off my Mustang, and I needed an activity where I could move a little slower and still enjoy the rich and interesting experiences in nature that I craved. It was then that I discovered birds and soon fell in love with all things birding.

I started birding the local hotspots in my hometown of Austin and soon fanned out across Texas with my husband, Thomas Nilles, and mother to discover more species. They were already avid birders and knew far more than I did. Within a matter of months, I was reading books at night about birds and listening to their calls on an app I downloaded on my phone. About the same time, I went back to work for Texas Parks and Wildlife in the communications division to manage the Texas Children in Nature program, and there I learned about the Great Texas Birding Classic. A birding competition! It was just what my overly competitive heart needed. That spring I talked my husband, mother, and my uncle, Phil Scott, into participating in the six-day competition, and we spent a week in April birding across the state. I was hooked, and four years later, in 2018, I was honored with the Most Valuable Birder award. In 2019, I achieved the honor again along with my husband and mother. Basically, that means we entered more competitions that any other person or team. We have yet to win the six-day competition; however, we will continue to compete, as hope springs eternal.

Along my journey I learned that habitat matters and is essential to supporting a healthy bird population. While conducting research for my first book, *Parking Lot Birding: A Fun Guide to Discovering Birds in Texas*, I stumbled into a few cemeteries while chasing a lead on a rare or interesting bird. I began to realize what famed naturalist Aldo Leopold meant when he acknowledged that cemeteries are an important piece of the conservation riddle, especially when native plants are allowed and encouraged to grow in them.

Older or more historic cemeteries in particular can be home to large, mature trees, open grasslands, or meadows of wildflowers that are attractive to insects, birds, and other wildlife. In many cases, the location of the graveyard was chosen for some element of natural beauty to honor the departed. For example, Fairview Cemetery in Bastrop is located on a peaceful hill just north of town where the breeze eases through the tall pine trees. The Pine Warblers and Eastern Bluebirds also ease through the tall trees along with a variety of other species.

The vast majority of cemeteries in Texas follow the rural cemetery concept, which was accepted as Texas was being settled. The concept followed the trend popular with communities in the eastern part of the United States that changed cemeteries from being just a place to inter the departed to also being a place for the living to gather and reflect in a natural setting that was located apart from a church and, when possible, outside town. Cemeteries were the first community parks for many cities and were developed as such. More on that topic later.

While some communities insist on mowing and manicuring every inch of a cemetery, others opt for a more natural system that allows the wildflowers and other native plants to flourish. Sometimes even in the most manicured cemetery, the fence lines offer a robust bird habitat if the shrubs, trees, or native grasses are allowed to grow along the edge and on the other side. It was these "unkempt" areas that first caught the eye of naturalist and personal birding hero of mine, Connie Hagar. Near her home in Corsicana, Texas, Connie frequently visited the local cemeteries to search for rare and local wildflowers and, later, to observe birds. She and members of her garden club adopted Oakwood Cemetery in Corsicana as a place to study and showcase native plants and flowers. The Texas Garden Clubs and Nature Clubs of the early to mid-1900s have a long history of caring for and studying the nature within cemeteries. It would be great to see that connection rekindled.

While the birds get a good deal when living or passing through a cemetery, it is the birders who get the best deal. Cemeteries have a lot to offer—easy walking, open spaces to peer into the trees and habitats—and they are quiet, which makes it easy to listen to distinctive bird songs. But wait, there's more. Each location offers a snapshot of the cultural history of the community, and often there are historical markers with information on local history. I continue to be fascinated by the window into the human heart that each tombstone reflects. From the larger-than-life marble angels to the simplest handcrafted marker, each monument has a tale to tell. It expresses the story of the person interred there, the ones they left behind, their community, and the artistic nuance of the monument maker.

I enjoy looking at the rows of headstones and observing the artwork and creativity put into crafting each one. They are rich with symbolism and meaning that tell us who these people were, the faiths they followed, the clubs to which they belonged, and the impressions they left on the community or family. I do not pretend to be an expert on symbolism, but I do enjoy noticing the similarities and patterns that flow throughout the various communities and time periods. The Texas Historical Commission has designated sixteen hundred cemeteries in Texas as historic and is always looking for volunteers to assist with the preservation of the designated and undesignated cemeteries. The Texas Historical Commission also provides and cares for the informative historical markers located at many of the cemeteries in this book. Not every cemetery has a marker, but with some effort citizens can apply for one to be placed at a gravesite or at the cemetery.

Texas has an endless cast of characters, and it has been a blast exploring deeper into the history of the Lone Star State. I have to admit I learned a great deal about some of the more interesting characters as well as the cemeteries from Bill Harvey's fun book *Texas Cemeteries: The Resting Places of Famous, Infamous, and Just Plain Interesting Texans*. I continue to learn something new from each location. While researching the book, I traveled to over 270 cemeteries to narrow it down to the 91 presented in this guidebook. I have come to understand the birds a little better too. Perhaps the reverence I feel when at a cemetery causes me to stand still a little longer and take the time to observe the bird's habits and characteristics. I enjoy thinking about the past and knowing that the birds I see today are pretty much the same species that were living among the Native Americans and early pioneers. Granted, we have lost some important species along the way, and today more are in peril than ever before. For both those reasons every bird I see is valuable and important, as is every acre of habitat.

The combination of the natural and cultural history creates a unique sense of place. In a time when we are distracted by media and overscheduled, I find myself craving things that anchor me. Cemeteries help me remember our collective human history, while being outside helps me remember I am part of nature. While I hope you enjoy the birds at each location, I also hope you will learn something new about Texas' unique history and let yourself be immersed in the sense of place each cemetery offers.

I encourage you to use this book as a guide to some of the best birding and best cemeteries in Texas. *Now let's go explore!*

Eastern Meadowlark on tombstone

Angel at Old Brownsville Cemetery

Cemetery Birding

Bluebonnets in bloom at Oakwood Cemetery in Austin

Rural Cemetery Movement, Parks, and Birds

Like noted Texas geographer and author Terry Jordan, I too once held the assumption that graveyards were spaces designed for the dead, and I felt a twinge of guilt for exploring them to understand their natural and cultural secrets. I was relieved to read Terry's revelation in his book *Texas Graveyards: A Cultural Legacy*: "Graveyards, I learned, are not primarily for the dead, but are for the living" (1).

Cemeteries, especially the ones that rose out of the rural cemetery movement in the early 1800s, with their looping pathways, reflecting ponds, works of art, and intimate gardens, are indeed designed for the living. During the Industrial Revolution cities became choked with pollution from new factories, wood- or coal-burning stoves, poor sanitation, and human waste. In this environment, diseases would sweep through cities such as Boston, causing much death and leaving an additional issue of what to do with all the bodies. In Boston, they drew from a fresh European trend of placing new cemeteries outside the city limits instead of next to a church, which was typically located in the center of town.

Established in 1831, Mount Auburn Cemetery outside Cambridge, Massachusetts, is credited with being the first rural cemetery in the United States. Mount Auburn is also credited with being one of the earliest parks and is still managed for its dual purpose of being a space to honor the dead and providing a place for the living to grieve, reflect, and connect with the departed and with nature. A quotation on the dust jacket of James R. Cothran and Erica Danylchak's *Grave Landscapes: The Nineteenth Century Rural Cemetery Movement* comments on the movement: "These burial landscapes became a cultural phenomenon attracting not only mourners seeking solace, but also urbanites seeking relief from the frenetic confines of the city. Rural cemeteries predated America's public parks, and their picturesque retreats helped propel America's public parks movement."

The first waves of people heading into the cities were, in essence, escaping the uncertainty of living with nature. The Age of Reason or the Enlightenment of the 1700s tried to bring order to the chaos of nature through physical and social paradigms that elevated humans out of the animal or natural world and into their own realm.

However, the constructs of humans proved to be equally as dangerous in the new, factory-driven cities. As a result, a fascination with nature began to emerge in art, philosophy, poetry, and even in elements such as furniture and fixtures that filled the crowded homes of the wealthy and newly emerging middle class. Out of the austere Age of Reason came a new age in which the heart ruled in harmony with the head and nature was to be celebrated. Romanticism invited people to explore their feelings, express their imagination, and surrender to their emotions. A fixation with death and grieving influenced social norms as the idea of being melancholy, or having deep feelings, became popular. Nature offered a place to contemplate and feel. Surrounding a graveyard with nature, especially natural elements that evoked a direct emotion— well, that was the Holy Grail of melancholy for the Romantics.

Mount Auburn Cemetery was established by the Massachusetts Horticultural Society to be a cemetery and experimental garden. For almost two hundred years the cemetery has held true to its vision of a dual purpose and today offers thoughtful burial services and 175 acres of gardens, open spaces, and forests. The Massachusetts Horticultural Society works to maintain the space as viable habitat for urban wildlife in partnership with several universities and has established the Ecological Education and Biodiversity Studies Fund to financially support the ongoing studies and improvements. The Friends of Mount Auburn's website has an entire page dedicated to the wildlife that lives in and is studied at the cemetery. The group even offers bird walks organized through its office of Wildlife Conservation and Sustainability.

As Texas was becoming a state, the Romantics were contemplating the mysteries of nature and how best to design a cemetery that could evoke all the right emotions. Most of the early Texas cemeteries followed the grid pattern, which brought order to the chaotic pioneer life. German cemeteries of Central Texas are especially fixed in an orderly grid pattern. In many cases the grid was incorporated into the newly designed cemeteries to retain a traditional element while also incorporating new styles that took visitors on an emotional journey and created spaces for people to gather, reflect, and express their feelings. They were places to be one with nature.

One of the earliest and most prestigious professionally designed cemeteries in Texas is the eighty-eight-acre Glenwood Cemetery in Houston. It was endowed with all the elements of melancholy, from a multitiered or weeping fountain, to looping pathways lined with a canopy of trees that lace together in an embracing arch, to grieving angels and rolling hills. In fact, the cemetery was considered the first park in Houston and was a recreational destination for many years. The Glenwood Cemetery Historic Preservation Association website states:

> Glenwood shares characteristics of other 19th century romantic garden cemeteries: it was established in a rural area (as Houston existed in 1871). It was built on

a site with a distinguishing natural feature. Glenwood's design takes advantage of the ravines leading to Buffalo Bayou to create a rolling landscape unique in Houston. It was landscaped in a naturalistic style with curving roads and walkways. Newspaper accounts of 1871 compared Glenwood to such well-known garden cemetery parks as Mount Auburn in Cambridge, Mass. (1831), Laurel Hill in Philadelphia (1836) and Green-Wood in Brooklyn (1838). Architectural historian Stephen Fox has written that Houstonians of the late 19th century considered Glenwood to be not only a cemetery but also a landscaped park. Improvements in streetcar transportation brought increasing numbers of visitors to Glenwood on pleasant Sunday afternoons.

Oakland Cemetery in Dallas was established in 1891 and was designed with the forest-and-lawn concept that also celebrated nature with open prairies encircled by more wooded spaces. Members of Audubon Dallas have been conducting bird counts at the cemetery since 1957. Both Glenwood and Oakland Cemeteries were celebrated as parks when they opened and still serve the community in that way, even though the two could not be any more different in how they are maintained. Glenwood offers lush, manicured spaces, while Oakland is allowed to be more natural and even overgrown in some portions of the cemetery.

The Glenwood Cemetery Historic Preservation Association also shares another idea on its website that the Romantics understood—nature has a profound effect on our mental health and well-being. I am pleased that we are arriving at this concept again today. When I was working for Texas Parks and Wildlife on the Texas Children in Nature program, I vetted multiple research studies that made the connection between the concept that nature benefits the physical and mental health of children and adults. Thankfully, Richard Louv brought this concept back to public view in 2006 with his watershed book, *Last Child in the Woods: Saving Our Children from Nature Deficit Disorder*. Even the name of the book evokes a visceral response. Louv sparked an international movement to reconnect children and families with nature.

As part of my career with the Children in Nature movement, I worked on a program in Austin to evaluate and rethink how school campuses were used and could be transformed into outdoor classrooms to increase a child's connection with nature. It was an intense project that brought together our national partners at Children & Nature Network and National League of Cities, along with local partners at the City of Austin, Austin Independent School District, and Children in Nature Collaborative of Austin. The "green school parks" model went even further than just planting a few trees on the school grounds. It opened those campuses to the local communities as a park during out-of-school time. I did not come up with the idea, but once I saw the value, I hunkered down to find all the leverage points to help make it a reality. I even took an online course from the University of North Carolina through the

Natural Learning Initiative to understand best practices to design outdoor learning environments and natural play areas. Later, I was lucky enough to be part of a similar collaboration with the Texas Department of State Health Services to rethink how child-care centers use their outdoor spaces. All of this land-use rethinking got me, well, thinking.

During the process, I began to explore all the green spaces cities manage that are not typically considered parks but still offer ecosystem services. Thanks to one of my interns, Sean Vallefuoco, I started thinking about how these nontraditional green spaces support birdlife. For example, the main purpose of a school is to educate students. But what do the grounds of the school do all day and night? When managed properly, those campuses can be used as outdoor classrooms and spaces where native trees and plants can be cultivated to support birds and wildlife. They can reduce heat-island effects in urban areas and can slow storm-water runoff so it absorbs into the soil instead of disappearing down storm drains or into overloaded creeks.

Cemeteries offer a similar service to a community, especially in a large urban city. Older ones in particular often have mature trees, shrubs, and grasses that support insects, birds, reptiles, and mammals. In urban areas in Texas where heat islands are common, large trees become even more important as a tool to help reduce the impact of our rising temperatures. A heat island occurs in heavily developed urban areas where temperature builds, which in turn can increase air pollution and heat stress on all animals, including people, and water pollution in the form of toxic algae blooms.

One of the top recommended methods for reducing heat islands is to cultivate a healthier tree canopy and native plants. I personally would like to see more native trees and understory bushes planted in cemeteries that have the space, especially to replace the older trees that might be nearing the end of their life. Many of the cities that manage cemeteries through their parks departments now have master plans that include an inventory of the plants and trees, as well as make recommendations for the replacement of aging trees. I personally would like to see a broader sharing of best practices in cemetery management among cities that improve the cultivation of native plants to reduce heat islands and support birds.

I will even plant the seed (pardon the pun) by saying I would love to see the Texas Master Naturalist program and Texas Garden Clubs work with the cemetery associations and cities to help create best-practice guidelines for properties in their communities as spaces where birds and pollinators can thrive.

I'm not the only one who understands that a cemetery can be an ecological wonderland for both plants and wildlife. Famed conservationist Aldo Leopold wrote passionately in *Sand County Almanac* about the relationship he had with the plants in the cemetery in his community:

Every July I watch eagerly a certain country graveyard that I pass in driving to and from my farm. It is time for a prairie birthday, and in one corner of this graveyard lives a surviving celebrant of that once important event. It is an ordinary graveyard, bordered by the usual spruces, and studded with the usual pink granite or white marble headstones, each with the usual Sunday bouquet of red or pink geraniums. It is extraordinary only in being triangular instead of square, and in harboring, within the sharp angle of its fence, a pin-point remnant of the native prairie on which the graveyard was established in the 1840's. Heretofore unreachable by scythe or mower, this yard-square relic of original Wisconsin gives birth, each July, to a man-high stalk of compass plant or cutleaf Silphium, spangled with saucer-sized yellow blooms resembling sunflowers. It is the sole remnant of this plant along this highway, and perhaps the sole remnant in the western half of our county. What a thousand acres of Silphiums looked like when they tickled the bellies of the buffalo is a question never again to be answered, and perhaps not even asked. This year I found the Silphium in first bloom on 24 July, a week later than usual; during the last six years the average date was 15 July. When I passed the graveyard again on 3 August, the fence had been removed by a road crew, and the Silphium cut. It is easy now to predict the future; for a few years my Silphium will try in vain to rise above the mowing machine, and then it will die. With it will die the prairie epoch.

This is one little episode in the funeral of the native flora, which in turn is one episode in the funeral of the floras of the world. Mechanized man, oblivious of floras, is proud of his progress in cleaning up the landscape on which, willy-nilly, he must live out his days. It might be wise to prohibit at once all teaching of real botany and real history, lest some future citizen suffer qualms about the floristic price of his good life. (44–46)

The more than fifty thousand cemeteries in Texas collectively constitute hundreds of thousands of acres of land that make them worth considering when thinking about our natural spaces. Texas is 268,596 square miles big; however, 94 percent of that land is privately held. Since only 6 percent of land in the state is public and there is a rapidly growing population of over thirty million people, it becomes imperative that we consider how every acre is used to support our human needs as well as the needs of wildlife.

As you explore the cemeteries featured in this book, I hope you will consider how you can contribute to the improvement of these spaces through volunteering with a cemetery association or working to connect the associations with local birding or garden clubs, Master Naturalists, or other conservation-minded groups. I will also stress that it is important to be respectful of the established rules and guidelines of the cemetery and never try to plant or remove plants at a cemetery on your own.

Texas Cemetery Birding Locations

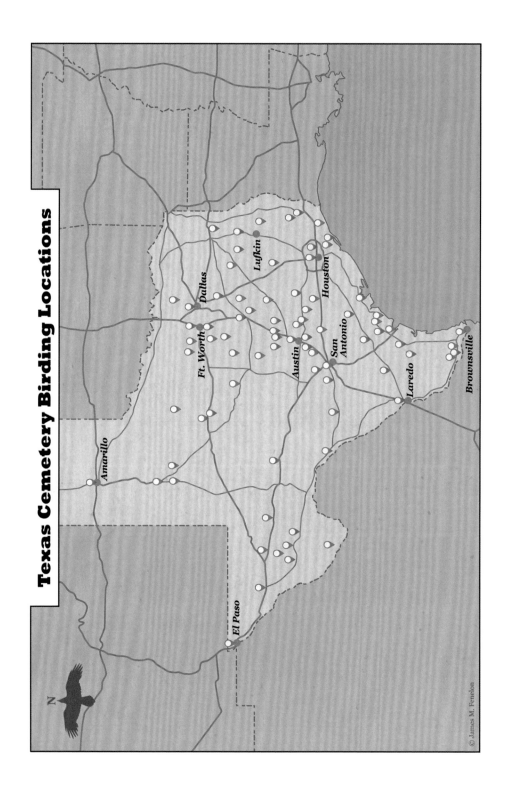

N

Amarillo

El Paso

Ft. Worth

Dallas

Lufkin

Austin

Houston

San
Antonio

Laredo

Brownsville

© James M. Fenelon

Things to Know before You Go

Ethics

Bird-watching in cemeteries is different from birding at a park, at a nature center, or on private property. I cannot stress enough to the reader how important it is to be respectful and mindful because you are birding on sacred ground. When I am at a cemetery, I follow a strict ethical code that I will share.

When arriving at a cemetery, you can either park your car or bike outside the gates and walk in or park along the cemetery roads, or in the parking lot if there is one available. Many of the cemetery roads are not very wide, so be attentive to find a place where your vehicle does not impede other visitors. And most of all, do not ever park on a gravesite. If there is a person visiting a grave or if there a service in progress, please park on the opposite side of the cemetery to give those who are grieving their space.

Cemeteries offer acres of easy walking. While out birding, please do your best to stay on the roads or designated paths and do not walk across the graves. Experienced birder and friend Javier DeLeon, with the Texas Parks and Wildlife Department, advises that he tries to walk along the backside of the headstones if he ventures off the road to observe something and he never walks across a grave. I agree with his advice.

Many headstones or grave markers are not as strong as they might appear, so please never lean or sit on them. If you want to sit to watch the birds, consider packing a camp chair or use a bench located in the cemetery. Not every location has benches, but many do and some are even built into a family plot.

Loved ones often decorate gravesites with mementos, trinkets, and flowers both real and artificial. Each gift left on a gravesite has meaning, so please do not remove items or rearrange things. If there is obvious trash like a beer can or plastic bag, I will pick up those items and recycle or throw them away; otherwise, I leave everything as I find it. Just as one might follow Leave No Trace practices when visiting a park, the same principle can be applied while birding at a cemetery.

If I see someone visiting a grave or clearly immersed in grief, I stop my bird-watching and give the individual space. I have never encountered someone who is annoyed that I am nature watching at the cemetery, and I hope to keep it that way through offering my respect and compassion. I recognize that it might seem odd that I am there enjoying the beauty of nature while they are there for a far less pleasant reason.

If I am birding with friends or family and there are other people in the cemetery, we speak in soft voices. I come from a long line of loud talkers, so that rule is hard to follow, but we do so out of respect and reverence. And if there is an active ceremony, I just avoid it altogether by either coming back later or going to the opposite side of the cemetery.

Always be respectful of the posted hours of operation. You do not want to get locked in if the gates are closed at dusk or at a set time. If you ever observe someone vandalizing a monument or other criminal activity, please head to your car or to a safe place and call 911. If someone has decided to vandalize a grave, chances are that you do not want to come into direct contact with that person, so please let the police address the vandal.

I also want to stress the importance of giving the birds their space while they are nesting, teaching their fledglings to fly, or feeding. I have seen people go to extreme lengths to get the "perfect" photo of a bird or wild animal. Please be mindful that they too are living creatures who see humans as predators, and if we push too far into their purpose-driven life, we only create unnecessary stress for the wildlife.

Ecoregions of Texas

An ecoregion is an ecologically unique area with a defined geographical space. You do not need to be an expert on ecoregions of Texas to go birding and have a great time. For the most part I try to line up the chapters of this book with the Texas Parks and Wildlife (TPWD) ecoregions and a major metro area if possible. As I selected the cemeteries for each region, I tried to include a variety of habitats the area has to offer. My desire is to make it easy to travel from one cemetery to the next as you are out exploring.

It is useful to understand the land, especially in the context of how it has shaped the human existence since the first Indigenous people set foot on what is now the state we call Texas. The ecoregions absorbed the waves of people and often defined how they lived. For example, the Caddo people arrived in the eastern part of Texas around AD 800. The rich soils, consistent rainfall, and abundant wildlife supported the development of fixed communities. By 1200 the Caddo were cultivating crops, including maize, beans, and squash. The Karankawa, who lived along the coast, created lightweight portable pole and skin housing structures that they could move easily as they traversed the barrier islands or moved inland to avoid coastal storms. The sandy soils and marshlands did not provide fertile grounds for crop cultivation for the Karankawa; instead, they mastered hunting, fishing, and gathering techniques that supported their culture.

Gould Ecoregions of Texas. With permission, Texas Parks and Wildlife Department.

Once the Europeans introduced domesticated species such as horses and cattle, the ecoregions again shaped the human experience. The grasslands that once supported the vast herds of American bison were transformed into cattle country. TPWD defines those ecoregions as Piney Woods, Gulf Prairies, Post Oak Savanna, Blackland Prairie, Cross Timbers, South Texas Plains, Edwards Plateau, Rolling Plains, High Plains, and Trans-Pecos.

The ecoregions are important to the birds, as they have adapted to, and prefer, particular native plants, insects, aquatic life, or prey that occupies certain regions. For example, all Golden-cheeked Warblers are native-born Texans, and their preferred nesting habitat is along the cedar and oak canyons of the Edwards Plateau. They utilize the bark from mature Ashe junipers to construct their nests and feed voraciously in the spring on caterpillars that emerge on the oaks. The colonial wading birds, with their long legs, are concentrated around the wetlands of the Gulf Coast Prairies and

Marshes. Cactus Wrens, as the name suggests, are attracted to the cactus in the Trans-Pecos and South Texas Plains regions to build their nests and feed.

Since the European arrival, the land has been forever altered to meet the demands of the populations through agricultural production, oil and gas extraction, mining, logging, and the constant urban sprawl. Despite all of our human demands, the ecoregions remain a constant, as do the needs of the migratory and resident birds.

Migratory Flyways

Texans have front-row seats twice a year to one of the largest winged migrations in the world. Each spring and fall, hundreds of species of birds, butterflies, moths, and bats fly into or across the state as they follow their ancestral routes to the places best suited to breed and to raise their young. Starting in March, the birds from Central and South America begin to arrive as they cross overland or make a leap of faith to fly across the Gulf of Mexico. Around the same time wintering birds begin their journeys north. As the birds come into Texas, they follow either the Central or Mississippi Flyway. Occasionally, a bird from the Pacific Flyway will veer off course and arrive in Texas, which causes much excitement to us birders.

Birds following the Central Flyway might nest in Texas or continue farther north. They fly along the longest stretch of land uninhibited by mountain ranges in the world, known as the Great Plains. Some travel even farther into the boreal forests of Canada or to the Arctic Circle. Birds that follow the Mississippi Flyway travel through or even nest in East Texas or disperse into the eastern parts of North America.

Beginning as early as July, the migration starts all over again. The Purple Martins are among the first to announce the fall migration as thousands of them gather in massive roosts. Travis Audubon and several other Audubon societies in Texas even host Purple Martin parties to celebrate the "hurricane of birds" as they gather for several weeks before collectively making the flight south for the winter. For me, one of the announcements of the fall migration that I never tire of hearing is the distinctive call of the Sandhill Cranes as they fly over my home in Central Texas in their distinctive V-formation.

Cemeteries offer a quiet space to enjoy the passing and resident birds in all seasons, especially if they offer mature trees or are buffered by additional natural spaces. I will never forget an early-morning visit in May to the Macedonia Cemetery outside Granger, where I was treated to an amazing thirty-seven species, including the Magnolia, Yellow, and Black-throated Green Warblers; Yellow-billed Cuckoos; and one of my favorite prairie birds, the Dickcissel. That's the splendor of birding; you never know what you might see until you walk out the door.

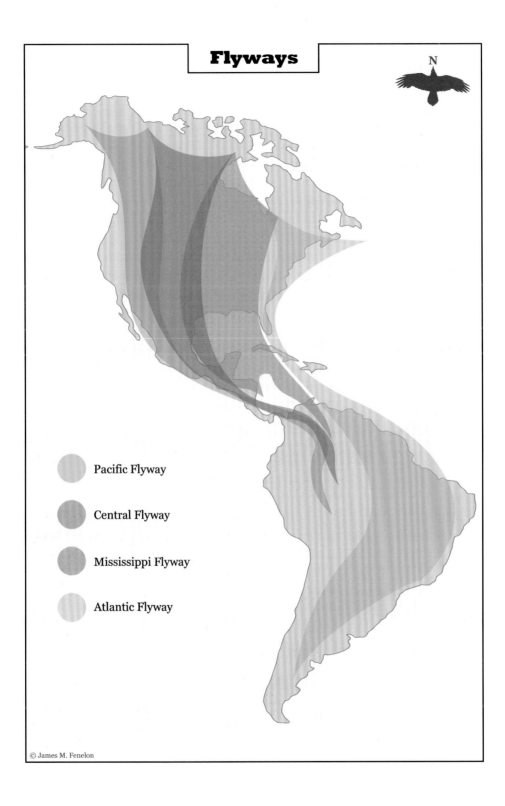

Flyways

N

Pacific Flyway

Central Flyway

Mississippi Flyway

Atlantic Flyway

Cemetery Selection

According to the Cemetery Preservation Program of the Texas Historical Commission there are an estimated fifty thousand cemeteries in Texas that range from a single grave on private property to larger sites that have thousands of burials. I chose the cemeteries featured in this book based on a few simple criteria. First, the site has to have a strong variety of birds and habitat to sustain that diversity throughout the year. Second, it has to be open to the public and located in an area that is safe and easy to access. Third, it has to be interesting. Not all cemeteries are created equal, and some are not much more than a heavily mowed field with in-ground headstones or are so overly decorated with artificial flowers that it can feel unnatural.

One of the reasons I love birding in cemeteries is that there are so many interesting things to look at and learn about in addition to the birds. The headstones offer insights into the past through their symbolism, lettering, names, materials, and even the placement. Since the headstones and monuments are part of the attraction, I tried to focus on places that feature an interesting variety of birds, habitat, headstones, and history.

Not all cemeteries are created equal is also a true statement when it comes to habitat. I tried to find locations that offered a mix of native mature trees, understory bushes, grasses, and a water source. Water sources can range from fountains, to ponds and reflecting pools, to creeks and rivers, or even a view of the Gulf of Mexico. Many cemeteries do not have a noticeable water source, such as Chamberlain Cemetery in Kingsville; however, the grass is watered, which creates little pools for the birds to enjoy and is attractive to insects that sustain a healthy population of South Texas birds. I can say without hesitation that the cemeteries that offer a greater variety of native plants and trees sustain a greater variety of birds. I will also add that mowing matters. Cemeteries that allow the wildflowers to bloom in the spring and wait to mow until the flowers have gone to seed offer amazing habitats for the birds, as they support a greater variety of insects, including butterflies and moths. For those that do offer perpetual mowing care, I would love to see more cemetery associations set aside a few areas for pollinator gardens with native plants.

Sometimes a cemetery abuts an adjacent park or nature center, which is an added bonus that contributes to the abundance of birds. A few cemeteries are even located in a park or wildlife refuge. And just in case the birding is not coming together at the cemetery, I have listed nearby birding locations that might also be of interest.

Did I mention that not all cemeteries are created equal? This also applies to the division of races, cultures, social clubs, and religions. Many of the early cemeteries set aside land for African Americans and people of color so they could have a place to be honored and buried that was separate from where White people were buried. When possible, I use the terms that the communities used to describe the cemetery sections or separate cemeteries. Also, I make note of segregation policies that were later changed, as all public spaces were legally bound to be more inclusive starting in the 1960s. I use their words, even if distasteful, to try to capture a snapshot of what it was like during a certain period in time. I do not judge how things were conducted in the past; however, I do try to provide context and acknowledge that we humans have not always gotten things right—but at least we are trying to learn from past wrongs; however, sometimes we backslide as we continue forward. I subscribe to the view that we must understand and learn from the past if we are to improve our personal and collective existence.

Tombstone Tales

My delightful husband suggested I add a tombstone tale and a tombstone tail for each location, and I thought it was a mighty fine suggestion. At the beginning of each cemetery description a symbol and its meaning are presented. While there is general consensus on the meaning of most symbols or traditions, there is always room for interpretation both from whoever placed it as well as the current onlooker. I do my best to decode the past as a means to understand more about the culture and individuality of each community.

Before the days when people left a digital footprint or were remembered in piles of photos in scrapbooks or online, a tombstone was often the last-chance reminder of who they were and what made them unique. Perhaps the difference they made mattered only to the members of their family, or perhaps their impact had a greater value to the community, state, or even the nation. Possibly they dared to cross an ocean to seek a better life, fought in a war, started a business, served as an elected official, fought for civil rights, invented a better way of doing things, created a great work of art, served to enforce the laws, healed the sick, or taught generations of children. The days that they filled while on earth mattered to someone, and the tombstones are a perpetual reminder of their existence.

With limited space on a tombstone, its message had to be conveyed through size, construction material, the symbols, words included, and even placement in the cemetery itself. While some had resources in life and wanted to leave a reminder of that fact in death, countless others were buried with no final reminder of their existence, save for their remaining family and friends. While those people mattered to those they loved, the burden of a marker was all too often an expense countless millions could not afford. I am always pleased when I see a newer gravestone placed at a grave by that person's children or family at a later date and once they had the means to do so. In older cemeteries, there are often unmarked graves, and we will never know anything about that person's joys, hardships, or legacy. Sometimes those graves have a simple stone or wood stake to mark the spot where the person was put to ground. For that reason, it is important not to move or pick up stones or other objects when visiting a location, as those objects could be the only reminder that there is a grave located there.

As I mentioned, I do not pretend to be an expert on tombstone symbolism; most of what I know comes from observation, online research, Terry Jordan's book *Texas Graveyards*, or James R. Cothram and Erica Danylchak's *Grave Landscapes*. I also found Tui Snider's *Understanding Cemetery Symbols: A Field Guide for Historic Graveyards* to be helpful. Part of the joy of visiting cemeteries is discovering the mysteries of the past, and I invite you to do a little investigating on your own.

Starting in the mid-1800s, some secular orders assisted with the purchase of a gravestone or provided insurance policies that included one. The expense of funeral services and a headstone was often a financial burden that many could not afford until the introduction of benevolent society insurance. While the Freemasons, Independent Order of Odd Fellows (IOOF), Benevolent Protective Order of Elks (BPOE), and others included a blaze or symbols on the headstone, the Woodmen of the World (WOW) provided unique log-themed monuments. All of the benefit organizations have a long and interesting history in Texas. Throughout the years, the various organizations provided plots of land to be used as cemeteries for their members, assisted the widows and children of their members, and worked to benefit the communities they served.

Soldiers of various wars have methods of showing their service too. Many Union and Confederate servicemen have a metal marker placed next to their headstones. Union soldiers often have their name, birth and death dates, and rank etched into the symbol of a shield; however, the shield was also used for veterans who served in the Spanish-American War and War of 1812. Some Confederates have the Confederate Cross, also known as the Southern Cross, etched into their marker. Family members often place the Confederate flag on their graves during Memorial Day or Veterans Day, although this is becoming less popular. Memorial Day used to be known as Decoration Day and was a time to honor the dead by decorating their graves and performing maintenance at the cemetery. Communities would gather at the cemeteries to hold picnics, share stories, and place mementos on the graves.

The Daughters of the American Revolution and the Daughters of the Texas Revolution also place a metal marker at the graves of their members, or the members can have it engraved on their monument.

Servicemen and servicewomen from all armed forces, regardless of their periods of service, are eligible for a government standard-issue headstone or marker in line with the other issued markers of that particular public cemetery. According to the US Department of Veterans Affairs, spouses and dependents are also eligible for a headstone as long as they are buried in a public cemetery. The white upright markers are easy to spot, while the ones that lie flat on the ground are a little harder to find.

Religious orders have their own symbols as well. Catholics often have a simple cross or something more elaborate, such as a statue or etching of Jesus, Mary, Our Lady of

Guadalupe, or a preferred saint. Jewish cemeteries or graves often display the Star of David or a menorah, and many headstones have small pebbles placed on top of them by family members who want to share that they have visited their loved one's final resting place. Both Catholic and Jewish cemeteries are often set apart from those of other denominations and might even be fenced from the rest of the cemetery, as they prefer to lay their dead to rest in consecrated ground. Most Protestant cemeteries in Texas did not require the ground to be sacred even though some are located next to a church.

There is so much more symbolism that is fascinating and tells the story of the person lost or the friends and loved ones left behind. Angels, flowers, shrouded columns, doves, lambs, hearts, skulls, shells, books, hands, stars, urns, and even anchors all convey a meaning or feeling. Newer gravestones can initially seem plain compared to the older, more ornate ones, but then you might come across one that is etched with the San Antonio Spurs logo, a bull, a man fishing, or a semi-truck, and you know symbolism is still alive and well.

Bird Lists

For each location I mention a variety of birds sighted in various seasons or that commonly occur at the cemetery. As always, I make the disclaimer that there is never a guarantee that every bird listed will appear when you visit. The bird lists come from my personal observations, talking to locals, and www.eBird.org, which is powered by the Cornell Lab of Ornithology.

The eBird website allows citizens to log birds they see any time of year and any time of day. The entries are vetted by the team at Cornell and by volunteer local biologists to ensure that people are not posting observations of birds that do not occur in that area. The data are used to help scientists and conservationists focus on where critical habitat is located and what is in need of protection. It also helps them better understand the migration patterns of birds all over the world and how they might be affected by climate change and habitat loss. There are some really cool interactive maps on the website to show the migration routes and timing of specific birds.

I do not list every bird that can be seen in the area; however, I do try to capture a good spectrum of what might exist at a location during each season. Some cemeteries do not have eBird lists other than what I have entered on my personal account. In those cases, I pulled data from nearby locations that share similar habitats. My hope is that as you visit and bird the locations listed in this book, you will record your observations on eBird to ascertain how these spaces support avian life. If you really want to be a citizen-scientist, you can also record animals, plant, and insect sightings on iNaturalist.org.

As mentioned, I try to report what birds are seen in each season. The year-round birds are the residents that generally do not migrate and stay in a fixed range the majority of their life. Some days it can feel like spring and summer occur in one day in Texas as temperatures swing from hot to extra hot. For birds, spring starts in March in Texas, with the migration extending to late May or early June. Some birds have a spring migration range that brings them to Texas to breed and nest. For example, the Northern Parula migrates from South and Central America and nests in Central and East Texas, as well as the eastern parts of the United States. Many species of warblers and other songbirds show up for only a few weeks in April and May as they pass through on the migrations, sending birders from across the state rushing out their front doors to try to see their favorites or even spy a rare bird that has ventured off course.

Summer can linger until October with temperatures that can still be in the nineties on Halloween, but in general for the birds, summer ends around August. The Purple Martins and hummingbirds begin their journeys from Texas to Central and South America in mid-July to mid-August. Ducks, geese, and songbirds will pass through Texas from August to November, with many species remaining in Texas for the winter.

Winter birding, especially along the Gulf Coast, is exceptional as the shorebirds, ducks, geese, and cranes all gather along the marshes, bays, and beaches. There is an overlap in the seasons since the timing of the migrations can vary depending on the weather. Songbirds generally molt after the breeding season ends and don a duller version of their brilliant spring fashions, so it is a little trickier to identify them as they pass through in the fall or come to winter in the state.

Tombstone Tails

Like the feather facts in *Parking Lot Birding*, tombstone tails highlight a few fun facts about a bird you might see at one of the 91 locations. Tombstone tails include facts about a bird's migration pattern or home range, nesting and feeding habits, preferred habitats and other tips that are useful to identify and understand the species. I also try to include the season in which you are most likely to see that bird.

There's an App for That

I really like the Find a Grave app and website to locate cemeteries and learn about the people interred there. While researching this book, I cross-referenced the Find a Grave website with the eBird website to find graveyards with good bird counts or in an area with steady bird activity. I also called on the hive mind of the Texbirds Facebook group to ask them to share what cemeteries they enjoyed birding and was deluged by great suggestions.

I use the iBird Ultimate app to help me identify birds when I am out in the field. There are also good apps offered by Audubon, Peterson Bird Field Guide, iBird Pro, and Merlin Bird ID by Cornell Lab of Ornithology. EBird also offers an app to record observations while in the field. The app is cool because it will track the distance you cover, which helps scientists understand exactly what you are seeing and where. I don't always want to be part of Big Brother and Big Data scenarios and often return to my trusty field guides, small notepad, and camera to record what I observe and make notes about the cemetery. I'm a fan of Sibley's birding guides, but there are many other books on the market to choose from. Gary Clark's *Book of Texas Birds* is also one of my favorites.

Safety

Just like all outdoor recreation activities, birding is best when you take a moment to plan for your safety at all times. Texas is hot—there is just no way around it. But don't let that stop your outdoor fun; just be prepared by knowing your limits, wear a hat and lightweight clothing, and carry plenty of water. Cemeteries do not have gift shops to purchase water, nor do they offer drinking fountains. A rare few might have a chapel that has a place to get water, but for the most part the ones listed in this book do not. Be sure to take water with you. I have also found most locations do not have restrooms, so take the time to make a pit stop before you get immersed in an active cemetery birding situation.

The weather in Texas is fickle and can change moods faster than a teenager. Make sure you check the weather and have a good weather app on your phone before you walk out the front door. If it looks like there might be a change in the weather, especially in the spring, be sure to take several layers of clothing. I cannot count how many times I have loaned out extra layers of clothing to friends and family on outdoor adventures as an unanticipated blustery cold front blasted through. In my birding backpack I keep my camera gear, binoculars, bottle of water (in a reusable container), light snack, light rain jacket, scarf, sunscreen, notepad, pen, and of course my lipstick. My grandmother lived by the creed that a good southern girl should never be more than lunging distance from her lipstick at all times. It is about the only beauty tip I follow, as you never know whom you might run into while out birding, especially in a cemetery. During COVID-19, I added an extra protective face covering and hand sanitizer to my pack.

I usually enter in the address and get the directions set on my phone the night before so they can sync up with my navigation system in the car and I'm not fumbling through that process down the road. If I do need to change course, I always pull over somewhere safe and get the directions reset before motoring on. The Find a Grave app has a feature where you can click on the map of an individual cemetery and it will give you directions in the mapping system. For your convenience I have included the address of each cemetery at the beginning of each location description.

Just as when visiting a park, it is always a good idea to carry your cell phone with you at all times. You can use it to take pictures or look things up, but it is always good to carry it for safety too.

I'm not the most graceful person, so hear me when I say, watch your step. Cemeteries can often have uneven ground and hidden things in the grass to trip over; so literally watch your step. I can also tell you from experience that marble is a very hard object and hurts when you stumble into it. It is always safest to stay on the roads or beaten path if your balance is a little off or you are tragically ungraceful like me.

Accessibility

Birding is a wonderful pastime for people with limited and full mobility alike. When possible, I mention if the location is accessible for people using a wheeled mobility device such as a wheelchair or walker or are birding with small children in a stroller. Many of the older cemeteries have gravel or dirt roads that are not suitable for all mobility types. While the unpaved roads might be a limitation, I say all the time that my van makes a great bird blind. Some cemeteries have accessible parking spaces and restrooms, but they are few and far between. For the most part the accessible spaces are paved roads. I added these notes after having a wonderful conversation with Virginia Rose, founder of Birdability.

Now let's go birding.

Male Bronze Cowbird preforming mating dance

Upper Gulf Coast Prairies and Marshes

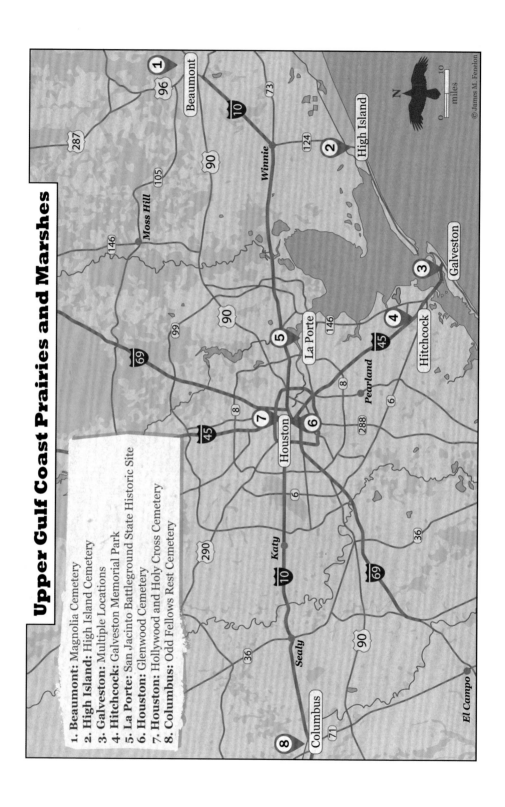

1. **Beaumont:** Magnolia Cemetery
2. **High Island:** High Island Cemetery
3. **Galveston:** Multiple Locations
4. **Hitchcock:** Galveston Memorial Park
5. **La Porte:** San Jacinto Battleground State Historic Site
6. **Houston:** Glenwood Cemetery
7. **Houston:** Hollywood and Holy Cross Cemetery
8. **Columbus:** Odd Fellows Rest Cemetery

© James M. Fenelon

Upper Gulf Coast Prairies and Marshes

The Texas Parks and Wildlife Department website sums this expanse of the state succinctly when it states that "the region includes barrier islands along the coast, salt grass marshes surrounding bays and estuaries, remnant tallgrass prairies, oak parklands and oak mottes scattered along the coast, and tall woodlands in the river bottomlands." Basically, the Gulf Coast is a mix of habitat that supports some of the best birding in the world.

This was the homeland of the Akokisa and Karankawa, who lived nomadically across the region starting about AD 800 to 1,000. Archeologists date the earliest humans in the area to around ten thousand years ago; early nomadic tribes had little impact on the wildlife or landscape. Once the waves of European explorers and settlers began to arrive, the coastal plains were plowed into agricultural fields and the forests were logged for their timber. After oil was discovered, the entire area was transformed even further by derricks and refineries as it became one of the largest oil producers in the world.

Since the dawn of time, there has been conflict between the power of water and humans. The massive rivers of this region empty into bays and estuaries and often jump their banks to flood crops, fields, and cities. Nature recently reminded the city of Houston that despite our best efforts, water has the power to defy dikes and level levies as Hurricane Harvey dumped thirty inches of rain in parts of the city. The coastline has seen its share of hurricanes and tropical storms. The barrier islands not only offer great birding habitat but also function as a buffer to protect the mainland from raging storms and rising storm surge. When it is not storming, the entire coast is an exciting place to bird in every season.

Beaumont: Magnolia Cemetery
2291 Pine Street

Laid to rest in the sprawling seventy-five acres of rolling hills, magnificent magnolias, and whispering pines are some of Texas' wealthiest wildcatters, timber tycoons, and stalwarts of shipping. Resting peacefully next to them in simple graves are thousands of people who helped the emperors of industry make their millions.

Texas Revolution hero and pioneer William McFaddin gave the original land for the cemetery in 1847. By that time, he could afford to give a little land away as he had already amassed a headright (approximately 1,280 acres) of land in Williamson County and an additional 1,000 acres in Jefferson County for his service in the Texas Revolution. He was only seventeen when he ended his military service. He and his son, William Perry Herring McFaddin, started the McFaddin Ranch of Beaumont, which was one of the first cattle operations to use Brahman cattle imported from India. In addition to running the cattle ranch, the McFaddins were industrious rice farmers and at one time had the largest muskrat-pelt operation in the world. The McFaddin family lands also just so

Tombstone Tale

The virtue or angel holding the anchor represents that person's devotion to faith, steadfastness, and hope. The anchor can have a more literal meaning if that person was lost at sea, served in the navy, or just enjoyed boating.

happened to be where Anthony Lucas leased a parcel and drilled an oil well into the salt dome and hit what later came to be known as the Spindletop Oil Field.

The land McFaddin selected for the cemetery is located on the highest hill in Beaumont, which overlooks a finger of the Neches River. The river is visible from the cemetery in only a few places because of the dense forest. However, its proximity to the wetlands and woodlands that surround it makes for stellar birding habitat. The open fields dotted with the majestic pines, oaks, cedars, and magnolias provide excellent spaces for the birds to nest, perch, and feed. There are several things that look like trees that also make great perching places, but they are, in fact, Woodmen of the World (WOW) headstones. The Ogden family-tree marker wins the prize for the largest WOW headstone I have ever come across. If you explore the older part of the cemetery, I guarantee you cannot miss it.

This is also the final resting place of one of my nature heroes, Corrie Herring Hooks (1876–1963). She was a charter member of the Texas Ornithological Society, East Texas Nature Club, Magnolia Garden Club, Louisiana-Texas Horticulture Club, and Texas Federation of Women's Clubs. Corrie was also a founding member of the Big Thicket Association and is reported to have had a deep knowledge of the plants and wildlife of the area. She invited ornithologists, naturalists, and friends to her hotel on High Island to observe the wonders of the spring migration and establish the island as an important stopover for migrating birds. The Corrie Herring Hooks Bird Sanctuary at High Island is part of this dynamic woman's legacy.

Speaking of birds, some of the year-round avian residents at the cemetery include Eastern Bluebirds, American Robins, American and Fish Crows, Northern Cardinals, and Northern Mockingbirds. With the return of spring this cemetery is a good place to watch for warblers of every variety, especially along the edge of the thicket. Just north of the cemetery at Collin's Ferry Park there are reports of the Prothonotary, Hooded, Common Yellowthroat, and Magnolia Warblers along with American Redstarts and Northern Parulas. On my visit in April, I was impressed with the number of Barn, Northern Rough-winged, Tree, and Cliff Swallows all zooming in and out of the headstones and feeding on the endless supply of insects. This is also a good place to look for Brown-headed Nuthatches and Brown Creepers. During the winter, watch for Brown Thrashers, Hermit Thrushes, and American Robins to be feeding in the leaf litter along the edges of the forest. I look forward to more bird checklists being submitted on eBird for this location.

One portion of the streets at the cemetery is paved and suitable for people using a wheeled or seated mobility device. However, you can use your car as a bird blind and view most of the wonders of this location from a vehicle. For those who wish to walk the grounds, the rolling hills and looping roads create an easy walking space.

If you are in the area birding, I hope you will take the time to explore the Cattail Marsh Scenic Wetlands and the Big Thicket National Preserve or the McFaddin

National Wildlife Refuge. The Forest Lawn Memorial Park near Collier's Ferry Park is also worth checking out. As a side note, Forest Lawn has paved roads and is less hilly, which might be better suited for a person with limited mobility.

Tombstone Tail: Magnolia Warbler

The male is a striking yellow, black, and gray with a distinct black necklace that decorates its lemon-yellow chest. Magnolia Warblers breed in the dense boreal forests of Canada and winter in Central and South America, with a migration route that passes through most of the eastern part of Texas. In 1810, Alexander Willison originally named them the "black-and-yellow warbler" when he first saw them feeding in a magnolia tree; later the name Magnolia Warbler seemed more fitting. During the spring migration, look for them feeding on insects on the outer edges of trees and shrubs as they head to their breeding grounds in Canada and the Great Lakes region.

High Island: High Island Cemetery
Fifth Street and Gulfway Lane

There might not seem to be much to this small cemetery at first; however, have a walk along the edge and peer into the woods from March into May. As the migrants arrive during the spring migration, the tall thicket of trees and vegetation is a welcome sight for the weary travelers who dare to cross the Gulf of Mexico or travel overland from South and Central America. Along the edge of the woods is a small drainage ditch that provides fresh water for the birds to bathe and drink. When I arrived on a warm spring day in April, I was drawn to the edge of the woods by the joyful song of the Swainson's Thrush.

The manicured lawn attracts Indigo Buntings in the spring and is visited daily by European Starlings. The birds that arrive during the spring migration can change daily, and for that reason I look forward to more observations being posted from this location. During the short time that I visited in April 2020, there were Baltimore Orioles, Summer Tanagers, Rose-breasted Grosbeaks, Northern Cardinals, and Black-throated Green Warblers all feeding in the woods along the edge of the cemetery or in the large magnolia tree near the street. In the wetlands beyond the cemetery I could easily see Great, Snowy, and Cattle Egrets along with Great Blue Herons moving slowly through

CHARLES CRONEA
JAN. 14, 1805.
MAR. 4, 1893

Tombstone Tale

Hip tombs are not common in Texas but are very distinctive. This is a variation on the chest box with angled sides like the hipped roof of a house. A hip tomb such as the one at Charles Cronea's grave is useful in the Gulf Coast region to keep the coffin from rising in a storm surge.

the marsh. During the spring migration, keep an eye on the trees for the more than thirty types of warblers that pass through. A few other spring treats include Scarlet Tanagers, Painted Buntings, Wood and Gray-cheeked Thrushes, veeries, and Eastern Kingbirds. Winter brings the return of Savannah, Song, and Swamp Sparrows; Hermit Thrushes; Brown Thrashers; Gray Catbirds; and Yellow-rumped Warblers. There are well over 320 species of birds that visit High Island throughout the year, which makes it interesting in any season.

High Island is the highest point along the Gulf Coast between Mobile, Alabama, and the Yucatán Peninsula. The raised land sits on top of a massive salt dome and is surrounded by marshes, coastal prairies, sandy beaches, and the Gulf of Mexico. Native Americans frequently came to the area for the mineral springs and fresh water that the landmass provided. The fresh water still supports a large forest of coastal oaks, hackberries, willows, and other vegetation. This small cemetery is walk-in only and not suitable for people with limited mobility.

The cemetery is just north of the Corrie Herring Hooks Woods Sanctuary, which is operated by the Texas Ornithological Society. Houston Audubon and Texas Ornithological Society own and operate several nature preserves on the island and along the Bolivar Peninsula to protect the habitat and offer birders a place to observe the wonders of the region. There are plenty of great birding locations on High Island and along the Bolivar Peninsula, including Boy Scout Woods and Smith Oaks, where you can stop to get excellent birding advice from Houston Audubon volunteers and staff who run the sanctuaries. I have to admit that the parking area for the Boy Scout Woods offers some of my favorite birding during the spring when the mulberry trees have fruit. For more about the history of the region, check out Melanie Wiggins's *They Made Their Own Law: Stories of the Bolivar Peninsula*. The title pretty much says it all.

Tombstone Tail: Kentucky Warbler

This beautiful yellow-and-black warbler can be found feeding on the ground or in understory brush of forests or along the edges between forests and fields. These warblers winter in the Caribbean and Central America and nest in east and central North America. The males are not terribly musical birds, as they sing only one song their entire life. According to Partners in Flight, these warblers are on the watch list of birds of concern due to habitat loss of understory native plants in forests.

Galveston: Galveston Cemeteries

Multiple Locations

Galveston has a complicated and long human history that is difficult to tell in such a short space. Thankfully, the town is filled with historical markers and museums ready to be consumed by the eager mind. I think Gary Cartwright, author of *Galveston: A History of the Island*, captures the essence of the community in the opening line of his book: "I never go back to the island without sensing the ghosts. I can't think of a place where they run thicker."

Indeed, death is no stranger to the barrier island that has been inhabited for almost ten thousand years. Prior to the European exploration and then exploitation, the cannibalistic Karankawa inhabited the island for part of the year as they migrated between the mainland and the barrier islands. The cemeteries do not hold the remains of any of the Karankawa, as they were effectively considered, by many, an extinct culture by the time the American Civil War erupted. However, there is an Atakapan burial ground on the Bolivar Peninsula that dates back around five thousand years. The early explorers or pirates such as Álvar Nuñéz Cabeza de Vaca; René-Robert Cavelier, Sieur de La Salle; and Jean Lafitte are also not buried on the island. What you will find is one of the greatest collections of early Texas emperors of industry, banking, shipping, and

Tombstone Tale

The woman or angel clasping her hands at her chest, eyes turned toward the heavens, often represents the virtue of charity. This statue in particular is at the grave for the Dominican Sisters of Houston, many of whom were lost in the hurricane of 1900.

insurance resting peacefully next to nuns, teachers, artists, stonemasons, physicians, and children—so many children.

Death might arrive on the island to claim an individual, or it may sweep through in a wave of cholera, yellow fever, measles, Spanish flu, or COVID-19. Nature also doles out a blow from time to time in the form of hurricanes or floods. The hurricane of 1900 is still considered the most devastating storm in American history, with between six thousand and ten thousand people lost; many were swept out to sea, never to be seen again. The island community has also paid its fair share of human capital by sending off men and women to fight in every US war since the Texas Revolution.

The cemeteries carry the collective memories of each life lived and lost along the way. They also tell the stories of the cultures that passed through. When Galveston became one of the major ports in North America, it was also a point of entry for millions of emigrants from Serbia, the Czech Republic, Greece, Italy, Sweden, and South America: each culture an oddity on the first day and a neighbor by the second day.

Prior to the Civil War, Galveston also saw its fair share of enslaved persons disembarked from ships on their way to the plantations in Texas, Louisiana, and other places in the South. While Texas was still part of Spain, Galveston was the back door for importing enslaved people from Africa or the Caribbean Islands after other ports were closed to the insidious trade. Pirates active in the Gulf of Mexico during the early 1800s were after more than just Spanish gold from Mexico. A ship filled with slaves was worth far more than gold for pirates who participated in the morally bankrupt trade of humans.

After the Civil War, Galveston boomed again in the sale and transport of cotton and cattle to willing buyers in the eastern United States, Canada, or Europe. By 1874 it was known as the "New York of the Gulf." During the Prohibition era in the 1920s the island became a popular tourist destination, with gambling and drinking the main attractions. Today, it is a major hub for outdoor recreation, relaxing on the beach, history, and nature tourism.

The Broadway Cemetery Historic District runs between 40th and 43rd Streets and contains seven cemeteries: Old City (1839), Old Potter's Field, later called Oleander (1839), Old Catholic (1844), Episcopal (1844), New City or Yellow Fever Yard (1867), Hebrew Benevolent (1868), and Evergreen (1939). The grounds are thick with Gothic revival headstones and mausoleums, obelisks of every size, vaults, and gravestones made from shining white marble to simple concrete. The former citizens of Galveston rest peacefully under the blanket of wildflowers that bloom from March to June.

I hope you will visit the grave of one special citizen buried at this location. Cecilia E. Seixas (1883–1900) formed the first Audubon Society in Texas and one of the first in the country with her friend Estelle Cannon Hertford (1876–1946). Concerned about the loss of shorebirds and gulls to the millinery trade, the young women organized the society in 1898, and by 1899 they had seventy-five members and held meetings twice a month. Sadly, seventeen-year-old Cecilia Seixas died in the 1900 hurricane.

The Broadway Cemetery Historic District's flowers, native grasses, and scattered mature trees are inviting to spring migrants such as Yellow, Black-and-white, Hooded, and Black-throated Green Warblers. On a visit in May I watched a pair of Summer Tanagers build a nest in one of the hackberry trees. Spring can also bring Scarlet Tanagers, Rose-breasted Grosbeaks, Indigo Buntings, and Red-eyed and Yellow-throated Vireos.

Lakeview Cemetery complex is between 57th and 61st Streets and has an impressive WOW monument sculpted by famed artist Pompeo Coppini and is dedicated to the twenty-four Woodmen who were swept away in the 1900 hurricane. The graves seem slightly disorganized, as they rest between the looping roads. I get the feeling that the cemetery once had some lovely trees, but they must have been lost along the way since there are only a few remaining. There is a small pond with fresh water that is attractive to insect eaters that return in the spring, such as Barn, Cave, Cliff, and Tree Swallows; Purple Martins; Chimney Swifts; and Common Nighthawks. Because the grounds are close to the beach, the skies are busy with passing American White and Brown Pelicans, Roseate Spoonbills, White Ibis, and of course Laughing Gulls. Occasionally, Long-billed Curlews and White Ibis will feed in the grasses near the pond. Surrounding Lakeview are the Memorial, Municipal, Beth Jacob, and Serbian Orthodox Cemeteries. Each has a unique flare and style. However, none of them have mature trees or suitable bird habitat.

The Calvary Catholic Cemetery is worth a visit to see the Gothic revival vaults and grieving angels. The grounds are devoid of trees except along the edges, which offer good birding in the spring. The pond behind the columbarium is where you can find passing spring migrants such as Baltimore and Orchard Orioles, Gray Catbirds, and Yellow-billed Cuckoos. Great-tailed Grackles can be found year-round at this location; however, it is also a good place to find the less common Boat-tailed Grackles. Black-necked Stilts and Whimbrels wade along the shallow edges of the pond, while American and Least Bitterns hide in reeds with Common Gallinules and American Coots. A colony of Monk Parakeets has a nest in the cell-phone tower behind the shopping center adjacent to the cemetery, which makes it easy to spot the chatty green birds.

Each of the cemeteries offers easy walking; however, Lakeview and the Catholic cemeteries are better suited for people using a wheeled mobility device. Nearby birding can be found at Lafitte's Cove, Galveston Island State Park, and Moody Gardens. Galveston holds the FeatherFest birding festival each April during the spring migration, which is worth attending if you are in the area.

Tombstone Tail: Summer Tanager

The male Summer Tanager is the only all-red bird in North America. Males return to Texas with their yellow female mates to breed in parts of the state that have suitable woodlands. These long-distance migrants travel to Central and South America during the winter. They are considered a bee and wasp specialist and will separate the stinger from the insect by banging it on a branch. They also consume caterpillars, fruits, berries, and other insects. Like many red-colored birds, they are surprisingly challenging to see once they are immersed in the canopy; however, their lovely song will often give away their location.

Hitchcock: Galveston Memorial Park

7301 Memorial Street

Founded in 1925, this large park-like cemetery is flanked to the south and east by the Highland and Marchland Bayous. This is an active burial site, so please be respectful to the families at a service or visiting a loved one. I also recommend giving yourself plenty of time to stroll along the multitude of looping streets and study the birds in the mature magnolia, live oak, pine, and hackberry trees. The paved, shaded streets make this an excellent place for people with limited mobility or with children in a stroller to bird.

With only a few checklists submitted on eBird, it is difficult to gauge how many species actually live here or migrate through this location. However, when I visited in May, I was treated to eighteen species in an hour. A storm was rolling in, so I had only a short period of time to document what I was seeing and hearing. As the stormed approached, in I watched a flock of Common Nighthawks feeding on insects rising on the winds.

Down by the bayous, look for Belted Kingfishers, Ospreys, Great and Snowy Egrets, and Great Blue Herons to be feeding throughout the year. In the fall and winter the ducks return to the wetlands, and it is common to find Ring-necked Ducks, Redheads, and the ever-present Black-bellied Whistling-Ducks. The large canopy of live oak trees is attractive to a variety of warblers and vireos as they pass through in April and May.

Tombstone Tale

The Celtic cross is defined by the nimbus, a circle at the top of the cross that can represent either heaven and earth, or the moon and earth. The cross and nimbus are often artfully decorated with Celtic designs.

Winter brings the return of Pine and Yellow-rumped Warblers along with flocks of Pine Siskins and Cedar Waxwings.

With well over seventy acres of woodlands and wetlands to explore at this location, it is easy to spend several hours admiring the birds, habitat, and well-maintained cemetery. Nearby birding can be found at Jack Brooks Park and Carbide Park.

Tombstone Tail: Osprey

This large, fish-loving raptor can be found across East, Central, and South Texas during the winter and migrates north to breed. Ospreys can live about twenty years and will travel up to 160,000 miles in their lifetime as they migrate from their wintering grounds of Texas, Mexico, and the West Indies to breed in the northern parts of the United States and Canada. For many years they suffered a decline caused by the use of the pesticide DDT,

which weakened their eggs and made them susceptible to cracking. After the United States banned DDT, Ospreys made a surprising comeback and are still seeing a rise in population. They also benefit from the stocking of fish into rivers and lakes across Texas.

La Porte: San Jacinto Battleground State Historic Site

3523 Independence Parkway

Thanks to the Daughters of the Republic of Texas this historic battlefield became the first state-owned park in Texas and predates the Texas State Parks system. For most die-hard Texans, the San Jacinto Battleground and Monument are sacred lands where Texas was born out of the blood and sweat those men left on the battlefield that fateful morning on April 21, 1836. There are plenty of historical markers to enjoy that tell the

Tombstone Tale

Reflecting pools have been popular since the early Egyptian culture and are often paired with a tall structure such as an obelisk or monument. They are a place to reflect and remember and evoke a feeling of tranquility. Many smaller reflecting pools in cemeteries have been removed as the trend has fallen out of fashion. The San Jacinto reflecting pool is approximately 1,777 feet long and 219 feet wide and was constructed in 1936.

tale of the birth of the republic. There are also two small family cemeteries inside the boundaries of the twelve-hundred-acre State Historic Site.

In the midst of the grinding industrial complex, this point where the Buffalo Bayou and the San Jacinto River empty out into the bay is a welcome refuge for migrating and resident birds. The large oak trees, coastal prairie, and freshwater wetlands host more than three hundred species of birds. Oh, how the world has changed since those brave Texans and Mexicans clashed on that day in April.

April is the height of the spring migration, and I like to think that perhaps at least one soldier found comfort in the joyful song of the Orchard Oriole or beauty in the technical colors of a Painted Bunting as the Mexican army camped among the oak trees. The live oak grove is still one of the best places at this location to find the migrating Magnolia, Bay-breasted, Blackburnian, and Cerulean Warblers, as well as vireos and flycatchers. To see just about everything the location has to offer in every season, park by the monument and walk along the trail out to the boardwalks and pavilion in the marsh. During the fall and winter the wetlands host over thirty species of ducks and geese, including Northern Pintails, Blue-winged Teals, Hooded Mergansers, Eared Grebes, Gadwalls, and Redheads. In the shallows look for wading birds such as Dunlins, Little Blue Herons, Wilson's Snipes, and a horde of herons and egrets.

A grass path leads to the small Habermehl Family Cemetery by the reflecting pond. Located near the parking lot, the Zavala Family Cemetery and San Jacinto Battlefield Cemetery are easier to visit and have an accessible path that leads to the monuments. When visiting the Zavala Cemetery, you might notice it is oddly organized for such an old cemetery. That is because the headstones were moved to this location from the family plantation across Buffalo Bayou near the present-day city of Channelview. A storm destroyed parts of the original family plot, and continued subsidence threatened it until action was taken to move it.

The grassy areas around each of the cemeteries yield birds such as Sedge Wrens and Field, LeConte's, and Swamp Sparrows—to name just a few of the grassland birds at this location. The live oak grove around this area is a good place to look for many of the twenty-eight species of warblers reported here.

Portions of this location are suitable for people with limited mobility. However, some of the paved surfaces can be a little rough in spots. Additional nearby birding can be found at Sheldon Lake State Park and Environmental Learning Center, Baytown Nature Center, or Armand Bayou Nature Center. All three locations offer excellent birding as well as guided bird walks and classes.

Tombstone Tail: Wilson's Snipe

This medium- to long-distant migrant shorebird is actually a real bird and not some mythical creature. Although my brothers tried many times to get me to go "snipe hunting," I never fell for the prank. The birds' cryptic coloring makes them difficult to find as they weave in and out of the mudflats of wetlands. They thrust their long, straw-like beak into the mud to search for and then suck in invertebrates, larvae, and worms. They winter as far south as Venezuela and breed as far north as Alaska. Once the fledglings are ready to leave the nest, the parents divorce; the males take the older fledglings, and the females take the younger ones. During the nonbreeding season, they are widely spread across the United States into Central and South America where wetlands exist.

Houston: Glenwood Cemetery

2525 Washington Avenue

Glenwood Cemetery was established in 1871 and is Houston's first designed burial ground. Even today, it feels more like a Victorian-era garden than the final resting place for the titans of industry, commerce, politics, invention, and natural resource extraction. Set on a bluff above Buffalo Bayou it has a commanding view of the city that so many of the people buried at this location helped build. Glenwood is often referred to as the "River Oaks of the dead." For those not familiar with Houston's neighborhoods, River Oaks is at the intersection of the "haves" and the "have even more."

The cemetery association offers guided history tours, or you can simply walk the paved streets and read the various historical markers. Because of the well-kept, paved roads I highly recommend this location to people using a mobility device. According to the Texas State Historical Association, Glenwood opened at a time when other Houston cemeteries were filling up quickly because of a wave of yellow fever and other diseases. The original design followed the popular rural cemetery style that took advantage of the rolling hills and view of the bayou. Planner and horticulturalist Alfred Whitaker designed the grounds and drew on elements featured at Mount Auburn Cemetery in Cambridge, Massachusetts, and Greenwood Cemetery in Brooklyn. When the cemetery opened, it was heralded as Houston's first city park. The design makes for a pleasant walk that allows you to feel removed from the city when engulfed in the greenery and beauty of one of the many enchanting enclaves.

Tombstone Tale

The angel holding flowers is a reminder that life is fleeting. The lily often represents a life lived in purity, mercy, and innocence or a return to those values.

When Glenwood annexed the adjacent Washington Cemetery, it increased in size to eighty-four wooded acres. Washington Cemetery was founded in 1887, under the name German Society Cemetery; however, the name was changed in 1918, when all things German fell out of favor after World War I.

The giant oaks and other trees bring comfort and peace to those who visit, and they harbor a variety of bird species. Just down from the Skyline Meadow is Lake Whitaker and Buffalo Bayou, which provide sufficient wetland to support several types of wading birds, including Yellow-crowned and Black-crowned Night-Herons, Snowy and Cattle Egrets, and waterfowl such as Black-bellied Whistling-Ducks. When I visited in late May, the Blue Jay parents were trying desperately to get their oversized fledglings to leave the nest and take flight. It seemed every tree had a squawking pair of parents and a defiant youth who would rather have its breakfast in bed. There have been sporadic reports of Red-vented Bulbuls at the cemetery and nearby parks along the bayou; although these birds are not native, they are nonetheless pretty to see.

During April and May, look for Hooded, Nashville, Kentucky, Magnolia, and Worm-eating Warblers in the trees and at the birdbaths. Spring also brings the return of Gray-cheeked, Swainson's, and Hermit Thrushes, along with Ovenbirds and Northern Waterthrushes. The fall and winter see an abundance of small birds such as Pine, Orange-crowned, and Yellow-rumped Warblers; Cedar Waxwings; and Blue-gray Gnatcatchers.

Even on days when the birding is not great, you will not be bored, as there are so many historical markers and much exquisite art to see. For more information about Glenwood there is a wonderful book, *Houston's Silent Garden*, by Suzanne Turner and Joanne Seale Wilson with photographs by Paul Hester.

Nearby birding locations can be found along Buffalo Bayou, Memorial Park, and Magnolia Cemetery. I also enjoy birding at the Houston Arboretum and Nature Discovery Center.

Tombstone Tail: Yellow-crowned Night-Heron

This stocky heron has a large oval-shaped head with a distinct black-and-white mask and yellowish crown feathers. It is a treat to see the males fan out their long head and shoulder plumage during mating displays. Fossil records show that they have been stalking around the marshes and wetlands searching for crabs and other crustaceans of North America for nearly two million years. While it is most common to see them wading in the marshes, also look for them roosting in trees. These colonial wading birds can be found along the Texas coast year-round and in South, Central, North, and East Texas during the spring breeding season.

Houston: Hollywood and Holy Cross Cemeteries
3506 North Main Street

This historic fifty-five-acre cemetery complex is flanked by Little White Oak Bayou and Moody Park, which create a large habitat in the middle of the Houston sprawl. The cemetery is still quite active and was busy each time I visited. It is easy to log some miles here if you walk the endless loops that lace together along the contours of the land. I found the best birding to be up on the last hill where the bayou makes a ninety-degree turn. With large pine trees whispering in the breeze and plenty of understory bushes for the birds to dart in and out of, it is the most peaceful section.

Established in 1895, the cemetery was envisioned as serving a dual purpose of interring the dead and offering a park setting to the living. It featured a stranger's rest for anonymous persons and indigents and a baby's rest to receive young children lost during waves of disease outbreaks in the swampy early days of Houston's history.

When I visited just before Memorial Day, it was striking how many veterans are laid to rest here from the Texas Revolution to the War in Afghanistan. I am always taken aback by the toll of human life wagered and lost in the defense of our democracy and ideal of freedom. There are historical markers located at the graves of several of Houston's most noteworthy citizens, including Henry Philemon Attwater (1854–1931), conservationist and former director of the National Audubon Society. The Attwater's Prairie-Chicken is named for him.

Also buried here is one of my favorite Texas women, Mollie Arline Kirkland Bailey (ca. 1841–1918), otherwise known as the "Circus Queen of the Southwest." Mollie Bailey is the only woman to have successfully owned and operated a circus in the

Tombstone Tale

The lamb often adorns the top of a child's gravestone and is associated with purity and innocence.

United States. She intentionally took her circus to the smaller towns, as she felt they deserved entertainment too. Mollie and her circus walked across Texas from Houston to Amarillo and back each year until she finally bought a train to transport her troupe. To avoid the occupation taxes of the time, she purchased lots in over one hundred of the towns she visited. When the circus was not in town, she encouraged the town to use those lots as playgrounds or ball fields for children or a place to gather. Mollie was fascinated by the natural world and would often halt her red-and-white wagon train to collect a specimen of a flower or plant to send back home to her daughter or her one of her biologist friends. She is buried on the bluff that overlooks what used to be the winter grounds of her circus and is now Moody Park.

The habitat in and around the cemetery supports a number of year-round species, such as Blue Jays, Northern Cardinals, Red-bellied Woodpeckers, and Carolina Chickadees. Down by the bayou, look for Great Blue and Green Herons; Yellow-crowned Night-Herons; Great and Snowy Egrets; and Belted Kingfishers. I was a little saddened by how much trash was in the bayou; hopefully, the city or a conservation group will take action to clean it up, especially where it flows past the park where children play.

During the spring, look and listen for Ovenbirds and Black-and-white, Nashville, Kentucky, Hooded, Magnolia, and Chestnut-sided Warblers in the large trees and shrubs near the bayou. The spring also brings Orchard and Baltimore Orioles, Red-eyed and White-eyed Vireos, Barn Swallows, and Chimney Swifts. With the return of fall the trees come alive again with small birds such as Pine, Yellow-rumped, and Orange-crowned Warblers; American Goldfinches; Blue-headed Vireos; and Hermit Thrushes.

Nearby birding can be found next to the cemetery at Moody Park, which can be fairly busy on weekends and after school. Woodland and Hogg Parks are only a short drive away.

Tombstone Tail: Green Heron

This small carnivorous forager can be seen most often sitting motionless, staring into a shallow stream or pond waiting for a frog, fish, or worm to swim by. Green Herons are one of the few birds that use bait to catch a meal. They will drop seeds or smaller insects on top of the water to bring the fish up. They sit with their long neck tucked into their body until it is time to strike. Occasionally, they will dive into deeper water to forage. Cornell Lab of Ornithology notes that Green Heron populations are in steep decline because of habitat loss by filling in, channelizing, or draining wetlands.

Columbus: Odd Fellows Rest Complex

1518 Montezuma Street

Columbus is a beautiful, historic town set on the banks of the Colorado River. It is also a place that has always been a crossroads. It is here that the ecoregions of the Oak Savanna and the Coastal Prairies merge. Prior to the arrival of settlers, the land was shared, not always amiably, by the Tonkawa and Karankawa. In 1821, empresario Stephen F. Austin brought the first three hundred families to his colony south of what is now Columbus. As the families spread out looking for suitable lands to farm, several of them settled west of the Colorado River near Columbus. Mexican governor José F. Trespalacios ordered the colony to be divided into two districts, with Columbus being the dividing line and the anchor community for the western district. Today, it is at the intersection of Interstate 10, Highway 71, and Highway 90.

The large oak trees, historic homes, and businesses make it an interesting place to spend a day exploring Texas' past. Established in 1871, the cemetery is part of that past with older graves dating back to 1852. This is a great example of a lodge cemetery that was established by IOOF Lodge No. 51. The timing of opening the cemetery was good because just a few years later, in 1873, the community and much of Texas were hit by another deadly yellow fever outbreak.

The complex, which includes the St. Anthony's Catholic and Willing Workers Cemeteries, is also flanked by Cardinal Park and a local golf course, which has several

Tombstone Tale

The Independent Order of Odd Fellows (IOOF) is represented by three interlocking rings or chain links.

small ponds and a creek, providing excellent habitat for migrant and local birds. When I visited in early May, I was in a bit of a hurry because a storm was blowing in from the south; I was still pleased with the number of birds I spotted. A group of Mississippi Kites that were moving quickly as the storm approached caught my attention. Their steel-gray and white bodies and wings boldly stood out against the dark skies.

On that same visit, the Northern Cardinals were busily feeding their young chicks and warding off the bully Blue Jays. Scissor-tailed and Great Crested Flycatchers danced from the treetops while snatching insects, while Yellow-throated, White-eyed, and Blue-headed Vireos flitted around the interiors of the majestic live oak trees. During the fall and winter, look for American Pipits, American Goldfinches, and Orange-crowned and Yellow-rumped Warblers to return. With the abundance of Spanish moss draping from the trees, this seems like an ideal nesting area for Northern Parulas.

The roads here offer easy walking but are not accessible for wheeled devices. Nearby birding can be found at Beason's Crossing Park by the Colorado River.

Tombstone Tail: Northern Cardinal

This lovely red-and-black bird can be found east of the Rocky Mountains from Mexico to Maine. The females are not as colorful as the males, but both share an equally beautiful song, which is an unusual feature for a female songbird. Males will fiercely defend a territory and even defend the territory from themselves by attacking their reflection in a window or a car's rearview mirror. The cardinal's large bill allows it to eat a wide range of food that includes seeds, fruits, and insects. These tough birds are the mascot for Columbus. Healthy birds can live up to fifteen years.

Ancient live oaks at Columbus IOOF Cemetery

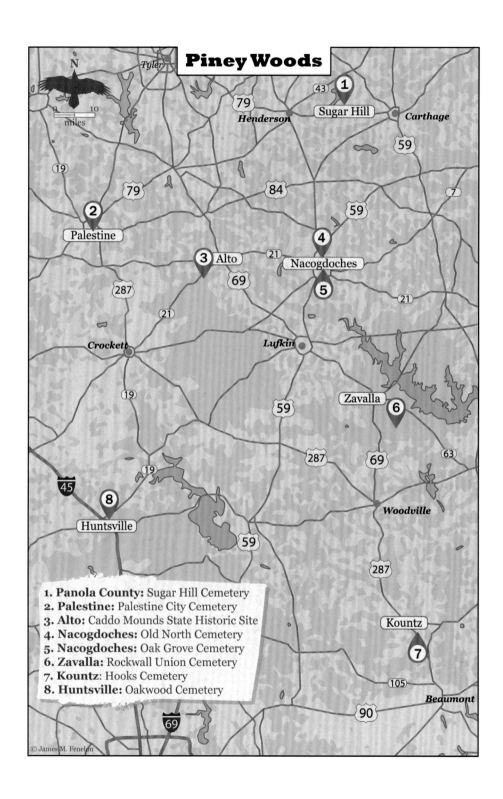

Piney Woods

N

0   10
miles

19

Tyler

79   Henderson

43   1   Sugar Hill   Carthage

59

79

2

Palestine

84

59

19

7

59

4

Nacogdoches

3   Alto

21

287

69

5

21

21

Crockett

Lufkin

19

Zavalla

59

6

19

287

69

63

45

8

Huntsville

59

Woodville

287

1. **Panola County:** Sugar Hill Cemetery
2. **Palestine:** Palestine City Cemetery
3. **Alto:** Caddo Mounds State Historic Site
4. **Nacogdoches:** Old North Cemetery
5. **Nacogdoches:** Oak Grove Cemetery
6. **Zavalla:** Rockwall Union Cemetery
7. **Kountz**: Hooks Cemetery
8. **Huntsville:** Oakwood Cemetery

Kountz

7

105

Beaumont

90

69

© James M. Fenelon

Piney Woods

The Piney Woods of East Texas are defined by massive pine-hardwood forests supported by an annual rainfall of between thirty-six and fifty inches that fills the endless matrix of creeks that flow into the mighty Trinity, Neches, and Sabine River basins. When I was a child, I would take a trip each year with my grandparents from Austin to Nacogdoches. I would wait with anticipation to see the first pine tree along the drive and blurt out "I see one" the instant the first one came into view. Having grown up on the Blackland Prairie around Kaufman, Texas, my grandfather had a deep and abiding reverence for trees, and the loblolly pine was among his favorites.

The abundant flora and fauna of East Texas have supported humans for thousands of years. Early Native Americans hunted the forests alongside or in competition with black bears and red wolves. There are reports of a few black bears returning to East Texas, but the red wolves have long since disappeared. Even with two of the large predators removed, there is an abundance of other wildlife both rare and common that roams the woods, wetlands, and fields. For example, the Red-cockaded Woodpecker is one of the endangered species that can be found in the Sabine and Davy Crockett National Forests and on private lands such as the Boggy Slough Conservation Area outside Lufkin. The bottomlands and wetlands support Wood Storks, Prothonotary Warblers, and other declining neotropical songbirds. There is a patchwork of national forests and preserves, state and local parks, as well as nature centers, that helps protect rare plants, animals, and ecosystems.

The long human history in East Texas has left the region full of family and small cemeteries, in addition to the larger ones, that are worth exploring to understand the layers of experiences incurred along the way.

Panola County: Sugar Hill Cemetery
County Line Road to County Road 242

According to the Texas State Historical Marker located at the cemetery, the first burial took place here in 1849; the land was later given for the purpose of a cemetery and community gathering place in 1855. The small farming community peaked in population in the 1880s and was abandoned by the 1930s.

To get to the cemetery, visitors drive along Martin Lake on County Line Road to County Road 242. Your birding adventure for this cemetery starts as soon as you turn onto County Road 242 and are surrounded on both sides by wetlands, forests, and pockets of prairie. The wetlands are most active from November to March when the waterfowl and shorebirds return. Watch for Northern Shovelers, Gadwalls, American Wigeons, Ring-necked Ducks, Greater and Lesser Scaups, and Blue-winged Teals. The grasslands of the cemetery and along the road support fourteen types of sparrows, including Lincoln's, Swamp, and Field Sparrows.

As spring returns, watch for Blue Grosbeaks, Dickcissels, Indigo and Painted Buntings, and Lark Sparrows to migrate into the area, with some remaining to nest. The forest around the cemetery supports year-round woodpeckers such as Pileated, Downy, Hairy, and Red-bellied Woodpeckers that are sometimes easier to hear than see. The Eastern Bluebird is also a beautiful resident and can be found perching, flying, and singing throughout the area. Some 147 species of birds have been recorded here, so you are sure to have a delightful day exploring, with most activity occurring

Tombstone Tale

The loss of a child is hard no matter the circumstances. Children's graves often show a child resting peacefully. In this case the child is sleeping in the shelter of a shell. This funerary motif can symbolize the child as a precious pearl. Sears, Roebuck and Company catalog offered a similar headstone in the early 1900s.

between October and April. The fall colors in this part of the East Texas forests are worth seeing. If you are out in the warmer months, please watch out for snakes.

I will be honest; this is in the heart of Texas' coal country. Martin Lake was established in the 1970s as the cooling lake for the large lignite-fed electric plant located on the opposite side of the lake from the cemetery. The Beckville Strip Mine is located on the same side of the lake just north of the cemetery. According to a 2019 article in the *Texas Observer* the power plant is one of the worst sulfur dioxide polluters in the state. We do not often talk about acid rain anymore, but the leading harmful chemical in acid rain is sulfur dioxide. The chemical irritates the lungs of all terrestrial and avian animals, including humans. It is also toxic to many types of plants as well. I mention this since there is no way of ignoring the giant power plant or the nearby mine as you explore the area. The mine was blasting when I was there, and it was slightly unnerving.

On the plus side, the Texas Utilities Generating Company gifted 286 acres on the north end of the lake for Martin Creek Lake State Park. At the entrance to the park is the Historic Harmony Hill Cemetery, which is interesting but does not offer much in the way of birds. Nearby birding can also be found at Martin Cemetery, also off County Line Road, or Conner Cemetery just north of Beckville.

Sugar Hill Cemetery is not suitable for people with limited mobility because it has only gravel and grass pathways. However, the drive along the lake and wetlands offers favorable car-birding opportunities.

Tombstone Tail: Swamp Sparrow

This rusty-capped sparrow has longer legs than most sparrows, which serve it well in the swamps and marshes it inhabits. These sparrows look similar to Lincoln's Sparrow but lack the streaky chest; both can be found at the edges of wetlands. They winter across the eastern and southern parts of the United States, in Texas, and into Mexico. When they are in Texas, they feed mostly on seeds and fruits. During migration they will consume insects for a protein boost as they head north to the boreal forests of Canada to breed. Despite the loss of so many wetlands across North America east of the Rocky Mountains, this hardy sparrow's population is stable.

Palestine: Palestine City Cemetery
Cemetery and Market Streets

This location has every feature I think an old rural southern cemetery should have—lush green rolling hills, old stone walls, towering trees draped with Spanish moss, a small creek, and monuments of every size and shape. When I visited on Memorial Day weekend, the flags were set out to mark the graves of those who had given service to their country from the Texas Revolution to the War in Afghanistan. The bold colors of the flags contrasted with the white and gray headstones and lush green grass.

The complex is three cemeteries that cover over fifty-five acres and are now operated as a single complex by the City of Palestine Parks Department. The looping roads and open fields offer the perfect vantage to peer into the thick East Texas woods that surround the cemetery on several sides. When I visited in the spring with my husband, we packed a picnic to enjoy while we sat and watched the birds. The white clouds billowed up for an afternoon rain shower against the clear blue sky. To say the whole thing was as pretty as a picture would be an understatement.

I was so pleased to see a royal-blue flash fly past me and land on a shrub just above the tall grass. Once the flash of feathers paused, I could see it was a beautiful male Blue Grosbeak. He was joined by a female as they continued to feed in the shrubs near the

Tombstone Tale

Ferns represent humbleness and sincerity, while ivy is an evergreen that symbolizes immortality and everlasting love. Ivy can also represent a binding or embracing love.

creek. The large field across from the stream is also a great place to look for birds such as Dickcissels, Eastern Phoebes, and Eastern Wood-Pewees in the spring and summer. During the spring migration, keep an eye on the willows along the creek to harbor Palm, Bay-breasted, Chestnut-sided, or Magnolia Warblers. When I returned in July the following year, I spotted both Indigo and Painted Buntings teaching their fledglings to fly.

While walking the multi-terraced grounds, look and listen for Yellow-bellied Sapsuckers; Northern Flickers; and Pileated, Red-headed, Red-bellied, Hairy, and Downy Woodpeckers from October to May. With so many large trees and cavities created by the woodpeckers, I would not be surprised if there were not an owl or two that frequent the cemetery. There is not much of a birding list for this location; however, the habitat is perfect for a host of migrants in both the spring and fall and plenty of room for the resident birds to feed, nest, and raise their young.

Several of the roads here are paved and suitable for a wheeled mobility device; however, the steep slopes might make it a challenge to navigate without assistance. Visitors with limited mobility are always invited to use the car as their bird blind, and this makes an excellent car-birding cemetery.

Nearby birding locations can be found at Davey Dogwood Park, Upper Lake Park, or the Gus Engeling Wildlife Management Area. The historic Memorial Cemetery off Moody Street is interesting and has moderate habitat for the birds. If you are interested in the history of East Texas, stop by the Museum for East Texas Culture.

Tombstone Tail: Blue Grosbeak

The males of this species are a brilliant royal-blue, while the females are a medium brown. Despite their brilliant coloring, they can be difficult to see as they move in and out of the grasslands and shrubs. Even though they are dispersed widely across North America during the summer, they are not an abundant bird since they require a fairly extensive range for each breeding pair in their preferred habitat. They often use snakeskins in the construction of their nests as a way to deter predators and because it is an easy material to weave into the nest. Data from the Cornell Lab of Ornithology show that this species has expanded its range north over the past few decades to include North Dakota in the Midwest and northern New Jersey in the East. They winter in Central America and the Caribbean.

Alto: Caddo Mounds State Historic Site
1649 Texas Highway 21

The Caddo Mounds State Historic Site might not immediately come to mind as a traditional cemetery. However, one of the large mounds located at the site is a burial mound. Around AD 800, the Caddoan Mississippian culture extended to the region and started a permanent village on the bluff above Bowles Creek. As they made their way into the area, they followed and improved an ancient trail that traversed the land and treacherous rivers to trade as far south as the Gulf of Mexico and east into the Mississippi River watershed.

The abundance of food and water allowed the Hasinai group of the Kadohadacho (Caddo) people to thrive. An elaborate hierarchy of religious and political systems emerged that utilized the mounds as part of their civic and religious ceremonies. They honored their dead, especially those who had reached an important level in society, with elaborate burial rituals that included interment in the mounds. In addition to building mounds, they were skilled craftspeople who built handsome beehive-type structures and cultivated maize, beans, squash, and even sunflowers.

Tombstone Tale

The early Caddoan Mississippian culture used burial mounds to honor the dead.

The mound-building culture of the Caddo halted around 1300 when the smaller tribes became self-sufficient and no longer needed the hierarchy of the religious and political systems on which they had previously depended. At the height of their culture, it is estimated that the Caddo numbered around two hundred thousand people living throughout the Angelina, Brazos, Trinity, Neches, Sabine, and Red River watersheds.

In 1542, a diarist traveling with the Spanish explorer Hernando de Soto described the Caddo as having a remarkable culture with large stores of maize. As the Spaniards and later the French entered into the Caddo's world, the newcomers were at first an interesting trading partner. However, the Europeans brought a terrible and unwanted gift in the form of Old World diseases. The first notable waves of disease occurred in the 1690s, with cholera being one of the worst killers. Native Americans simply did not have the immune systems to defend themselves against measles, smallpox, chicken pox, and other European illnesses that spread quickly. The Spaniards also brought to the New World another deadly weapon: the horse. Once the Comanche acquired and mastered riding the horse, they swept into Texas, and the farming Caddo communities were a favored target of their raids.

In the 1840s, after decades of conflict with the Europeans, other tribes, and loss from disease, the remaining Caddo moved to a part of their traditional range near the Red River, hoping to avoid further loss of life and lands. Finally, in 1859, the remaining approximately one thousand people were rounded up and moved to the Washita Reservation in Oklahoma. The Caddo Nation is recognized by the US government and now resides in Oklahoma.

The first professional archeologist explored the site in 1919, with following examinations occurring over the years until 1939, when the University of Texas, in conjunction with the Works Project Administration (WPA), started excavating and mapping the mounds. In 1974, the Texas Parks and Wildlife Department was able to purchase the seventy acres around the mounds to establish a park; an additional twenty acres were added in 1981. The Texas legislature transferred the management of the park to the Texas Historical Commission in 2008. In the fall of 2019, the legislature and the citizens of Texas voted to dedicate 6 percent of the Sporting Goods Tax collected by the state to fund historical sites, with the remaining 94 percent of the tax going to Texas state parks. Thanks to my father, George Bristol, and many others, this dedicated funding stream makes it possible to better care for our state parks and historic sites.

In the spring of 2019, two tornados ripped through the historic site and destroyed the Visitor Center and replicas of the Caddoan homes. The mounds remain intact, as does the ADA walking trail and interpretive panels. When I visited in 2021, construction was under way to rebuild the Visitor Center and other structures. It is worth the time to walk the short looping trail to the viewing platform that looks out over the woods and pond. The pond brings in a few waterfowl and wading birds, such as the

Pie-billed Grebe and Great Blue Heron; it also supports the Belted Kingfisher and is visited from time to time by a Bald Eagle. Red-winged Blackbirds, Wood Ducks, and Hooded Mergansers enjoy the wetlands as well. I also recommend either walking or driving the road that loops behind the historic site and bird along the road near the creek. There is an old orchard and lots of bottomland trees that support a good variety of forest-loving birds.

During the spring and summer, search the grasslands for Scissor-tailed and Acadian Flycatchers, Barn Swallows, and Dickcissels. This is also a favorable place to listen for the Eastern Meadowlark's sweet song that sounds like it is saying *spring-is-here*. The grasslands also support fourteen species of sparrows, including Fox, Savannah, Song, and White-throated Sparrows in the fall and winter. When I visited in January, there were two American Kestrels hunting in the fields and returning to their perch on the telephone wire near the road. Some of the resident birds include American Crows, Carolina Wrens, Northern Cardinals, and Blue Jays. Over one hundred species of birds have been identified at this location, with a good distribution in each season.

Nearby birding can be found at Mission Tejas State Park and Ratcliff Lake Recreation Area.

Tombstone Tail: American Crow

This large, intelligent black bird with a powerful beak can be found across most of the lower forty-eight states and parts of Canada. American Crows are highly social and will remain in family groups throughout their lives. During the winter they form massive roosts with hundreds or sometimes thousands of birds. When they are foraging, they spend a good deal of time eating and hopping on the ground looking for insects, seeds, small reptiles, fruits, and even bits of trash. They are one of the few birds that will use a tool to reach a piece of tempting food. Recent studies have been conducted with crows and found that they have long memories. Additionally, they recognize faces and will report to the flock if that face is a friend or foe. Many Native American cultures include this talkative bird in their stories and myths: sometimes as a trickster, other times as a protector. They can live up to sixteen years in the wild and have been reported to live more than fifty years in captivity.

Nacogdoches: Old North Cemetery

332 County Road 205

When I first visited this graveyard in December, I was not sure if it would make the cut for a cool place to bird. My uncle Steve Scott, my mother, and I wandered around marveling at the various tombstones and especially at the wooden grave house that encases the grave of Lucinda Lilly. Lucinda died at age forty after she lost two infants several years earlier. She must have been much loved by her husband to have such an elaborate grave house constructed for her.

As we moved to the edge of the site where the trees are tall and the undergrowth on the other side of the fence is thick, the birds revealed themselves. Dark-eyed Juncos, American Robins, Pine Siskins, and Northern Cardinals all scratched along in the deep leaf litter, while Pine and Yellow-rumped Warblers flitted about in the treetops.

Tombstone Tale

The tradition of a grave house comes from many cultures, including Native American, African, and northern European. Often associated with being protected or "gone home" to the afterlife, grave houses were popular in early East Texas cemeteries where the three aforementioned cultures blended.

In the African American section, White-throated and Chipping Sparrows foraged in the grass. During the spring, look and listen for Yellow-throated and Red-eyed Vireos, American Redstarts, and Yellow and Black-and-white Warblers.

The Old North Baptist Church, established in 1838, is the oldest active Missionary Baptist Church in Texas, with the graveyard predating the church. Legend holds that the first burial on the grounds was of a young girl who died while traveling through the area with her family. The land was given by the Sparks family to be used as a cemetery in 1836, making it the oldest Protestant cemetery in Nacogdoches. Prior to the Texas Revolution all colonists were part of Mexico and, therefore, part of the Catholic Church.

This is one of the few examples of a graveyard in this book. A graveyard differs from a cemetery in that is located next to and maintained by a church. A cemetery is located away from a church. The graveyard was laid out in a traditional grid, with family plots lined with curbing or iron fences; however, the contour of the land and shifting soils have caused the grid to become a somewhat disjointed patchwork of squares, which makes walking the grounds challenging. The cemetery is still divided into two sections, which was part of the original design. One section of the grounds was reserved for members of the congregation and their families who were enslaved or of African descent. Of the very first founding members of the congregation, two men, Anthony and Chancy, were recorded as being slaves. (Their last names were not recorded.) Many of the names of those buried in the African American section were also not recorded or were marked simply with a stone or numbered marker. Many of the older headstones lie flat on the ground, so watch your step and be respectful. This section of the graveyard is worth strolling through because it is surrounded by excellent habitat.

This graveyard is not accessible for people with limited mobility, as there is not a paved path. Nearby birding can be found at Oak Grove Cemetery, Pecan Park, and Bonita Creek Preserve in Nacogdoches. I look forward to more bird counts occurring at this graveyard to better understand what the ten acres and the woods beyond the fence support.

Tombstone Tail: Eastern Bluebird

The male Eastern Bluebird is a royal-blue, rust, and buff color, with the female being a duller version of the male. These birds generally nest in cavities and respond well to nesting boxes that are specific to their species. The males will dance around the nest cavity and fill it with nesting materials to attract a mate during the spring. A successful pair can lay two clutches of eggs in a season. Many of these insect- and fruit-eating birds migrate; however, they can be found in most parts of Texas year-round. Their populations have made a strong comeback after dwindling due to the introduction of the aggressive European Starling, which takes over their nesting cavities. Conservation efforts have included introducing "bluebird" trails that placed nesting boxes in parks and schools around the country. I have come across a few cemeteries that have bluebird boxes, and I would love to see more.

Nacogdoches: Oak Grove Cemetery
200 North Lanana Street

I have traveled to Nacogdoches my entire life to marvel at the loblolly pines on our family's little slice of the great forest. The town has always felt old and even mysterious to me—not frozen in time or stuck in a particular age but simply from another time altogether. I am sure I feel that way because my family has repeated their stories and the history of early Texas to me for so long that they tend to blend together. My grandparents' stories capture the essence of the town as it has dealt with the eternal struggle of the hierarchy of families; discrimination against race, ethnicity, religion; and a struggle between using the land for production or managing it in conservation. Drought, floods, snakes, bugs, feral hogs, unruly livestock, stray dogs, and the ever-present red soil are all cast members in my family's stories and have been present since humans started inhabiting the region.

The only remains of the earliest people to settle the area can be found on Mound Street, so named for the burial mounds the Caddo built between AD 800 and 1200. Originally, there were three of these mounds, but their significance was not understood when the first university was built, and two of the mounds were lost. And that is what Nacogdoches is about: layers. The name of the town and county is a testament to those layers, as it was named for the Nacogdoches, a smaller group of the Caddo.

Around 1716, Europeans arrived when the Spaniards founded Nuestra Señora de Guadalupe de los Nacogdoches and five other missions in East Texas because they

Tombstone Tale

In 1936, to celebrate the one-hundred-year anniversary of the Texas Revolution, the State of Texas placed markers at the graves of all the men and women who served in the fight for independence. The markers are generally made of gray granite and bear the state seal.

feared the French would try to claim the land as theirs. In 1825, empresario Hayden Edwards was allowed to bring eight hundred families to colonize the area, thus establishing it as an important city in the eastern part of the soon-to-be republic.

The first recorded burial at Oak Grove Cemetery was in 1837, long after the town was established. There are older Spanish graves in the cemetery that date back to the early 1700s. Those graves were moved from their original burial place where the current courthouse resides. Did I mention the layers? Since the cemetery opened, those interred represent the business leaders, rebellion organizers, funders of the Texas Revolution, signers of the Texas Declaration of Independence, religious leaders, veterans of wars, teachers, farmers, civic leaders, artists, and one famous poet—Karle Wilson Baker (1878–1960).

Karle was not only one of the country's most celebrated poets, novelists, teachers, and essayists of the first half of the twentieth century; she was also an avid birder and naturalist. Her home located off Mound Street was known as Tanglewood. She wrote a lovely book, *The Birds of Tanglewood*, in which she eloquently describes the avian life of East Texas during the early 1900s. There is a statue of her at the corner of North Mound and Hughes Streets that has one of the most beautiful poems I've ever read inscribed on it. Karle is buried in her family plot under a magnificent magnolia tree.

The cemetery is approximately twelve acres, which are easy to explore with plenty of shade from the mature trees that represent some of East Texas' finest species. The backside of the property is flanked by Lanana Creek and the Lanana Creek Trail, which provide a good water source and additional cover for the birds. When I visited on a misty morning in December, I was treated to seventeen species of birds in less than an hour. The next afternoon when the sun returned, that number climbed to twenty-three species, including a male White-throated Sparrow whose colors were so rich that he seemed to already be sporting his breeding plumage. The Cedar Waxwings and Yellow-rumped and Pine Warblers were feeding voraciously on one of the large cedars at the end of Oak Grove Cemetery Drive. As spring returns to the area, so do the flashy warblers that dance through the tops of the trees. There are reports of the beautiful Cerulean Warblers in the area, and the cemetery has the proper habitat to support them as they migrate through along with Magnolia, Chestnut-sided, and Yellow Warblers. The spring also brings the return of Mississippi Kites, Ruby-throated Hummingbirds, and Gray Catbirds. I have also come across Brown Thrashers, American Crows, Red-headed Woodpeckers, Eastern Bluebirds, and American Robins that stay in the area year-round.

Birding in the thick woods of East Texas can be challenging, which makes the open spaces of the cemetery a tranquil place to observe them. The paved road makes this an accessible birding location. Nearby birding can be found at Pecan Park, Tucker Woods, and Lanana Creek Trail.

Tombstone Tail: Hermit Thrush

This small thrush has brown upperparts and a spotted chest. Hermit Thrushes return to Texas in the fall and stay until late spring. They can often be found scratching the ground or even vibrating their feet on a leaf to bring insects to the surface and snatch them up. Most nesting pairs east of the Rocky Mountains build their nests on the ground, with some building nests in low shrubs in the forests of Canada or west of the Rocky Mountains. They have a flute-like, somewhat mournful song that makes them an enjoyable bird to encounter during the spring in Texas or across their breeding range. The thrush's song has captivated American poets such as Walt Whitman and Karle Wilson Baker.

Zavala: Rockwall Union Cemetery (also known as Boykin Cemetery)

County Road 9 to County Road 14 North

The journey to get to this cemetery is worth the experience. Driving the dirt county roads is like boring through the deep East Texas forest. Because we live in a state with more paved roads than most countries, the long dirt road feels like a teleporter to another time. Since it is dirt and can quickly turn to mud, I recommend a higher-clearance vehicle for this adventure.

Traveling to the small cemetery, visitors will pass through the Angelina National Forest and Upland Island Wilderness to arrive at the edge of the Catahoula and Frazier-Runnels Preserve. The Angelina Forest was established in 1938 in an effort to conserve some of the last remnants of the mixed-pine forests in Texas. The woods contained in the Upland Island Wilderness are said to be some of the most ecologically diverse in the state, with more than 450 plant species and eleven unique habitats, which support over 170 species of birds, including the endangered Red-cockaded Woodpecker.

Dessor Ree Frazier (1918–2004) donated twenty acres to the Catahoula and Frazier-Runnels Preserve. Dessor gave the land in memory of her grandfather, a freed slave, who owned and retained the land for decades. She was born on the farm that

Tombstone Tale

A coffin case is a decorative metal casket case that serves to protect those entombed from the shifting soil or a high water table.

her grandparents owned and held a special connection with the land. Dessor saved up enough money to go to Prairie View A&M University nursing school by working six days a week for many years. After graduating, she found segregation applied even to the highly educated. She was denied entrance to most hospitals simply based on the color of her skin until she finally gained acceptance at the University of Texas Medical Branch in Galveston—where she worked for thirty-three years. Dessor, her grandparents, and many of their extended family are buried in the cemetery. Her gift of the land to the preserve is a notable example of how individuals can contribute to conservation on a scale that is meaningful to them.

Next to the cemetery is a marker designating the edge of the Catahoula Preserve, which was purchased by the Texas Land Conservancy (TLC) in 1984 under the direction of Ned Fritz. The property was the first land that TLC purchased and was an inholding in the national forest. TLC now holds 126 properties totaling 91,539 acres of conserved lands in Texas.

The cemetery offers an open space to peer into the dense woods. I suggest packing a lunch, some chairs, and a lot of bug spray so you can sit peacefully to enjoy the breeze whispering through the pines or to listen for the drumming of the Pileated Woodpecker or the high trill of the Pine Warbler. Woodpeckers are abundant in the forest, with Red-headed, Red-bellied, Downy, and Hairy all existing here alongside Yellow-bellied Sapsuckers and Northern Flickers. Look for Hermit Thrushes, American Robins, and Northern Cardinals scratching through the leaf litter for insects or Brown Creepers scooting up the trunks of the trees. When I visited in November, the Carolina Wrens and Carolina Chickadees were up in arms about something and were issuing a warning to the forest. I could not see what they were upset about but suspect it was either a hawk or an owl, as they mobbed the upper parts of the canopy. The cemetery has some magnificent trees within the fenced area that are worth scanning for nesting birds in the spring. The best time to visit is between October and April when the bugs and snakes are less intense.

Nearby birding can be found at the Boykin Springs Recreation Area on Blue Lake or the Cassels-Boykin Park on Lake Sam Rayburn. Or just enjoy exploring the Angelina National Forest and Upland Island Wilderness.

Tombstone Tail: Carolina Wren

This rust-colored, compact bird with a dramatic white eyebrow can be found in the wooded areas of Texas and eastern parts of the United States. The males sing loud and often year-round, with greater frequency in the spring. Females of this type of wren do not share the gift of song. I like what Cornell Lab of Ornithology says about these bouncy, bold birds: "Pairs stay bonded year-round, with no vacation from singing or defending territory." My friend says she thinks it sounds like they are saying *cheese-burger, cheese-burger, cheese-burger*, which is an easy way to remember their call. They are attracted to wood and brush piles in yards where insects are abundant and will come to bird feeders for suet or mealworms. Healthy birds can live up to seven years.

Kountz: Hooks Cemetery
Highway 287 and Hooks Cemetery Loop

This is a great example of a family cemetery. East Texas is full of these types of small family cemeteries that served the communities for generations. There are over one thousand people buried here who were relations of the Hooks or their friends. Many of the graves are not marked; however, it seems the family has done some recent work to identify and mark some of the graves that were previously unidentified. The Hooks family has lived in the Big Thicket forest since the mid-1800s, and their descendants can still be found in the area.

It can be tough to see the birds here because they disappear into the dense forest. The openness of the cemetery allows you to peer into the forest to catch a glimpse of Eastern Towhees, American Robins, Hermit Thrushes, Brown Thrashers, or Chipping Sparrows. When I visited in February, I took a moment to close my eyes and listen to the forest. Pine Warblers, Carolina Wrens, and Northern Cardinals joined the chorus of rustling leaves and the passing breeze. As I continued my walk, a Red-shouldered Hawk passed overhead, and within seconds the Blue Jays began mocking the sound of the hawk to alert the others of its presence.

I was drawn to this cemetery because it is the final resting place of one of my nature heroes—Bessie Reid (1880–1962). Bessie and her best friend, Corrie Herring Hooks, advocated for the preservation of the Big Thicket forest and were astute, self-taught ornithologists and naturalists. (Corrie is buried at Magnolia Cemetery in Beaumont.) Bessie and Corrie were both founding members of the Big Thicket Association and

Tombstone Tale

Everything about this headstone suggests the person buried here was a life cut short. The open book suggests there were still chapters left to live. The falling rose in bloom suggests this was a female taken before she had a chance to bloom and mature.

Texas Ornithological Society. Bessie was also a folklorist who captured many Native American legends of Texas and the South in a book coauthored with Florence Stratton called *When the Storm God Rides: Tejas and Other Indian Legends*. Of modest means, Bessie and her husband, Bruce Reid, gave the land around their home near Village Creek to the Big Thicket National Preserve.

There are no paved or accessible paths at this location. Nearby birding can be found at Big Thicket National Preserve Headquarters and Visitor Center, Village Creek State Park, or Roy E. Larsen Sandyland Sanctuary near Silsbee.

Tombstone Tail: Red-shouldered Hawk

This talkative raptor can be found in the forested parts of Texas and the southeastern parts of the United States. Look for the distinct red shoulders and banded black-and-white tail when these hawks are in flight. Red-shoulders prefer to live and hunt near water and nest in tall trees, but they are not fish eaters. They prefer to dine on small mammals such as mice and rats or reptiles such as lizards and snakes. They return to the same nesting site year after year. When the parents are coaxing the fledglings out of the nest, they talk even more than usual, and they usually talk a lot. Blue Jays can mimic the calls of the Red-shoulders. Healthy birds can live up to twenty-five years.

Huntsville: Oakwood Cemetery
Ninth Street and Sam Houston Memorial Drive

Give yourself some time to immerse in Texas history at this location. The birding is fair, but the history is off the charts. As you enter, I recommend picking up a walking tour booklet at the kiosk to learn about the men, women, and children buried in the cemetery. There are also historical markers located throughout the grounds.

When you arrive off Sam Houston Memorial Drive and enter through the small gate to the walking path, you are greeted by the impressive monument of Sam Houston. The paved path meanders through the tall pine trees and past headstones of all sizes that represent the families of Huntsville. Perhaps one of the more interesting and peaceful places along the walking tour is the Rawley Rather Powell Memorial Park, otherwise

Tombstone Tale

The monument of Sam Houston was created by Pompeo Luigi Coppini (1870–1957), a prolific sculptor who immigrated to the United States from Florence, Italy. His work can be found in front of the Alamo in San Antonio and in several cemeteries listed in this book.

known as Wildwood Sanctuary. The sanctuary is about four acres and was given by the Powell family in memory of their five-year-old son, who died of complications from a tonsillectomy in 1923. Rawley Powell's mother, Marian Rather Powell (1881–1974), is credited with helping establish the state park system in Texas during the 1920s. She was also a champion of the suffrage movement in Walker County and active in the Federation of Women's Clubs. Marking the Powell family plot is a life-size bronze monument of *Christus* or *Comforting Jesus*, which is a replica that was originally designed by the famous Danish sculptor Bertel Thorvaldsen. The benches near the statue offer a comforting retreat to watch the birds.

The opulence of some of the memorials stands in stark contrast to the rows of crosses that mark a few of the unknown graves of enslaved people and early African Americans living in the county. The African American section is about three acres and was in use prior to the establishment of Oakwood. It is not known how many unmarked graves actually exist here, as it was overgrown with thick vegetation for many years.

As you meander down the paved historic walking path, be sure to look up into the towering trees during the fall and winter to watch for Red-breasted, White-breasted, and Brown-headed Nuthatches and Brown Creepers gleaning insects from the trunks. Northern Flickers and Yellow-bellied Sapsuckers also return in the fall to join the Red-headed, Red-bellied, Downy, and Hairy Woodpeckers that live in the area year-round. When I visited in February, the newer section of the cemetery across Martin Luther King Drive was busy with Chipping, White-crowned, and White-throated Sparrows; Pine Siskins; and Cedar Waxwings.

During the spring, the woods fill with the sights and sounds of resident birds such as Tufted Titmice, Carolina Chickadees, Northern Cardinals, and Blue Jays. The spring also brings the return of Northern Parulas, Yellow-billed Cuckoos, Mississippi Kites, and Ruby-throated Hummingbirds, all of which breed and nest in the area. I look forward to more checklists to be submitted from this location, as I suspect that Brown Thrashers and Hermit Thrushes could also be found here.

This cemetery has a designated parking area and paved walking path that make it accessible to people with limited mobility. Nearby birding can be found at Eastham Thomason Park or Huntsville State Park.

Tombstone Tail: Blue Jay

This noisy, large songbird can be found across most of the central and eastern parts of the United States. In Texas, Blue Jays are most abundant in the central, northern, and eastern parts of the state, with large populations living in urban areas. Northern birds occasionally migrate in large groups, while southern birds tend to remain in an area as long as the food is plentiful. These blue, black, and white birds mimic other birds, especially Red-shouldered Hawks, as a way to communicate danger to their social groups. When a warning signal is given, they will collectively mob a bird, snake, cat, or other predator. The brilliant blue color is achieved by refracting light from special cells on the barbs of their feathers. These intelligent birds can live more than twenty years and will form social groups called parties or scolds.

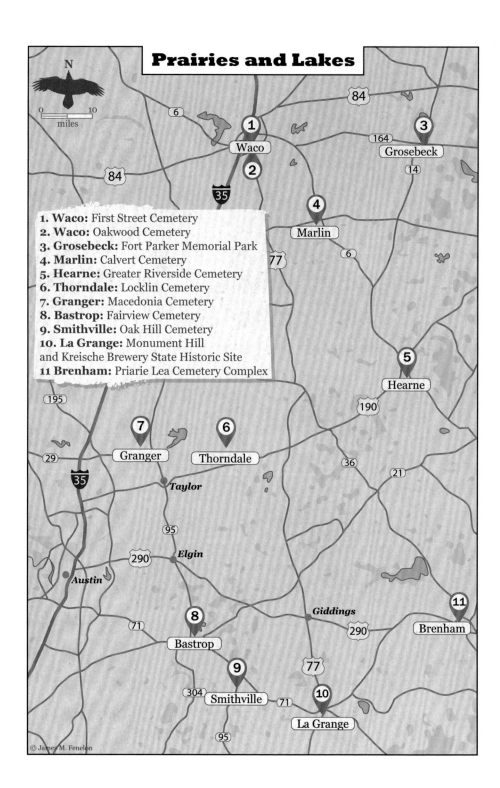

Prairies and Lakes

1. **Waco:** First Street Cemetery
2. **Waco:** Oakwood Cemetery
3. **Grosebeck:** Fort Parker Memorial Park
4. **Marlin:** Calvert Cemetery
5. **Hearne:** Greater Riverside Cemetery
6. **Thorndale:** Locklin Cemetery
7. **Granger:** Macedonia Cemetery
8. **Bastrop:** Fairview Cemetery
9. **Smithville:** Oak Hill Cemetery
10. **La Grange:** Monument Hill
and Kreische Brewery State Historic Site
11 **Brenham:** Priarie Lea Cemetery Complex

© James M. Fenelon

Prairies and Lakes

The Prairies and Lakes region is nestled between the Piney Woods to the east, the Hill Country to the west, and the Gulf Coast to the south. It comprises two ecoregions: Blackland Prairie and Post Oak Savanna. Prior to Anglo settlement there were not large lakes in this region; instead, the creeks and rivers made their way uninhibited to the Gulf of Mexico. Since that time, many of the rivers and creeks have been dammed to form reservoirs to supply the thirsty urban population with water. According to the Texas Water Board, there are 196 reservoirs in Texas at this time, with more being considered. The lakes also provide year-round recreation opportunities for people and habitat for waterfowl and inland shorebirds. However, the reservoirs also flood millions of acres of bottomlands that were rich habitats for birds, wildlife, timber, and agriculture.

The Blackland Prairie has rich soil that can grow most anything with a little irrigated water supplied from the reservoirs. Texas Parks and Wildlife describes the region as having "luxuriant native grasslands" that attracted early settlers. The large prairies were easily turned into fields of cotton, corn, wheat, or pasturelands for cattle and horses. Prior to Anglo settlement the tallgrass prairies were home to the Wichita, Tawakoni, Caddo, and Bidai nations. Once the Comanche acquired and mastered the horse, they moved through parts of the region as they followed the migrating herds of bison.

TPWD describes the regions as historically having "wide vistas of tall-grass—little bluestem, Indiangrass, switchgrass and a myriad of wildflowers were broken only by the occasional motte of trees giving the landscape a park like atmosphere." The open spaces are punctuated with stands of blackjacks and post oaks, pecans, and cedar elms, which is an excellent mix for wildlife. The forests, grasslands, and variety of water sources support an exciting mix of birds in all seasons.

Waco: First Street Cemetery
100 Texas Ranger Trail

First Street Cemetery is Waco's first and oldest public cemetery. This is a unique location in that many of the headstones and coffins were relocated to Oakwood Cemetery to make room for the interstate, park, and later the Texas Rangers Hall of Fame and Museum. There are still headstones and graves left of the original Masonic and Odd-fellows cemetery that was established in the 1850s. The connecting Hebrew cemetery is completely intact. Both the cemeteries and the park have majestic live oak and pecan trees that were there long before the first settlers were interred along the banks of the mighty Brazos River.

The first people to live in the area were the Hueco, a minor tribe of the Wichita. When Stephen F. Austin's scouts first came across the Hueco, they noted that the tribe was small, lacked warriors, but had crops and livestock that were easily sustained by the fertile land and fresh water. The scout also reported that the Hueco had access to a clear, cold-water spring in the vicinity of what is now Indian Springs Park.

By the 1860s, Waco was a booming town and an important crossing of the Brazos River for the Chisholm Trail cattle drives. In 1866, some innovative folks from the Waco Bridge Company constructed a 475-foot long suspension bridge across the

Tombstone Tale

The menorah is one of the most recognizable Jewish symbols. The seven lit candles in the candelabrum represent unity, devotion, and the divine light of God.

expansive Brazos to charge tolls to the cattle drivers. Some paid the tolls, while others risked swimming their cattle across the river. By 1871, more than six hundred thousand head of cattle had stomped their way through town. The bridge still exists and is just north of the cemetery along the Waco River Walk. The cattle drive was a short-lived industry for Waco, while cotton was the economic king for many decades until fires and crop failures finally forced the area to diversify. The Cotton Palace opened in 1909 and hosted an annual fair that attracted thousands of people from around the country. In 1923, more than one hundred thousand people attended the fair in a single day.

The other big economic and social powerhouse in the region was education. Baylor University moved from Independence, Texas, to Waco in 1886 and is the oldest continuously operating university in Texas. It was also the first university in the state to offer a degree in law. Women were allowed to attend the university starting in 1887 but did not have access to all the courses offered until much later. In 1964, African Americans were finally allowed to attend. Many of Waco's founders are buried along the life-giving river in the First Street Cemetery.

The proximity of the cemetery to the river offers birders access to a fair amount of ducks and shorebirds that can be seen from the cemetery and connecting park. The proximity to I-35 does make it feel like an urban space, but I have been pleased with the number of species I have observed on each visit. During the spring and summer, look for Scissor-tailed and Great Crested Flycatchers, Western and Eastern Kingbirds, White-eyed and Red-eyed Vireos, and Northern Shrikes to launch from the trees or headstones as they chase after insects. The fall and winter bring the return of Chipping, White-crowned, Harris's, White-throated, Song, and Lincoln's Sparrows. If black-birds are your thing, then you are in luck, as Red-winged Blackbirds, Brown-headed Cowbirds, Common and Great-tailed Grackles, and Baltimore Orioles all frequent the grounds during migration or as residents.

This cemetery is not suitable for people with limited mobility since there is not a paved or hard-surface path or road. Nearby birding is good year-round at Oakwood Cemetery, Cameron Park, Woodway Park, and Waco Mammoth National Monument.

Tombstone Tail: Great-tailed Grackle

This iridescent black-and-purple social bird forms large flocks that come to roost on winter evenings in cities across Texas except in the far east or west. They are expressive birds that are constantly chattering to each other in loud, cackling calls. Great-tailed Grackles were not common in Texas until the 1960s, when agriculture and development expanded, thus expanding their range north from Mexico. Now they can be found in multiple states north and east of Texas. They are opportunistic feeders; watch for them to be feeding and strutting along in parks, neighborhood lawns, school campuses, or parking lots searching for bugs, tidbits of trash, frogs, or lizards. I often refer to them as parking lot birding royalty.

Waco: Oakwood Cemetery
2124 South Fifth Street

This large, 157-acre cemetery was established in 1878 on a plot of land outside town on a defunct fairground and racetrack. Some of the headstones have older dates, as they were relocated here from the First Street Cemetery. There are two adjacent cemeteries, Holy Cross Cemetery and McLennan County Restland Cemetery, which add to the suitable habitat for birds and offer more opportunity to explore.

Tombstone Tale

Rustic-style headstones and architecture were popular at the turn of the nineteenth century. As part of the arts and crafts movement, the rough-hewn style often incorporated elements of nature, including lettering that seems to be made of sticks. The rustic elements can also be paired with elegant pieces such as a marble angel or polished scroll to represent the meeting of the perfect world of the afterlife with the rougher world of the living.

As soon as visitors pass through the gates, they will notice that the grounds are meticulously maintained. Since 1898, the site has been cared for by the Oakwood Cemetery Association, which is made up solely of women, as directed in the original bylaws. The main drive is surrounded by a tunnel of green formed by planted rows of live oak trees. The original part of the cemetery is laid out in a traditional grid with curbed and fenced family plots alongside individual graves surrounded by a grid of paved streets. The newer section features looping streets that weave in and out of groves of trees and several open grass lawns.

There are hundreds of stunning headstones that are truly works of art along with an entire city of angels that graces the grounds along with obelisks, statues, and even a few modern art pieces. Oakwood, like so many early Texas cemeteries, is filled with first- and second-generation immigrants who wanted the community to know they had "made it." Having a large or custom headstone was a symbol of wealth and societal importance—two things they could not have achieved in the socially static countries of Europe. The names on the headstones reflect the waves of immigrants who arrived in Texas from England, Scotland, Germany, Sweden, Russia, Greece, Italy, Spain, Mexico, and beyond. Many of the headstone inscriptions note where the individual was born or came from. Not all moved directly from a foreign country; many new Texans arrived from other states hoping for an opportunity to seek their fortune or join a family member. One of the more well-known people buried here is Pat Morris Neff (1871–1952), the twenty-eighth governor of Texas. Neff pushed for the creation of the state park system in Texas in the 1920s. He and his mother, Isabel Neff, gave a portion of their family lands to form one of the first state parks. Mother Neff State Park is located just down the road outside Moody.

The large live oak, pecan, magnolia, and pine trees offer good habitat for migrating warblers and vireos, as well as for many of the resident birds, including a healthy variety of woodpeckers such as the Red-bellied, Hairy, Ladder-backed, and Downy. Some of the other resident birds include Carolina Chickadees, Carolina Wrens, and White-winged Doves. During the spring and summer, Chimney Swifts, Purple Martins, and Common Nighthawks return to the area to nest and feed. If you are lucky, you might also catch a glimpse of Painted Buntings, Blue Grosbeaks, and Dickcissels feeding on the native grasses just beyond the fence line at the back of the cemetery. Scissor-tailed Flycatchers use the open grasslands, and the telephone wires above, from May to September. During the winter, look for the return of Blue-gray Gnatcatchers, Cedar Waxwings, Ruby-crowned Kinglets, and Blue-headed Vireos. It is common to find over twenty species of birds at this location during the spring and fall migrations.

The shaded, paved roads of Oakwood make for excellent birding for people with wheeled mobility devices. Nearby birding locations can be found at the First Street Cemetery and Fort Fisher Park, Cameron Park, and Lake Waco Wetlands.

Tombstone Tail: White-winged Dove

This bird is one of the conservation success stories of Texas. As I stated in *Parking Lot Birding*, "This bird, which seems so abundant now, was once down to just around five hundred thousand birds. In the 1920s and 1930s heavy agriculture (especially in the Rio Grande Valley) reduced the traditional nesting habitats by 90 percent. Overhunting also reduced the populations; however, through conservation efforts and regulated hunting the birds have made a comeback and are thriving. Their range now covers most of Texas and Mexico. By the 1980s the birds started expanding their range and can now be found as far north as Maine in limited numbers. I love to hear them cooing during the spring in my yard in Austin" (121).

Groesbeck: Fort Parker Memorial Park

Two miles northwest of Groesbeck on FM 1245

I was pleasantly surprised by this cemetery at every level. The cedar-lined drive offers a welcoming entrance to the cemetery and adjacent park. In the center of the cemetery is a larger-than-life statue representing the pioneer Parker family who settled the area in 1833. The base of the statue, known as the Pioneer Monument, was installed in 1922 when the citizens of Limestone County convinced the Texas legislature to appropriate a portion of the funds to create the granite columns and pedestal. The statue of Silas, Lucy, and Cynthia Ann Parker was added in 1932.

In 1836, Fort Parker was attacked by a group of Kiowa and Comanche. The attack left two wounded and five settlers taken. One of those taken was Cynthia Ann Parker, who later married the Comanche chief Peta Nocona and had three children. One of

Tombstone Tale

It is unusual to have so many graves marked with a headstone that simply reads "Unknown." According to the Limestone County Historical Commission, there are hundreds of unmarked graves in the cemetery. The headstones were placed to represent a section of them; however, it is unclear how many actually exist.

those children became the last free Comanche chief, Quanah Parker. The saga of the Parker family has captured the imagination of storytellers for generations. There are dozens of books, both fiction and nonfiction, written about them.

The birding is good from the second you pull through the gates to the time you drive past them on your way out. The drive from the gates to the cemetery is lined with cedars and flanked by fields that host a variety of birds throughout the year. When I visited in January after a snowstorm had blown through two days before, I was pleased to find flocks of birds voraciously feeding. Savannah, White-throated, and White-crowned Sparrows; Dark-eyed Juncos; Yellow-rumped Warblers; Pine Siskins; and American Robins all pecked along through the dormant grasses while Eastern Bluebirds and Eastern Phoebes perched on the headstones waiting for insects to emerge as the day warmed. As I walked around the looping road, I spooked up a Great Horned Owl that swooped out of a large pecan tree. The owl was instantly mobbed by a pair of Blue Jays and a Northern Mockingbird.

In the fields beyond the cemetery there were a substantial number of Eastern Meadowlarks and Killdeers scampering along the ground. At the back of the cemetery there is a pasture with a stock pond that hosted Canada Geese, American Wigeons, Northern Shovelers, and one other species of duck that I was unable to identify. A Great Blue Heron, warming in the sun, rested on the edge of the pond. There is an additional pond at Todd Park, which is connected to the cemetery and offers picnic tables where you can sit and watch the birds or just listen to the breeze roll across the plains.

On my visit in January, I spotted thirty-six species of birds and would have kept making observations if I had not been pressed for time to return to Austin. When I visited again in June, a Crested Caracara launched from the road as I entered the gates. I was also pleased to observe Painted Buntings, Yellow-billed Cuckoos, and an Acadian Flycatcher on that visit. I have returned to this location six times and am always pleased with the abundance of birds. There are now fifteen checklists with seventy-three species recorded on eBird.

There is not an accessible parking space here, but the paved roads are acceptable for people with limited mobility. The roads of the cemetery are narrow, so it is best to park near Todd Park and walk the grounds. Nearby birding can be found at Fort Parker State Park, Trading House Creek Reservoir, and several points along Lake Limestone.

Tombstone Tail: Yellow-rumped Warbler

This is one of the most abundant winter birds in Texas. While wintering, and in nonbreeding colors, these warblers can appear to be a nondescript little brownish bird with one distinct marking—the yellow spot on its rump. When the males don their breeding plumage, they are sharp-looking birds with slate-gray, black, and white on their heads and body and yellow patches just under the top of the wing. The Myrtle subspecies of this warbler has a black mask and white throat, while the Audubon's has no mask and a yellow throat. There is talk about separating the subspecies into their own species as they are visually quite distinct from one another. Yellow-rumps winter farther north than most warblers and will migrate to Canada and Alaska to breed. These small birds have adapted well to a variety of habitats as they are able to consume a wider array of food that includes insects, seeds and fruits.

Marlin: Calvary Cemetery
Fortune and Burnet Streets

There is a lot to like about this rural cemetery. The rolling hills, majestic live oaks, looping roads, and lovely headstones all create a tranquil setting where you can listen to the symphony of birds on a warm spring morning. The cemetery is flanked on two sides by a wet-weather creek that has a respectable number of willow trees and understory brush to support a host of migrating and resident birds. I suggest taking your time exploring the entire cemetery, with special attention to the perimeter road that allows you to peer into the dense woodlands along the creek.

The creek area is a good place to look for Lincoln's Sparrows, Hermit Thrushes, and American Robins in the fall and winter. During the spring migration watch for passing American Redstarts and Nashville and Black-throated Green Warblers. Watch the tops of the pecan trees for Yellow-bellied Cuckoos and Yellow Warblers. Up on the hill in the open spaces is where you will find some of the resident birds such as Killdeers, Northern Cardinals, Blue Jays, and Northern Mockingbirds. During the spring and summer, the open spaces are host to Barn Swallows gracefully sweeping past the headstones looking for insects.

There are several live oak trees that are well over two hundred years old that were full of Blue-gray Gnatcatchers and Ruby-crowned Kinglets feeding voraciously on

Tombstone Tale

There are plenty of headstones that convey what the departed did professionally. This creative headstone is shaped like a power pole with a cameo of the lineman.

insects when I visited in April. The Tufted Titmice and Carolina Chickadees were feeding in the live oaks as well, but they were not moving nearly as fast as the gnatcatchers or kinglets. On that same visit the White-eyed Vireos and Lark Sparrows were busy singing from the treetops.

The twenty-five-acre cemetery was formally established in 1862; however, there were several burials in the "old section" that date back to the 1850s. I was surprised that there was not a historical marker at the front gate or at any of the graves. There is an unofficial historical marker at the graveside of Senator Thomas Connally. This is also the final resting place of a nature hero of mine—Jeffie Davis Pringle Wardlaw (1878–1968). Jeffie was a teacher for many years and was active in the Federation of Women's Clubs. In 1940, she joined the Big Bend Park Association, which was tasked with making the case to turn Big Bend into a national park. Jeffie rode her horse and camped in most parts of what is now Big Bend National Park and was in high demand as a speaker to share her knowledge and passion about the wild spaces of the region. Jeffie and the Big Bend Park Association were successful, and in 1944, just six days after the D-Day invasion of Normandy, Big Bend was officially made Texas' first national park. Jeffie is buried next to her husband, Judge Louis Wardlaw.

The streets are paved and accessible in most of the cemetery. There are several steep hills that might make it difficult to maneuver a wheelchair alone or without an able assistant. Nearby birding can be found at Marlin City Park, which has a pond and walking trails, or at Falls on the Brazos Park.

Tombstone Tail: Carolina Chickadee

Central Texas is considered the western edge of this forest-loving little black, gray, and white bird. Carolina Chickadees look very similar to the Black-capped Chickadee, which lives in the northern United States and parts of Canada. Pairs do not mate for life; however, research shows they will stay together for many years. They typically nest in small tree cavities or will use birdhouses and on average will raise one clutch each year. They are one of the easiest birds for children or beginner birders to learn to identify, as they frequently visit bird feeders. When I am filling my feeders, I love to hear their joyful calls. Some think their calls say *chick-a-dee*, but I think they say *time-to-eat* or *look-at-me*.

Hearne: Greater Riverside Cemetery
Old Mumford Road

This burial ground has served the African American community of Hearne since 1894, when it was known as the New Colored Cemetery. The Old Colored Cemetery was actually located in what is now considered "old town" in Hearne. The Old Colored Cemetery now consists of a single grave belonging to a former enslaved woman, Hollie Tatnell (d. 1911). Her children refused to move her grave when developers bought the property and forced the other families to move their loved ones. Hollie's family believed deeply in the sanctity of burial and purpose of place, forcing the developers to build around her grave.

The plantation system arrived in the 1830s in Robertson's Colony with the new influx of farmers who had worn out their lands in other parts of the country. For over thirty years enslaved people toiled in the fertile but treacherous bottomlands of the Brazos River. Even after the abolishment of slavery, the Reconstruction-era

Tombstone Tale

The finger pointing upward to the crown means the departed has returned to the kingdom of heaven.

tenant farm system and Jim Crow laws continued the oppression of African Americans. Eventually, farming did become a profitable endeavor for many of the African American families who stayed in Robertson County, and many of those families are represented at the cemetery alongside the teachers, preachers, business owners, and a multitude of those who served in the military.

Greater Riverside is a large twenty-four-acre cemetery with plenty of native grasses, shrubs, and trees to support a variety of year-round and seasonal birds. When I first arrived, I did not see many birds along the main road. It was not until I walked along the edges where the open space of the cemetery met the woods that I started to see flocks of White-crowned Sparrows, Dark-eyed Juncos, Pine Siskins, and Cedar Waxwings. The sky was bluebird blue that day in November, and I watched a Red-tailed Hawk circle and pass out of view, only to be replaced by a pair of Red-shouldered Hawks. Speaking of bluebirds, there were plenty of Eastern Bluebirds perching on the post oaks and blackjack trees, while American Robins and Northern Cardinals hopped around on the ground. I watched a little brown bird scoot along the trunk of a tree and at first thought it was a wren, but after further investigation determined it was a Brown Creeper. When I returned in June, I was dazzled by the number of Scissor-tailed Flycatchers and Western Kingbirds. On that visit I also spotted Lark Sparrows, White-winged Doves, and a male Painted Bunting.

The gravel and dirt roads make for easy walking but are not suitable for a wheelchair or wheeled walker. That said, it is easy to see all that the location has to offer from a vehicle. Nearby birding can be found at Ruben Gomez Eastside Park in Hearne or Lake Bryan in Bryan.

Tombstone Tail: Downy Woodpecker

This is the smallest woodpecker in North America and can be seen foraging for insects on trees or at feeders that offer suet or a seed mix it prefers. Males tend to feed higher on a tree, while females feed on the middle and lower parts. Males have a small red rim on the back of their black-and-white head—a feature the females lack. They do not migrate and can be found across the forested regions of North America. Because they are adapted to living around people, they are frequently found in city parks, neighborhoods, and cemeteries. They have an advantage over larger woodpeckers in that they can nest in smaller cavities and smaller trees.

Thorndale: Locklin Cemetery

4903 FM 486

I was exploring the prairies east of Austin during the spring migration when I stumbled on this small, remote cemetery situated on a low hill just south of the San Gabriel River. From atop the rise it is easy to peer into the prairie that surrounds the cemetery and to view the small pond located just beyond the fence.

The wetlands have several large willow trees that are a good place to look for migrating warblers. The wetlands also support Great Blue and Green Herons, Great Egrets, and Red-winged Blackbirds. During the spring migration, the grasslands are filled with Dickcissels, Scissor-tailed and Great Crested Flycatchers, and Eastern Meadowlarks. When I visited again in November, I was pleased to find sixteen species in my short visit, including Vesper and Chipping Sparrows, Killdeers, and a Loggerhead Shrike. Some of the raptors include Red-tailed Hawks, Crested Caracaras, American Kestrels, and Cooper's Hawks.

The cemetery was established in 1844 by the Locklin family. The first burial on the site took place around 1840 after the local blacksmith died. Prior to the arrival of Europeans, this was the land of the Bidai, Deadose, and Akokisa tribes, who shared a common language and were part of the Atakapa. When the Spaniards established three missions along the San Xavier River (San Gabriel River) in 1749, they began converting the Native Americans to Christianity and used them as slaves on their farms. The cultivated lands and clusters of people became a target for the nomadic Apache. In 1755, after several raids and internal conflict among the missionaries, the missions were abandoned. The Bidai and other tribes suffered more from diseases introduced by the Spaniards than they did at the hands of the Apache and later the Comanche. W. W. Newcomb Jr. reports in *The Indians of Texas from Prehistoric to Modern Times* that the Bidai numbered only around one hundred men and women by 1830, with

Tombstone Tale

The horse or pony is often associated with courage, strength, and generosity. It can also mean the person buried had a strong relationship with this elegant, powerful creature.

some intermarried to the Koasati. With the Native Americans removed from the area by the 1840s, the lands opened up to the waves of American and European families such as the Locklins. There is a book at the pavilion that tells more about the history of the families.

This cemetery offers easy walking along the gravel roads but is not suitable for wheeled mobility devices. There is a pavilion that offers a relaxing, shaded space to look for birds. Nearby birding can be found at Apache Crossing Park or the many parks around Granger Lake. The IOOF Cemetery in Rockdale is also a nice placed to bird; however, the species will be similar to those at Locklin.

Tombstone Tail: Killdeer

The males and the females of this plover share the same distinct black-and-white neck rings and headband. While they prefer feeding in the grasslands of parks and pastures, they are also proficient swimmers and will wade into shallow water to feed. They lay their eggs in swallow depressions in the ground, which makes them susceptible to being stepped on by livestock or mowed over with lawn mowers and agricultural equipment. Parents will try to lure predators away from their nests by pretending to have a broken wing. They can be found year-round in Texas, with some migrating to parts of the northern United States and southern Canada.

Granger: Macedonia Cemetery

401 County Road 376

This might be one of my favorite cemeteries to bird, as I have recorded over sixty species here and discover more each time I visit. My highest count came on a cool day in May when I observed thirty-seven species in two hours. During the early, uncertain months of the COVID-19 pandemic, I visited here many times to escape to a peaceful space away from other people where I could tune out the constant barrage of doom-and-gloom news.

Macedonia is a great example of an early-Texas farm community that has gone by the wayside. All that remains to tell the town's short-lived tale are the headstones and descendants of the pioneers. In the 1870s, a number of German families moved to the area to establish a community on the banks of Opossum Creek just west of the town of Granger. In its heyday it had a church, gin, schoolhouse, store, and even a Masonic Lodge. Macedonia Lodge No. 443 was established in 1874, but after the town declined, the lodge was moved to Granger. What the simple country cemetery lacks in grand monuments, it makes up for in enchanting peacefulness.

Tombstone Tale

A lychgate, or corpse gate, is an Anglo-Saxon tradition, most popular in the Victorian era. The funeral procession would enter through the ceremonial arched gate. The meaning is unclear, but most evidence points to the idea that it symbolically separates the land of the living from the land of the departed. Everyday visitors were invited to enter through a smaller gate.

At the cemetery I find the most birds along the western fence line and in the large pecan tree near the back. Dickcissels and Eastern Meadowlarks can be found in the field, which has an abundance of prairie grasses and flowers that waver in the breeze. Because it is the prairie, keep an eye out for White-crowned, White-throated, Lincoln's, Song, Grasshopper, and Chipping Sparrows to be present during the winter and early spring. Northern Harriers often float along the fields just beyond the fence during the winter. The winter also brings large flocks of Brewer's Blackbirds and Common Grackles that can be seen moving as one across the landscape. On one of my visits in December I witnessed over two hundred Common Grackles roosting in the trees along the road. Check the telephone wires and fence posts for American Kestrels and Crested Caracaras.

On a visit in May 2020 I took one of my favorite photos of a Yellow-bellied Cuckoo that was hunting for caterpillars in the pecan tree. That same day I spotted a Common Nighthawk sleeping in the hackberry tree in the middle of the cemetery and an Eastern Kingbird calling from the top of the dead cedar tree. I took my time to observe each bird and felt a special connection with them on that morning.

Every time I visit the cemetery, I stroll down the country road and marvel at the giant pecan trees and look for Red-bellied and Ladder-backed Woodpeckers, Carolina Wrens, and American Robins. During the spring it is common to find migrants such as Nashville, Magnolia, and Yellow Warblers along with American Redstarts in the understory along the creek.

This location is not suitable for persons with limited mobility, nor does it have a restroom. Nearby birding can be found at Berry Springs Park and Preserve in Georgetown, Granger Lake parks outside Granger, and Murphy Park in Taylor.

Tombstone Tail: Dickcissel

This grassland bird breeds in Texas, across the Midwest, and in parts of the eastern United States and winters in Central and South America. The males and females have a flashy yellow chest with a distinct yellow eye bar. The males have a black V on their chest. Their song is a grassland classic and sounds much like their name. During the winter they will form large flocks that number into the millions. In their winter grounds in Venezuela, their roosts have been sprayed with poison in the past to kill the birds, as the government considered them pests. Like many grassland birds, habitat loss is a threat to their population as native prairies are converted into agriculture. They often place their nests near the ground, which makes them susceptible to being damaged by livestock and predation.

Bastrop: Fairview Cemetery
1409 Highway 95 North

Imagine taking a ship from Germany to Galveston in 1841 with dreams of a new life. After landing in Galveston, imagine walking or bouncing along in a wagon across the coastal plains through the post oak savannas all the way to Bastrop. Now imagine making that same journey with yellow fever. Crescentia Augusta Fischer, a German immigrant, died of yellow fever just five days after reaching the paradise of the Lost Pines of Bastrop. She is one of the first people to be interred at the newly formed Fairview Cemetery. Her grave sits at the top of the hill where she can listen to the breeze whispering through the large loblolly pines and blackjack oaks for all eternity.

The cemetery is home to a who's-who list of Texas pioneers, civic leaders, and war heroes spanning from the Texas Revolution to the War in Afghanistan. The pavilion provides information, and there are several historical markers throughout the grounds, including one for Robert Kerr, who served as the first African American representative for Bastrop County from 1880 to 1882. The cemetery is considered one of the most historic in the state.

Tombstone Tale

Metal fences were used by many cultures; however, in Texas it was most popular among German families. Fences offered protection for graves in a time when many cemeteries were not fenced and were open to livestock passing through.

During World War II over three hundred thousand troops trained at Camp Swift just north of Bastrop. Another large population existed at the German internment camp located next to the army base. As a result of this transitory population of young men, there were a number of unexpected children, many of whom died. Because of this sad fact, Hasler Brothers Funeral Home crafted small coffins for the children and even purchased doll's clothing to dress them in for a proper burial. They secured a space at the cemetery in an area watched over by the beautiful War Babies Guardian Angel. It is a sobering reminder of how that war touched communities all across the country.

On a lighter note, when I worked in the film industry, one of the movies I worked on filmed a scene at the cemetery, and my name was on one of the fake headstones. The movie was called *My Boyfriend's Back*, and it was a zombie love story. My brother, Mark Bristol, created the storyboards for the movie, and to this day it was one of the most fun projects we worked on together.

Because the cemetery is located on a hill, it provides a good vantage point to see migrating flocks of Snow Geese, Sandhill Cranes, or American White Pelicans. On a clear day in May at about two o'clock my mother and I watched hundreds of American White Pelicans twist and turn as they searched for the right thermal to take them north. I like to think they made it past Waco that day as they journeyed from the Gulf Coast toward the Midwest and Canada.

It is not uncommon to see Bald Eagles at this location, as they move back and forth from Lake Bastrop and the Colorado River. At the top of the hill, toward the fence line, there is a mulberry tree that was being mobbed by Cedar Waxwings, Baltimore Orioles, Northern Cardinals, and Blue Jays when I visited in April. The yaupon and brush on the other side of the fence provide decent cover for birds to hide in and then launch out to snatch a bug or feed along the ground. The large loblollys provide suitable habitat for Pine Warblers in the winter and spring and year-round for Pileated and Red-bellied Woodpeckers. During the winter, look for Field, White-crowned, White-throated, Chipping, and Savannah Sparrows to be feeding in the grasses or along the fence lines. The American Goldfinches, American Pipits, and Pine Siskins also return in the winter and can often be found in large flocks.

The roads here are paved; however, the steep slopes of the hills might make it difficult for someone using a wheeled or seated mobility device. Nearby birding locations can be found at Bastrop and Buescher State Parks, Lake Bastrop North or South Shore Parks, and the Colorado River Refuge.

Tombstone Tail: Pine Warbler

This yellow-and-buff warbler can be found year-round in the Lost Pines and East Texas forests. The populations increase in those areas during the winter as migrating birds arrive from the northeast. Their joyful, high-trill song can be heard throughout the tall pine forests in Texas and is something I associate with Bastrop. It is often easier to hear than see them as they work along the tops of the pines looking for insects. During the winter and in breeding season they will eat seeds and fruits, which means they will occasionally come to feeders. They spend the majority of their lives in or near pine trees; they build their nests in them from pine needles and bark, as well as forage for food in them. Deforestation is their greatest threat, although their populations currently seem stable.

Smithville: Oak Hill Cemetery
473 South State Highway 95

The earliest burials on this lovely hill date back to the 1880s. As you enter the gates, you will be greeted by the cemetery's namesake. The majestic live oaks grace the grounds along with blackjack oaks and cedars. The large trees support a plethora of resident and migrating birds year-round, with best birds and flowers existing from March to October. I love birding and exploring at Buescher State Park, especially since I used to work for the Bastrop and Buescher State Park complex. However, it is more difficult to bird in the dense forest and underbrush at the park. I enjoy the openness of this large, rural cemetery.

The town of Smithville has an interesting history, and many of its founders and their families are buried here. For example, one of those families is Emil (1864–1931) and Elizabeth Buescher (1874–1948), who gave the first 318 acres of land in the pine forest for the purpose of a state park. An article in the *Austin American Statesman* dated January 27, 1925, states that Emil Buescher, "president of the First State Bank here, has donated 100 acres of land a few miles from town for a state park. The deed

Tombstone Tale

The swastika is generally associated with the Nazi Party of Germany after its rise in the 1930s. However, the symbol has a longer history among religions such as Hinduism, Buddhism, and Jainism that are prevalent in India and Asia. The Greeks also used the motif to symbolize Zeus. The right-facing swastika often represents the sun, prosperity, and good luck. Variations of the symbol and its spiritual meaning can be found throughout cultures across the world.

has been sent to D. E. Colp of San Antonio, chairman of the parks commission." Under the direction of Governor Pat Neff, Colp and the newly formed State Parks Board were soliciting lands from willing donors to create a system of parks. It is reported that Governor Neff called Emil personally to request that he help preserve the natural beauty of the pines and prairie region and give a parcel of land. Emil Buescher was a businessman and president of the First State Bank in Smithville, and his wife was active in the garden club and a number of other community organizations. The garden clubs had long supported the establishment of a state park system and the concept known as the "Good Roads" movement (Colp was chair of the movement). The state parks were to be located along new good roads/state highways, a concept the Bueschers favored for their town. After the initial gifts of 300 acres of land between 1925 and 1930, the Buescher family gave an additional 318 acres once Emil passed away. Buescher State Park is now over 1,000 acres in size, with its headquarters located just off good road Highway 95.

I am not sure how many acres the cemetery includes, but if you walk the perimeter roads, it is a little over a mile. The perimeter is where the action is for the birds as they dart in and out of the brush that lines the fences or scamper through the grasses and wildflowers. During the winter, look for White-crowned, Savannah, Chipping, and Field Sparrows throughout the grounds, with the most activity occurring along the fences. The winter is also a good time to see American Kestrels, Red-tailed and Red-shouldered Hawks, and Crested Caracaras either perched along the electrical wires along Highway 95 or circling overhead. The pasture along the south side of the cemetery has plenty of Brown-headed Cowbirds, Killdeers, Eastern Meadowlarks, Cattle Egrets, and Common Grackles. The pasture also has a small creek that flows through it and a wet-weather pond that is attractive to spring migrants. Listen and look for the Pileated Woodpecker in the dead trees just past the creek. Northern Parulas, Summer Tanagers, and Painted Buntings all migrate to and nest in the area from April to September.

There is not a restroom at this location, but there is a nice pavilion that offers shade and a place to sit. The dirt roads are easy to walk; however, they are not ADA friendly. Nearby birding can be found at Buescher State Park or Vernon Richards Riverbend Park.

Tombstone Tail: Northern Parula

This bluish-gray, yellow, and buff-colored warbler builds its nest from Spanish moss and beard lichens. These warblers summer and breed in the eastern part of the North America from Florida to Canada. Due to increased pollution and clear-cutting, there has been a reduction in Spanish moss and beard lichens in forests within this warbler's range. Luckily, Smithville has an abundance of Spanish moss. It is not always easy to spot these warblers as they glean insects from the canopy of mature forests.

La Grange: Monument Hill and Kreische Brewery State Historic Site

414 State Loop 92

This is a place where Texas history and birding really come together in one great package. When you arrive, you will have lots of opportunities to learn about the men buried on Monument Hill, as well as the Kreische family, who built the brewery and stone house. Both state historic sites are surrounded by forty acres of rolling hills that have commanding views of the Colorado River and the town of La Grange. For many

Tombstone Tale

Large tombs are more common in the Mediterranean, pre-Columbian Americas, and Europe than in Texas. Tombs are often used to house the remains of one significant person or multiple people who suffered an unfortunate event together. This tomb is unusual because of its low, wide profile.

years, TPWD oversaw the management of the properties; however, during the 2000s the state legislature moved oversight and management to the Texas Historical Commission.

The birding at Monument Hill is good most of the year, with over 120 species of birds recorded at this location. In the spring, look for the return of Northern Parulas, which will nest in the live oak forest of the hill. The Painted Buntings also nest in the area, along with Purple Martins, Barn and Cliff Swallows, Chimney Swifts, Mississippi Kites, and Common Nighthawks. Spring migrants include Common Yellowthroats; American Redstarts; Chestnut-sided, Magnolia, and Yellow Warblers; and seven types of flycatchers.

During the fall and winter, look for the return of raptors. Many raptors live in the area year-round, including Bald Eagles, Red-shouldered and Red-tailed Hawks, Crested Caracaras, and Barred Owls. I did not find reports of Swainson's or Broad-winged Hawks on eBird for this location, which I find surprising since this area is on their spring and fall migration path. In the fall, keep your eyes on the sky to watch for migrating flocks of geese, ducks, and Sandhill Cranes. The treetops are busy in the fall and winter with Ruby-crowned Kinglets, Yellow-Rumped and Pine Warblers, along with American Goldfinches and Cedar Waxwings. While strolling along the ravine trail in the fall, watch for movement in the underbrush for Chipping Sparrows, Hermit Thrushes, and American Robins.

In December, the brewery and stone house are transformed into a winter wonderland. If you get a chance to do a little late-afternoon birding, stay for the holiday lights to come on at the brewery. It is an adventure worth experiencing.

There are paved, accessible trails, ADA parking, and a bathroom at this location. Nearby birding can be found at Buescher State Park, White Rocks Park, Lake Fayette Prairie Park, or Plum Park on the Colorado. The old city cemetery in the town of La Grange is worth a visit to learn more about the town and the people. The birding is not great there, but the history is rich, and the monuments are beautiful.

Tombstone Tail: Bald Eagle

This powerful raptor has represented the United States as the national bird since 1782. We did not always treat the eagles with the respect one might think a national bird deserves. As a result of the chemical DDT and overhunting, only four hundred nesting pairs remained in 1960 in the lower forty-eight states. Thanks to conservation efforts and the banning of DDT, the eagles made a comeback across North America. In Texas, they can be found in most ecoregions along rivers and lakes where fish are abundant. When hunting, they can reach speeds of up to two hundred miles per hour when in a power dive. Their nests can be up to six feet in diameter and weigh up to a ton, which means they need large mature trees near water to nest. Healthy birds can live up to forty years. They were removed from the endangered species list in 2007.

Brenham: Prairie Lea Cemetery Complex

1003 Prairie Lea Street

When most Texans think of Brenham, they think about indulging with Blue Bell ice cream on a hot summer day. But there's more to this moderate-sized town than ice cream and black-and-white cows that look like Oreo cookies. While there are several historic burial parks in the town, the oldest and largest park is the Prairie Lea Cemetery complex.

Prairie Lea sprawls out over a rolling hill and is joined by four other cemeteries: Willow Grove, Saint Mary's, Home Improvement Cemetery, and Bnai Abraham. While all of the cemeteries are adjacent to each other, some are separated by fences, which makes wandering through all of them more challenging. Prairie Lea was established in 1843 and is the largest, with the original twenty-two acres being added to throughout the years. However, it is not the oldest cemetery in town. That honor goes to the Masonic Cemetery on the other side of town. The Masonic Cemetery is also known as the Yellow Fever Cemetery after a wave of the deadly disease swept through in the 1860s.

Prairie Lea is the final resting place for many early Texas political leaders that you can read about as you crisscross the grid of graves while searching for birds. I have visited twice, and there are only four additional checklists on eBird for me to draw from. However, the mature live oaks, magnolias, and hackberries are busy with birds

Tombstone Tale

The angel reading or writing in a book is referred to as the "recording angel." This one is reading a book that is open to the middle to signify the person was in the middle of life.

each time I have visited. In addition to the beautiful trees there are a wetland and prairie that abut the back of the cemetery, which offer more habitat where you can make observations.

In the spring, watch for Painted Buntings, Summer Tanagers, and Northern Parulas to return and nest in the area. The grasslands at the back of the cemetery are a good place to look and listen for Dickcissels and Scissor-tailed Flycatchers during the spring and fall migration. As scorching summer melts into less-hot fall, look for the return of Cedar Waxwings, Dark-eyed Juncos, Eastern Meadowlarks, and American Goldfinches. When I visited in January, it seemed that every live oak was teeming with Yellow-rumped Warblers and Carolina Chickadees. Some of the year-round favorites include Northern Cardinals, Blue Jays, Red-bellied Woodpeckers, and Tufted Titmice. There are several bird feeders located throughout the grounds; however, they are not always filled.

The birds are not the only thing of interest with wings at this cemetery. There are some exquisite angels that are quite moving to gaze upon. One of the other things that captured my attention were the gravestones with epitaphs in German. The entire complex reflects the influences of the German and eastern European families that helped establish Brenham as a farming and commercial center. I invite you to explore the many historical markers at the cemeteries and throughout the community to learn more about this interesting, historic town.

The paved streets create an easy walking space for people with limited and full mobility. Nearby birding can be found at Lake Somerville State Park, Hohlt Park in town, and Washington-on-the-Brazos State Historic Site.

Tombstone Tail: Eastern Phoebe

This medium-sized flycatcher can be found year-round in Central and parts of East Texas. The birds winter in the southern and western parts of the state into Mexico and migrate as far north as Canada in the summer. Cemeteries are a great place to find these gray-and-black birds as they perch on headstones and hunt for insects in the open grasslands. You won't find them in large flocks because they are fairly solitary birds that come together in pairs only during breeding season. Their distinct call sounds as if they are saying their name: *Pho-ebe*.

Cross Timbers and Praries

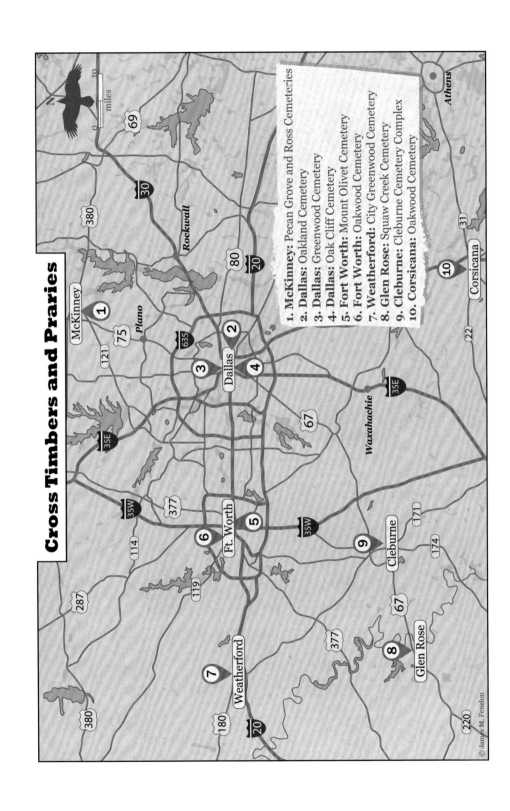

Cross Timbers and Praries

1. **McKinney:** Pecan Grove and Ross Cemeteries
2. **Dallas:** Oakland Cemetery
3. **Dallas:** Greenwood Cemetery
4. **Dallas:** Oak Cliff Cemetery
5. **Fort Worth:** Mount Olivet Cemetery
6. **Fort Worth:** Oakwood Cemetery
7. **Weatherford:** City Greenwood Cemetery
8. **Glen Rose:** Squaw Creek Cemetery
9. **Cleburne:** Cleburne Cemetery Complex
10. **Corsicana:** Oakwood Cemetery

© James M. Fenelon

Cross Timbers and Prairies

Ever since I was a kid, I've thought the term "Cross Timbers" seemed strange. I thought there must be a lot of fallen trees that cross each other or maybe it was how the ranchers made their fences—I wasn't sure. The reality is that the term was coined long ago when the area was first being explored. The early pioneers noted the stands of trees that lined the rivers and creeks or stood along small ridges that crossed the prairies and impeded their travel across the otherwise open mixed-grass prairies.

The prairies lined by wooded areas were a wonderland for wildlife such as American bison, white-tailed deer, antelope, coyotes, black bears, foxes, and a wide variety of birds. While the big herds of bison and antelope are gone, the birds remain fixed in their ancestral migration that crosses the region every spring and fall. The Wichita, Caddo, Tonkawa, and eventually the Comanche nations all hunted and lived in the region. Once horses and cattle were introduced to the Americas, this ecoregion supported vast herds of both that were fiercely guarded by the Comanche.

With the arrival of the Europeans the region was forever changed because the fertile soils supported crops of all sorts. Today, the Cross Timbers no longer slows travelers as they speed along the dizzying matrix of highways and roads that feed into Dallas–Fort Worth, one of the largest metro centers in North America. Many of the areas along the rivers have been dammed and flooded and turned into massive reservoirs to support the growing population and surrounding crop and pasturelands. For many generations, the prairies were not valued and were simply seen as land to be plowed, grazed, or turned into suburbs. Today, only remnants of the Cross Timbers and Prairies exist in protected spaces at state and local parks, wildlife management areas, and Nature Conservancy lands or private lands with conservation easements.

McKinney: Pecan Grove and Ross Cemeteries
1701 McDonald Street

There really is not a bad time of year to bird this historic cemetery, although its more open spaces might be pretty hot during the peak of summer. With that caveat, there are several species that nest in the region that would make an early-summer visit worthwhile. The flashy Prothonotary Warblers and Painted Buntings nest in the area after they arrive in late April or early May.

Pecan Grove and Ross Cemeteries merge to form a rather large complex that offers the birds a mix of mature trees, thickets, and grasslands. The combination of habitat makes the grounds a favorable place to look for Eastern Wood-Pewees, Great Crested and Scissor-tailed Flycatchers, and Eastern and Western Kingbirds as they arrive in the spring, with an occasional visit from an Alder or Willow Flycatcher. The Red-eyed and White-eyed Vireos also arrive in the spring and will nest in the area. Speaking of spring, keep your eye out for Black-and-white, Nashville, Yellow, and Wilson's Warblers to pass through from April into May or on their return journey in the fall. As summer passes into fall, look for Red-breasted and White-breasted Nuthatches, Brown Thrashers, and over fifteen species of sparrows. The mature trees are a haven for Yellow-bellied Sapsuckers; Red-headed, Red-bellied, Downy, Hairy, and Pileated

Tombstone Tale

The obelisk is an ancient monolith style that most notably comes from Egypt. It was made popular again in the 1700s in France when Napoleon brought one back from Egypt. There are many meanings behind the structure, with most aligning with strength, power, and a connection with heaven. The obelisk is often used to mark family plots or the graves of people who held a high station in the community.

Woodpeckers; and Northern Flickers. I would not be surprised if the old trees and quiet setting don't also harbor a Great Horned or Eastern Screech-Owl or two. During the fall, don't forget to look up and search the skies for Red-tailed, Swainson's, Broad-winged, and Cooper's Hawks, along with Mississippi Kites.

Pecan Grove was established in 1870 when twenty-one acres were surveyed and platted for the use of a cemetery. The original cemetery design included a Potter's Field for economically disadvantaged citizens (now one of the better places to bird). The cemetery association later added several acres of land, and that section is still an active burial site. There are historical markers that give insights into the people interred at Pecan Grove, including the twelfth governor of Texas, James Throckmorton. For the most part, the departed here are farmers, shopkeepers, teachers, firefighters, elected officials, health workers, military veterans, and at least two blacksmiths.

The two blacksmiths were James (Scotty) Forsyth (1860–1942) and his son-in-law Charles Bristol. Scotty is my great-great-grandfather, and Charles is my great-grand-father. Scotty emigrated from Scotland in the 1870s with little more than a letter of recommendation in his pocket and the dream of making a life in America in his head. I was visiting their graves with my father, George Bristol, when I noticed this location also offered a good assortment of birds.

In 1895, Ross Cemetery was opened under the original name of "Colored People Cemetery." The name was changed to honor a successful and well-respected African American woman, Hannah Ross, who lived in McKinney and passed away in 1902. Ross Cemetery was originally three acres and later expanded to eight acres. There are over one thousand burials in the relatively small cemetery, with many of them unmarked or unrecorded.

There is ADA parking near the chapel, and some of the roads are paved while the rest are a hard gravel surface that is not ideal for wheeled mobility devices. There is a restroom at the chapel when it is open. Nearby birding can be found at Heard Nature Science Museum and Wildlife Sanctuary, where over 240 species of birds have been recorded. Towne Lake Park is another nearby location that offers good birding year-round.

Tombstone Tail: Dark-eyed Junco

This pretty little slate-gray-and-white sparrow can be found in forests or along woodland edges across most of North America. Look for these birds in Texas in the winter, scratching or hopping through the leaf litter in search of seeds or small insects. During the winter they form large flocks and can be found feeding with other sparrows. They are one of the most abundant birds in North America and can live at sea level or all the way up to eleven thousand feet. Their tail feathers are bright white on the underside, and they will use them to flash a warning to other birds.

Dallas: Oakland Cemetery
3900 Oakland Circle

When I drove through the gates of Oakland Cemetery on a warm December after-noon, I felt like I had stumbled into a secret, enchanted Victorian garden. The unkempt grounds might be off-putting to some, but to me it was a wonderland of angels, monu-ments, native plants, and birds. A magnolia tree embraced the statue of Gabriel, while vines crawled up the body of one of the many angels, and lichen patinaed many of the headstones. Even the unpaved roads highlight the otherworldly feeling of a time that has slipped past.

George Loudermilk purchased the land for the purpose of a cemetery in the 1890s. The design the early cemetery association chose represents the popular Victorian-era, forest-and-lawn theme that called for open meadows surrounded by shaded woodlands where people could gather. The naturalistic style creates enchanting green spaces that enhance the stark white and gray headstones and monuments. When the grounds were originally laid out, they included a Potter's Field, a "Negro Cemetery," and a Confederate Cemetery that rimmed the edges. Oddly enough there is an ad-ditional Confederate Cemetery across Pine Street. The separation of Anglos, African Americans, Hispanics, Protestants, Jews, Catholics, and the haves and have-nots is

Tombstone Tale

The angel with a bowed head represents reverence, sorrow, and grief.

reflected in cemeteries established prior to the 1960s and is for the most part true here too: separate in life, separate in death. The designed landscape of the cemetery was always intended to serve the dual purpose of a burial ground and park. In the early days, families would pack a picnic and take the family to the grounds to tell stories and escape the rapidly growing city. By the mid-1920s the population of Dallas had grown beyond 150,000. In 1925, the Dallas City Council ordered construction of a rail line to connect downtown with the popular outdoor destination.

There is a large obelisk in the center of the grounds, where I recommend parking to start your walk in any direction around Oakland's many loops contained in the sixty acres. Some of Dallas's most famous emperors of industry, civic leaders, servicemen and servicewomen, farmers, oil barons, and hardworking citizens lie beneath the rich soil and towering trees. Between 1918 and 1919, more than two thousand victims of the Spanish flu were laid to rest in Oakland.

Dancing through the trees, shrubs, and grasses are a mix of migrating and year-round birds. In the winter look for American Robins, Dark-eyed Juncos, and Chipping and White-throated Sparrows picking through the leaf litter around the more forested sections. The large cedar trees can be busy with Blue-gray Gnatcatchers, Cedar Waxwings, and Yellow-rumped and Pine Warblers. I watched a murder of American Crows fiercely guard their territory and take up arms against a Red-tailed Hawk that passed overhead. They mobbed her as she fought to gain altitude in the still December air. Once she had achieved enough height to turn around and retaliate, the crows quickly retreated to the post oak tree to talk about their gallantry in battle.

During the spring and summer, watch the ground and lower bushes for Brown Thrashers, Swainson's Thrushes, and Gray Catbirds. The larger oak and pecan trees support Magnolia, Mourning, and Wilson's Warblers as well as Summer Tanagers and a variety of flycatchers. From April to August, Common Nighthawks race through the evening air. I have not seen an owl reported in the area, but there are several trees with large holes that seem perfect as a nesting cavity for a Great Horned or Barred Owl.

The Audubon Dallas has been conducting bird counts at this location since 1957; however, those counts are not recorded in eBird. As a side note, it would be great if volunteers with Audubon or Texas Master Naturalists could team up with the cemetery association to remove some of the invasive plants from the grounds.

Some of the roads here are paved, while others are compacted gravel, which makes it easy for walking and suitable for people with limited mobility. The cemetery is flanked on two sides by Opportunity Park, which displays several interesting modern art sculptures and interpretive panels that tell the story of some of Dallas's pioneer African Americans. Additional nearby birding can be found at Texas Discovery Gardens or the Trinity River Audubon Center.

Tombstone Tail: Common Nighthawk

This bird does not have a very fitting name as it does not typically fly at night, is not a hawk, and is becoming less common as the population is declining. Use of pesticides and loss of safe nesting habitat are noted as causes of this bird's decline. Common Nighthawks nest on the ground or even on flat gravel roofs, making their eggs and clutches susceptible to predation or being destroyed by lawn mowers and agricultural equipment. They have long migration routes from South America to North America in the spring, and some use a route over the Gulf of Mexico. When flying, they can look more like a giant bat as they chase insects at dawn and dusk.

Dallas: Greenwood Cemetery

3020 Oak Grove Avenue

Resting peacefully in the shadow of the ever-growing Dallas skyline lie many of the mavericks and pioneers who helped shape and build the city out of the vast prairie. The grounds are beautiful and filled with mature live oaks, magnolias, cedars, pines, and a variety of shrubs; many of the shrubs are not native to Texas. As you stroll along the dirt roads, you might become overwhelmed by virtuous feelings, which is all part of the design as the streets are named for the virtues. Greenwood is part of a complex of cemeteries including Calvary, Freedman's, and Temple Emanu-El that forms a green oasis that provides good cover and shelter for a pleasant mix of resident and migrating birds.

Tombstone Tale

The wreath is an ancient symbol that can represent victory over death, the circle of eternal life, and immortality through remembrance. The roses are a sign of hope and love. The urn and Greek column give the headstone a Greek revival flare.

Established in 1861, the Freedman's Cemetery has served an African American community that was once the largest segregated enclave in Dallas, if not the country. The North Dallas and Oak Cliff African American communities were the social and economic centers of black life from the Civil War forward. Freedman's is worth a visit to admire the memorial and learn more about this piece of Dallas history.

Originally named Trinity Cemetery when Greenwood was founded in 1874, the new site was located outside town and surrounded by farms. By several accounts, the cemetery had fallen out of favor and into disrepair by the late 1890s. Cattle roamed across the graves since there was no fence to keep them out. Thankfully, several concerned citizens came together to form the Greenwood Cemetery Association to care for the burial park. I invite you to take the time to enjoy the walking tour at the cemetery, which features dozens of interesting characters.

The best birding occurs along the edges where the woods are dense and there is plenty of leaf litter to harbor bugs for American Robins, Northern Cardinals, Eastern Bluebirds, or flocks of Dark-eyed Juncos during the fall and winter. Listen and watch for the resident Red-tailed Hawk that lives in the area and is frequently seen flying over the cemetery complex and adjacent buildings. On a visit in late December, I was treated to a glimpse of a Blue-headed Vireo snacking on a bug. I enjoyed watching him for some time as the leaves had fallen off the trees and I could see him better than when the leaves are thick during the spring. Speaking of spring, the roses and other flowers support Ruby-throated Hummingbirds, while American Redstarts, Common Yellowthroats, and Black-and-white Warblers feed on the insects on the mature trees.

The hard-packed gravel roads make for easy walking but might be a challenge to some mobility devices. Nearby birding can be found at Reverchon Park, Turtle Creek Park, and Oak Cliff Cemetery. The parks surrounding White Rock Lake are also worth a visit from October to May.

Tombstone Tail: Red-tailed Hawk

This large raptor is the most common hawk in North America and has adapted well to urban living. These hawks mostly consume small mammals such as squirrels, rats, and rabbits but will also eat slower-moving birds such as Rock Pigeons and doves. Pairs mate for life and can often be seen hunting together when one is not sitting on the nest. Healthy birds can live up to thirty years. As I said in Parking Lot Birding, "Their shrill call is used in movies for just about every type of bird from eagles to ravens and always seems to be present when a Native American enters the scene" (42).

Dallas: Oak Cliff Cemetery

1300 East Eighth Street

Established in the 1830s, Oak Cliff is generally considered to be Dallas County's oldest public cemetery. Set on a small hill rising out of the vast Blackland Prairie and Trinity River bottom, it provides a peaceful glimpse into the past. William S. Beaty moved to the area soon after the Texas Revolution to settle a 640-acre tract that rambled down to the Trinity River. In 1846, he gave ten acres of land to be used as a cemetery, as there were already people buried there. His settlement grew slowly and did not adopt the name of Oak Cliff until 1887. Dallas annexed Oak Cliff in 1904 and soon after constructed an improved bridge over the Trinity to better connect the affluent community to the growing city.

Even though the cemetery sits in the shadow of one of the ten most-populated cities in the United States, it feels like a country cemetery complete with tree-lined dirt roads. A dirt road in the middle of a city filled with pavement is an unusual thing. The trees along the fence line buffer the space from the adjacent neighborhood and

Tombstone Tale

The double-headed eagle goes back to ancient Mesopotamian mythology and appears frequently in various cultures across Europe, the Middle East, and Central Asia. The triangle in the middle with the number 32 is the mark of the 32nd Degree Scottish Rite Freemasons.

businesses, which further enhances its rural feel. The fence, trees, and shrubs also offer good habitat for birds, so keep an eye on them as you wander around the grounds.

In 1993, the Dallas Genealogical Society cross-referenced all the inscriptions on the headstones with Texas death certificates and other records to identify approximately twenty-five hundred marked graves and three thousand unmarked graves. Many of the unmarked graves are in the Strangers Rest, Potter's Field, or African American sections of the cemetery. The African American section located on the south end provides good habitat for Hermit Thrushes, American Robins, Gray Catbirds, and other woodland-edge birds that feed in the leaf litter.

When I visited in December, I was welcomed by a very bold Ruby-crowned Kinglet that was flashing his ruby-red crown as he darted in and out of a cluster of shrubs. On that visit I spotted sixteen other species as I explored the grounds. During the fall and winter it is easy to find large flocks of Cedar Waxwings, American Pipits, American Goldfinches, and Yellow-rumped Warblers. Brown Creepers can also be found scooting along the tree trunks during the winter. Once spring arrives, look for the return of Eastern and Western Kingbirds, Great Crested and Scissor-tailed Flycatchers, and the always graceful Barn Swallows to be ravenously feeding on insects. The grounds do not have a water feature; however, they do have a good mix of grasses, bushes, and mature trees that attract birds year-round. Due to the proximity of the Trinity River it is common to see flocks of geese, ducks, or even gulls flying overhead.

This cemetery is not suitable for wheeled mobility devices; however, it does offer easy walking along the central loop. The entrance into the cemetery and the roads are narrow with limited spaces to park, so plan accordingly. Nearby birding locations include Oakland Cemetery, Lake Cliff Park, and the Trinity River Greenbelt Park. I am also a fan of the Trinity River Audubon Center located a few miles southeast of this location.

Tombstone Tail: American Pipit

This small brown-and-buff bird can be found across most of Mexico, Texas, and the southern part of the United States during the winter and will migrate as far as the Arctic islands and northern Canada to breed. While foraging on the ground for insects, American Pipits continually bob their tails. Because they are ground feeders, they prefer areas such as agricultural fields, prairies, tundra, and cemeteries. When feeding, they can often be seen strolling along the open edges of creeks, rivers, and lakes. They build small nests on the ground that make them susceptible to predation; however, their populations are strong as humans continue to replace forested areas with lawns, golf courses, agricultural fields.

Fort Worth: Mount Olivet Cemetery
2301 North Sylvania Avenue

Founded in 1907 by Flavious McPeak and his wife, this cemetery is now managed by Greenwood Funeral Homes and is still an active burial park. One of the pieces of history at this location that captured my imagination is the cadaver vault. Grave robbing to sell cadavers for medical research was popular in the early 1900s. To prevent the potential for thievery, the McPeaks built a stately looking vault to house incoming bodies until they began to decay and were no longer of value to nefarious grave robbers. Sadly, the expense of building the vault bankrupted the McPeak family, and in 1917, William Bailey, who also owned Greenwood Cemetery, purchased Mount Olivet. The cadaver vault had to be destroyed in 1983, when it was deemed unstable for use.

From the beginning the cemetery was touted to be a park-like setting, and the Mount Olivet Cemetery Association helped establish a bus service from downtown Fort Worth in 1914. In 1918 and 1919, the buses were filled with grieving passengers when nearly six hundred people fell victim to the Spanish flu pandemic and were buried at Mount Olivet.

In the late 1920s, the grounds were transformed yet again by William Bailey's wife, Susa, an active member of the Garden Club in Tarrant County who brought in Hare and Hare Landscape Designer from Kansas City to design the new sections of Mount Olivet and Greenwood. The looping roads, grand monuments, and mature trees are still striking at both locations. The women of the garden club were impressed by the renovations and hired the same company to design the new Botanical Gardens of Fort Worth.

Not all things were created equal, as was common in those days in the South, and the original articles of incorporation stated that "no negro or African descendant shall

Tombstone Tale

I have not come across many dogs standing guard over a grave; however, they generally represent loyalty and protection.

ever be interred on said lots." Thankfully, the articles were found to be unlawful and were amended in 1969. Many cemeteries had such rules that were undone by the Civil Rights Act of 1964.

The cemetery has a rather large pond that attracts ducks and geese in the fall and winter, although the Canada Geese and Muscovy Ducks seem to linger all year. I should note that the area near the pond has some of the most frequently visited graves, so please exercise best ethics when near this section. The fall and winter bring in smaller birds such as Cedar Waxwings, Dark-eyed Juncos, and American Goldfinches. During the same season raptors are abundant here; Red-shouldered, Red-tailed, and Cooper's Hawks all frequent the open spaces and perch in the mature trees. Through-out the spring and summer this is a good place to look for Mississippi Kites, Common Nighthawks, and a variety of migratory songbirds, including Yellow Warblers and Summer Tanagers.

The birding here is not off the charts; however, the species that do exist at this location are abundant. I would like to see more data collected by citizen-scientists and logged into eBird to get a better understanding of the migrants that pass through this large cemetery. For example, not far away at the Fort Worth Nature Center and Ref-uge, fifteen types of sparrows and three types of towhees have been recorded during the winter and early spring. I believe the wooded space and fields along the back fence near the railroad tracks could harbor more species of sparrows and warblers than have been reported. There are several bluebird nesting boxes located along the back fence as well.

When you are birding this location, keep in mind that it is an active cemetery, so please give the bereaved their space. The grounds are also quite manicured as author Bill Harvey can attest. During the 1970s, Bill spent his high school summers hauling water hoses and pushing a lawn mower around the grounds.

There is accessible parking at the funeral home at the entrance of the cemetery and plenty of paved roads to explore by people with all types of mobility. Nearby birding can be found at Oakwood Cemetery, Fort Worth Botanical Gardens, and Fort Worth Nature Center and Refuge. The Colleyville Nature Center in Colleyville is also worth a look.

Tombstone Tail: American Robin

Whoever first penned the saying "early bird catches the worm" surely must have been referring to the American Robin. The early bird's arrival often signals the end of winter for many northern states. Not all robins migrate, but the ones that do appear early in the spring and start having clutches promptly. A breeding pair can have three clutches in a season; however, only a moderate number of the chicks will reach adulthood. Robins form large flocks, some consisting of several thousand, in late winter and early spring as they prepare for migration. When stalking a worm, robins turn their heads as they listen to the ground. They are members of the thrush family, characterized as mostly ground-feeding birds that consume earthworms, caterpillars, grasshoppers, fruits, and berries.

Fort Worth: Oakwood Cemetery
701 Grand Avenue

This sixty-two-acre cemetery comprises three burial grounds: Old Trinity for African Americans, Calvary for Catholics, and Oakwood for everyone else. And I mean everyone else who called Fort Worth home or those who passed through on the cattle drives or in search of a better life. Walking the tree-lined gravel streets, visitors will come across Bricklayer's Row, Confederate Row, and even Bartender's Row. Then there are rows of the emperors of industry tucked away in their beautiful mausoleums, as well as political pioneers endowed with great monuments. There are paupers, soldiers of almost every war, nurses, teachers, gunslingers, actors, musicians, bankers, firefighters, police, and lawyers all resting peacefully on the bluff above the Trinity River with a commanding view of the city.

The oak-filled bluff is also prime real estate for the birds. If you park near the chapel, look for the feeder and birdbath near the office. If there is food in the feeder, the Carolina Chickadees, Lesser Goldfinches, House Finches, and Northern Cardinals can be found flittering around. Just beyond the office you will find most of the historical markers and larger monuments; it is also where you can check the fence line for flocks of Cedar Waxwings and Pine Siskins in the winter and Nashville Warblers during the spring. The edges of this area are great for seeing birds, but I have found that the trees on top of the hill yield a plentiful number of species as well. During the winter it seemed that there was either an Eastern Phoebe, Eastern Bluebird, or Red-bellied Woodpecker in every tree.

Tombstone Tale

The calla lily often represents beauty, resurrection, and purity and is associated with marriage. The calla lily was a popular motif on Woodmen of the World headstones.

The most impressive views of the river and the city can be found from the Calvary Cemetery. It is the best vantage point to watch for ducks, geese, and wading birds such as the Great Blue Heron and Great Egret moving along the river. Search the skies for Red-tailed and Cooper's Hawks or Mississippi Kites circling effortlessly overhead during the fall raptor migration. Scissor-tailed and Least Flycatchers and Eastern and Western Kingbirds feed on insects during the spring and summer as they launch from the headstones or large trees.

As you look out over the city from this peaceful place, it is hard to imagine what the town must have been like in 1879 when the cemetery opened. Part of the impetus for opening Oakwood was that the original city cemetery, now called Pioneers Cemetery, had filled rather rapidly. When Fort Worth was still a Wild West cattle town, death was about the only sure thing. There were plenty of ways to die in those days, and wealth was not a protective shield against things like falling off your horse, getting trampled by cattle, being gunned down after a not-so-friendly game of poker, or dying in childbirth. Waves of diseases such as cholera, dysentery, measles, syphilis, and later the Spanish flu swept through the region prior to the establishment of clean water systems and adequate medical services. The cattle drives of the late 1800s brought waves of cowboys to the infamous brothels and bars of Hell's Half Acre, where many a gunslinger was sent to his grave, but the prostitutes fared the worst, with suicide the most common means of death.

Despite the hardships of being a "cow town," the city progressed and is now home to close to nine hundred thousand people and some of the finest arts and cultural museums in the state. My personal favorite is the Cowgirl Museum.

The gravel roads and shade of the mature trees make this an easy spot to walk in most seasons. However, the rough surfaces of the roads are not suitable for wheeled mobility devices. Nearby birding can be found at Mount Olivet Cemetery, Greenwood Cemetery, Botanical Research Institute of Texas, and Fort Worth Nature Center and Refuge. The Fort Worth Nature Center offers birding education programs and has a new ADA-friendly boardwalk to explore the wetlands.

Tombstone Tail: Scissor-tailed Flycatcher

This elegant flycatcher with its long, forked tail is easily recognizable as it perches on telephone wires and fences throughout Texas, Oklahoma, and Kansas during the spring and summer. During breeding season, males perform elaborate sky dances to attract a mate. These birds eat so many grasshoppers that their presence is considered an economic benefit to the agricultural industry in Oklahoma. In late fall they return to Central America, via Texas, to spend the winter.

Weatherford: City Greenwood Cemetery
400 East Water Street

The first recorded burial at this location dates back to 1859 when A. J. Johnson laid his young, twenty-two-year-old wife to rest. The town had just been incorporated the year before and was little more than an outpost on the frontier. Some might say it was too far out on the frontier at that time, as raids and attacks from the Comanche were a constant threat. The town was little more than a place of protection where farmers and ranchers could retreat during raids or offer a drink of water and a wish of good luck to passengers moving between Fort Worth and Fort Belknap. The city grew after the Civil War and as the final push to exterminate the remaining Native Americans or remove them to reservations was in full swing. Once the railroads arrived, it became an important shipping center for agricultural goods.

The Comanche left behind a legacy that is still the center of the town's worth and fame: the horse. Over time, Weatherford has become the "Cutting Horse Capital of the World," complete with a life-size bronze statue of a horse and cowboy outside the

Tombstone Tale

There are many types of handshakes that appear on gravestones. This one is clearly a man and woman holding hands and bound by a rope, which indicates they are bonded in marriage for all eternity.

Chamber of Commerce in town. The cowboy heritage is strong in this community and arises, in part, from famed cattle drivers Oliver Loving, who is buried at Greenwood, and Charles Goodnight, who is buried at the Goodnight Cemetery east of Amarillo.

Bose Ikard is also buried here. Bose was born into slavery in Mississippi and was in his twenties when he went to work as a free man for rancher Oliver Loving in 1866 on the first cattle drive that established the Goodnight-Loving Trail. He was considered one of Loving and Goodnight's most trusted cowboys. There is a statue of Bose Ikard at the Fort Worth Stockyards, and he was part of the inaugural class of the National Multicultural Western Heritage Museum in Fort Worth. His legacy and likeness live on in Larry McMurtry's famous Texas tale *Lonesome Dove* as the character Deets.

This is also the final resting place for several well-known public figures, including Tony Award–winning actor Mary Martin, mother of Larry Hagman, the star of the 1980s television show *Dallas*; former governor Samuel Lanham; and James Claude "Jim" Wright, former US congressman and US Speaker of the House. And look for the witch's tomb. You will know it when you see it, and you will certainly understand why this strange-looking in-ground tomb is the topic of ghost stories and urban legends.

Once you have had your fill of beautiful monuments and Weatherford history, have a look along the edges of the cemetery that border Town Creek. The riparian area and thick understory provide habitat for Spotted Towhees and Harris's, Song, Field, and White-throated Sparrows. The sparrows can often be found feeding in the grasses of the cemetery yard and then dart back into the cover of the brush from October to April. During the spring, look for Brown Thrashers and Swainson's Thrushes in this same space.

The large mature trees are attractive to the White-eyed, Red-eyed, and Blue-headed Vireos during the spring and summer. The trees and sizable monuments make great perching places for Western Kingbirds, Eastern Phoebes, and Great Crested and Scissor-tailed Flycatchers when they arrive in April and feed and nest in the area until September or October. During the mornings and at dusk the open spaces of the cemetery are alive with insect eaters such as Purple Martins and Barn and Cliff Swallows.

During the winter, the Northern Flickers return, along with Cedar Waxwings, American Goldfinches, and Dark-eyed Juncos. When I visited in February, I watched a couple of determined American Crows try to pull Mardi Gras beads off a tombstone. They probably would have succeeded in capturing their prize had a Red-shouldered Hawk not appeared overhead, causing the crows to scramble off, squawking as they went.

The combination of paved and compacted gravel roads and big shade trees makes this a wonderful space to bird for people with all mobility types. Nearby birding can be found at Holland Lake Park in town or at several locations around Lake Weatherford northeast of town. The floating bridge and boardwalk at the northern end of Lake Weatherford offer some solid birding during the winter months when the ducks and geese return.

Tombstone Tail: Indigo Bunting

This brilliant blue bird is one of the crown jewels of the spring migrations. During breeding season, the male's specialized feathers refract and reflect blue light to give it a rich indigo coloring. Like most blue birds, they do not have a blue pigment. In the fall the special feathers molt off, and they return to their dull brown coloring, which makes them tricky to identify in the fall migration. They breed across most of Texas as well as the central and eastern parts of the United States and winter in Central and South America. During the spring migration they generally travel in large flocks and can be found foraging on the lawns of nature centers, parks, cemeteries, or wherever there is a mix of fields and woodlands. Like most migrating songbirds, they travel at night, which makes them susceptible to colliding with high-rise buildings clad in glass.

Glen Rose: Squaw Creek Cemetery
County Road 303 off Highway 67

I stumbled into this cemetery one mild July day on the drive back from visiting my father in Fort Worth. It is a wonderful place to stop and stretch your legs and do a little birding. The cemetery is flanked on three sides by a forested area and golf course. The golf course has plenty of ponds to support a year-round flock of Canada Geese. On my first visit, I was treated to seeing an Orchard Oriole in the shrubs and sunflowers along the northern fence.

If you like evening-oriented birds, this is a great place to visit from April to August to listen and look for Chuck-will's-widows, Common Poorwills, Common Night-hawks, Chimney Swifts, Eastern Screech-Owls, and Great Horned Owls. During the spring migration, the large live oak and elm trees support Black-and-white, Nashville, and Orange-crowned Warblers. Summer Tanagers, Painted Buntings, Blue Grosbeaks, and Dickcissels all nest in the area from April to August.

While spring and summer bring in the flashy birds, the fall and winter bring in the majority of the species that frequent the rolling hills between the Paluxy and Brazos

Tombstone Tale

A coffin stone is a stylized type of ledger stone that comes from a German tradition. The word *ledger* comes from the German word *legen*, which means "to lie." The heavy stone helps secure the body from being dug up by wildlife or grave robbers, who used to remove cadavers from the graves and sell them for medical research.

Rivers. In October Hermit Thrushes, Spotted Towhees, American Robins, and over fifteen species of sparrows return to the area to stay until mid-April. During the fall the Yellow-bellied Sapsuckers and Northern Flickers also return to join the Red-bellied, Downy, and Ladder-backed Woodpeckers.

When most people think about Glen Rose, they might think about swimming in the river or visiting Dinosaur Valley, Cleburne State Park, or Fossil Rim Wildlife Center. Long before the Spanish explorers crashed on the Texas shores, this was the homeland of the Tonkawa with some crossover from the Bidai tribes. Once settlers began to arrive in the 1850s, they soon established a mill along the Paluxy River that became the central gathering place for the small community. By 1910, the mineral waters of the rivers and multiple creeks became popular with the health crowd, and several sanatoriums and spas opened. The waters were said to have medicinal qualities that attracted both legitimate and pseudo-doctors alike. During Prohibition the town became known as the "whiskey woods capital of the state" and supplied a steady stream of bootleg liquor to Waco, Dallas, Fort Worth, and Austin.

The crushed gravel road makes for easy walking but might not be suitable for some wheeled mobility devices. That said, most of the birds the cemetery has to offer can be viewed from your car, especially along the back fence where the understory is thick. There is a nice pavilion where you can have a picnic in the shade if you are out for the day. With two state parks—Dinosaur Valley State Park and Cleburne State Park, plus Fossil Rim Wildlife Center—the area has become a major attraction for nature tourism and outdoor recreation. There are several nice local parks along the rivers, and Squaw Creek Reservoir is located just north of town. However, the reservoir is the cooling lake for the Comanche Peak Nuclear Power Plant. Each location offers interesting wildlife-viewing opportunities.

Tombstone Tail: Orchard Oriole

The male Orchard Oriole is a rusty-orange color with a black hood, wings, and tail, while the female is bright yellow with gray wings. These are the smallest of all the orioles. They nest in groups for safety as they breed across Texas as well as the mid- and eastern parts of the United States. They feed mostly on insects and nectar that they find in shrublands near ponds, lakes, and rivers. In their wintering habitat in Central America, they primarily feed on fruit and nectar. Their nests are parasitized often by cowbirds, which, coupled with habitat loss and pesticides, has caused their population to decline over the past few decades.

Cleburne: Cleburne Cemetery Complex
405 Waters Street

This thirty-six-acre complex combines the Confederate Memorial Park and Rose Hill, Greenlawn, and Chambers Memorial Cemeteries. The older graves can be found in the City Cemetery and at the Confederate Memorial Park. There are more than three hundred Confederate and seven Union soldiers buried at this location, which makes sense as the town served as a mustering point for young men wishing to join the Confederate Army.

In 1922, the Confederate Memorial Park Committee was formed with the intent of laying out the roads in the pattern of the Confederate Battle Flag, also known as the

Tombstone Tale

The Southern Cross of Honor was established in the 1890s by the United Daughters of the Confederacy to honor Confederate veterans. The cross encompasses a wreath and the Confederate motto *Deo Vindice*, which means "With God, Our Defender." Sometimes it has an image of the Confederate flag or the letters "CSA."

Stainless Banner. Two of the roads were cut in the formation, but the idea was eventually abandoned. The committee did create the Confederate Veterans Memorial and erected an arch leading into the Confederate Memorial Park, where most of the veterans are buried. The town itself is named for Confederate general Patrick R. Cleburne. If you cannot get your antebellum South fill at the cemetery, consider bopping over to the Gone with the Wind Museum and Gift Shop just down the road on East Second Street.

I found the birding at this location to be best in City Cemetery and across the street at Rose Hill. There are brush piles along the edges of both that were busy with a flocks of Chipping, Clay-colored, and White-crowned Sparrows and Dark-eyed Juncos when I visited in February. Just down the road at Buddy Stewart Park, fifteen species of sparrows are consistently reported, and I feel confident that the fields in the cemetery could yield as many sparrows with a little more investigation. In the same area where I observed the sparrows, I spotted two Northern Flickers feeding on the ground. In the live oak and pecan trees there were Red-bellied, Downy, and Ladder-backed Woodpeckers. Along the main entrance to Rose Hill there is a green tunnel of live oaks that hosts Black-throated Green, Yellow, Nashville, and Black-and-white Warblers during the spring migration and Summer Tanagers during the summer.

There is a restroom at Rose Hill. I missed that fact and drove into town to find a lady's room before returning to continue birding. I have to admit sometimes I can get lost in the small details of birds and headstones and forget to notice the large things like a building with the word *Restroom* painted in big, red letters.

The roads at Rose Hill are paved and suitable for wheeled mobility devices, while the roads at City Cemetery are gravel. Additional birding nearby can be found at Cleburne State Park, Buddy Stewart Park, and Hulen Park in town along the banks of West Buffalo Creek.

Tombstone Tail: White-throated Sparrow

It is hard to visit the forests of the Great Lakes region or Canada without hearing the high, whistling song of this distinct sparrow. While wintering across Texas, these sparrows typically do not sing until they are on their way north to breed. Females build their nests on or near the ground, which makes them susceptible to predation or being crushed by humans or livestock. Despite their nesting habits, their populations are reported by Cornell Lab of Ornithology and Partners in Flight to be stable. Look for the distinctive white patch on their throat and yellow patch on their crown as their defining physical features. They spend a good deal of time hopping and scratching through leaf litter for seeds or insects.

Corsicana: Oakwood Cemetery

700 North Fifteenth Street

Two things happened in my life in the spring of 2019. First, I spent an amazing morning birding at the Rose Hill Cemetery in Corpus Christi. Second, I read *The Life History of a Texas Birdwatcher: Connie Hagar of Rockport*, by Karen H. McCracken. Connie Neblett Hagar (1886–1973) grew up in Corsicana and spent time in Navarro County cemeteries in search of birds, wildflowers, and other native plants. After reading the book and visiting the cemetery, I began to understand that cemeteries made great places to see birds.

Tombstone Tale

The weeping willow was a popular symbol that appeared on many commercial or premade headstones during the Victorian era into the nineteenth century. In Greek mythology, the willow is associated with the underworld. The willow tree was often planted in cemeteries, dating back to early Chinese cultures, and was considered the ultimate melancholy tree that appears to weep for the departed.

Connie is often referred to as the "First Lady of Texas Birding" since she put Texas on the map as one of the best places in the world to bird, especially along the Gulf Coast during the spring migration. While Connie lived in Corsicana, she was active in the Garden Club and Federation of Women's Clubs. As part of the Garden Club, Connie and her sister formed a Nature Club and obtained permission to make Oakwood Cemetery a wildflower sanctuary where the eighteen members of the club transplanted native species to the hallowed hills and valley along the banks of the creek. I would have loved to have seen the cemetery with the splendor of the wild-flowers and native plants. Connie's parents are buried at this location.

The cemetery still offers good birding; however, I was greeted by a phalanx of lawn mowers and leaf blowers when I arrived. Sadly, most of the Nature Club's native flowers and plants are gone. But the large mature post oaks, live oaks, magnolias, and cedars still soldier on, providing habitat and shade. Even with the army of lawn mowers I still counted twenty species of birds on a sunny day in December, with most of them hanging out in the trees and shrubs near the creek. In places where the leaf litter was allowed to stay on the ground, the Dark-eyed Juncos, American Robins, and White-crowned Sparrows scratched and bounced along while looking for insects. During the spring and summer, the Philadelphia, Red-eyed, and Warbling Vireos can be found here along with Blackburnian and Chestnut-sided Warblers.

The Community and Jester Parks are adjacent to the creek, so there is a fairly large piece of habitat for the birds. The roads and paths are well maintained, if not overly mowed, which makes walking the rolling acres easy. Only a portion of the roads are paved and accessible for wheeled mobility devices. There are several historical markers throughout the grounds that I recommend reading to understand more about the citizens and culture of Corsicana. Nearby birding can be found at IOOF Park in Corsicana and Lake Halbert Park just south of the city.

Tombstone Tail: Blue-headed Vireo

This medium-sized vireo winters across much of the southeast into Texas and Mexico. During migration these vireos journey to the coniferous and mixed forests of the northeastern United States into Canada. They have olive-green upperparts, white underparts, a blue-gray head, a distinctive white eye ring that looks like spectacles, and a small hook at the end of their beak. When building a nest, the males start the construction by wrapping materials around a fork in a tree; the females then complete the nest by lining it with feathers, fur, grasses, and other materials until it is sturdy and ready to receive three to five creamy-white eggs. Cornell Lab of Ornithology reports that Blue-headed Vireo populations have increased since 1970 and still remain strong.

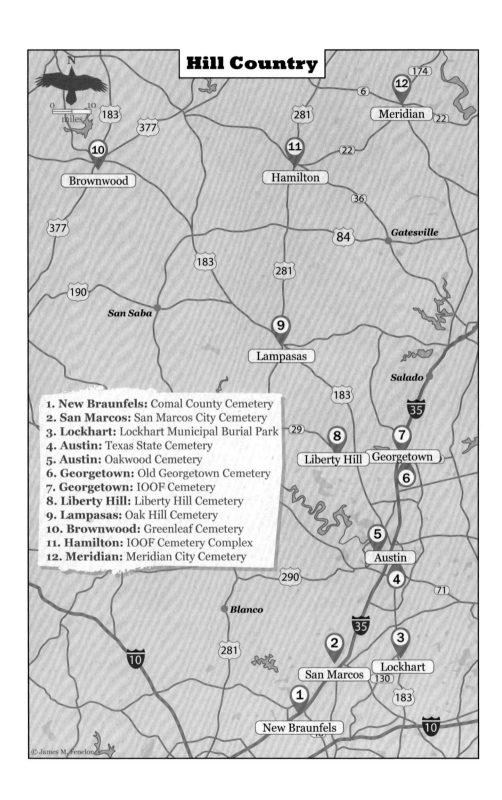

Hill Country

174
12 Meridian 22
6
281
11 22
Hamilton
36
84 Gatesville
377
377
183 281
190
San Saba
9
Lampasas
Salado
183
35
29 8 7
Liberty Hill Georgetown
6
5
Austin
290
71
Blanco
35
281
10 2 3
San Marcos 130 Lockhart
1 183
New Braunfels 10

1. **New Braunfels:** Comal County Cemetery
2. **San Marcos:** San Marcos City Cemetery
3. **Lockhart:** Lockhart Municipal Burial Park
4. **Austin:** Texas State Cemetery
5. **Austin:** Oakwood Cemetery
6. **Georgetown:** Old Georgetown Cemetery
7. **Georgetown:** IOOF Cemetery
8. **Liberty Hill:** Liberty Hill Cemetery
9. **Lampasas:** Oak Hill Cemetery
10. **Brownwood:** Greenleaf Cemetery
11. **Hamilton:** IOOF Cemetery Complex
12. **Meridian:** Meridian City Cemetery

N
0 10
miles
183
377
10
Brownwood

© James M. Fenelon

Hill Country

The Hill Country consists of the rugged limestone hills of the Edwards Plateau and the Blackland Prairie that rambles up to its edges. The plateau is home to clear, cool, spring-fed rivers and creeks that have been attractive to humans since the first Native Americans followed bison into the area some ten thousand years ago. The early Spanish, French, and later the German explorers and settlers found the springs a welcome reprieve from the craggy limestone slopes. Today, the region is one of the fastest growing in the country as people fall in love with the rolling hills, warm weather, parks and greenspaces, and steady economy.

The Edwards Plateau is also home to birds such as the endangered Golden-cheeked Warbler and threatened Black-capped Vireo, along with a host of endangered and threatened plants and insects. The growing human population puts pressure on these species and others that breed or live only in the Hill Country. Thankfully, some farsighted people took action, creating a network of parks and conservation lands to offer some protection for wildlife as well as for our own water resources. My mother, Valarie Bristol, was one of those people. She championed the Balcones Canyonlands Conservation Plan (BCCP) that brought together Travis County, the City of Austin, US Fish and Wildlife, several nonprofits, and private landowners to set aside over thirty-three thousand acres for the protection of seven endangered species and several more threatened ones in Travis County. The Balcones Canyonlands National Wildlife Refuge is separate from the BCCP lands but adds additional acreage to the conservation puzzle. Even with all this protected land, there is still a need for additional parks for people as well as wildlife and watershed protection and for preservation of the natural heritage of this unique region.

There is really no bad birding season for this dynamic region as flocks of wintering birds arrive in late fall, only to give way to waves of migrants passing through in the spring or nest in the region during the summer.

New Braunfels: Comal Cemeteries

301 Peace Avenue

New Braunfels sits on the edge of the Edwards Plateau and is often referred to as the gateway to the Hill Country. The large complex of three cemeteries sits on a bluff overlooking the clear, cool Guadalupe River. While visiting, I focused on the Comal Cemetery because of its size, proximity to the river, and favorable birding habitat. It is worth the time to visit all three cemeteries to fully understand the cultural history of the area.

The Comal Cemetery is a great example of the Texas-German-style cemetery that emerged in the late 1800s as more immigrants arrived in the German communities of Central Texas. There are interpretive panels and historical markers to offer some interesting facts about the people, wildlife, and plants found within the space. The New Braunfels Cemetery Committee prepared a master plan in 2010 that provides an interesting and comprehensive history of the cemeteries within the city limits. Additionally, Terry Jordan, author of *Texas Graveyards: A Cultural Legacy*, studied the German cemeteries of Comal County in great detail. I highly recommend his book if you are interested in learning more about the German burial rituals.

The Germans and people from other cultures often planted evergreen trees as a symbol of everlasting life. In the Texas Hill Country, the closest thing to an evergreen is the hardy Ashe juniper, which is found throughout the cemetery. A special public-

Tombstone Tale

The use of shells as a decoration on graves dates back to the early Egyptians and is associated with rebirth and the afterlife. The shell-covered cement graves were crafted by local cement artist Henry Mordhorst (1864–1928), who used Atlantic cockleshells. His work can be found throughout the cemeteries of Comal County.

service announcement: If you suffer from cedar fever, do not visit this location in late December and early January when the trees look like they are on fire as they explode with pollen. Unlike cedar-fever sufferers, the Cedar Waxwings enjoy the junipers and will feed on their fruits as they winter across the state.

After the cemetery was dedicated, the first recorded burial took place on a hot August day in 1873, a full thirty years after Prince Carl of Solms-Braunfels brought the first wave of immigrants to the area. The New Braunfels Cemetery was established in 1845 (predating the Comal Cemetery), and it got off to a busy start after a wave of cholera swept through, killing four hundred people between 1845 and 1846. The epidemic was so bad that there was not enough lumber to support the growing town and to make coffins, many of the fallen had to be buried, wrapped simply in blankets, in a mass grave. The deadly disease left a good number of orphans whom the remaining families took in as their own.

This is the final resting place of famed botanist Ferdinand Jacob Lindheimer (1801–79). Lindheimer is credited with documenting several hundred plant species, and his name is associated with forty-eight of those species, including *Lindheimer muhly*, which is a Hill Country specialty and one of my favorite grasses. For many years he was the editor and later became the publisher of the *Neu Braunfelser Zeitung* newspaper. He used the paper to express his views and also to celebrate the Texas-German community. When I visited his gravesite in February and again in March 2020, I couldn't help noticing that someone had recently planted nonnative plants in his plot.

The birding can be a little hit or miss depending on the season. Park your vehicle near the kiosk, have a look at the interpretive panels, and then walk toward the river. The best birding is along the cliff above the Guadalupe River and near the adjacent park. From that vantage it is easy to peer into the cypress tree canopy to see Belted Kingfishers waiting for a fish to pass by or to look for warblers and Summer Tanagers during the spring migration. The Green Kingfisher is seen on occasion from Cypress Bend Park, which flanks the cemetery to the southeast. There are over 150 species at Cypress Bend Park recorded on eBird.

The tangle of native vegetation along the fence is a good spot to look for resident birds such as Northern Cardinals, Carolina Chickadees, Black-crested Titmice, Carolina and Bewick's Wrens, and the flashy little Verdins. During the summer months, the tree canopy along the river hosts Yellow-billed Cuckoos, while the skies are alive with Chimney Swifts, Purple Martins, Barn and Bank Swallows, and Common Nighthawks. The trees along the river and in the cemetery support resident Golden-fronted, Downy, and Ladder-backed Woodpeckers. Most of the year Eastern Bluebirds, Northern Mockingbirds, and Loggerhead Shrikes can be found perching on the headstones as they scan for insects below. These insect eaters are joined in the spring by Great Crested and Scissor-tailed Flycatchers that return to the area to breed and nest.

There is ADA parking at the kiosk, and the paved roads make the cemetery accessible for people with all types of mobility. Nearby birding can be found next door at Cypress Bend Park, Landa Park, or the many parks around Canyon Lake just north of town.

Tombstone Tail: Yellow-billed Cuckoo

This long, slender bird is easier to hear than to see as it tends to creep along the canopy feeding on large insects and caterpillars—including the scary hairy ones. The cuckoo's distinct doorknocker or cooing sounds can be heard along woodlands surrounding rivers, ponds, and creeks of Texas from April until September when the birds are breeding and nesting. These long-distant migrants winter in the forested areas of South American and return to the forested parts of North America, mostly east of the Rockies, for the summer. They might migrate long distances and have a large distribution. Yellow-billed Cuckoos have a fairly short life span of around five years. Their populations in the western United States are in steep decline. Like many birds that migrate at night, they are prone to striking buildings, wind turbines, and other tall structures; however, habitat loss is their number-one enemy.

San Marcos: San Marcos City Cemetery
1001 Ranch Road 12

Established in 1876, this lovely cemetery sprawls out over forty-five acres atop one of the rolling hills of San Marcos. In 2019 the City of San Marcos approved $2.25 million to purchase and maintain an additional 4.21 acres of adjacent land. San Marcos is booming with growth, which makes it no surprise that it needs additional lands. The city was fortunate that there was a large parcel available, as Texas state law prohibits new cemeteries from being established within city limits. Only existing cemeteries can be expanded within a city.

When I visited on an unseasonably warm day in January, I was impressed with how many people were jogging and walking the grounds. I was also impressed by the number of white-tailed deer that lived in the cemetery. And then there is Pete the peacock, who hangs out under the large live oaks. I was taking photos of Pete when I noticed him perk up and watch a particular jogger cross the entire length of the cemetery. The man had a little bag of peacock treats and Pete knew it. The man did not know how Pete arrived at the cemetery, but he shared that Pete is much loved by the joggers and frequent visitors. I have to admit, he is a beautiful bird even if he is not native to North America.

Tombstone Tale

Bundled wheat usually symbolizes abundance or long life and is most associated with Ukrainian culture.

While visiting, I observed Golden-fronted and Ladder-backed Woodpeckers, Bewick's and Carolina Wrens, American Pipits, and White-crowned Sparrows in the majestic live oak trees and on the ground beneath them. Some of the year-round birds include Greater Roadrunners, Black-crested Titmice, Northern Cardinals, and Northern Mockingbirds. On one edge of the cemetery there is a thicket along the fence that offers good protection for the ground feeders such as Spotted Towhees and American Robins. A cell-phone tower just past the cemetery offers a perch for Turkey and Black Vultures as well as hawks that frequent the area. On a visit in April, I found the pecan trees and thicket along the edges of the cemetery busy with White-eyed Vireos, while Black-throated Green Warblers fed in the live oaks alongside Lesser Goldfinches. This location was designated a public hotspot in 2020 and already has sixty-five species recorded there, with more added each month. I was pleased to see that two Great Horned Owls were sighted at this location, as the habitat certainly seems favorable to support them.

The streets here are paved and accessible; however, some do have steep slopes. Most of the interesting birding locations can be viewed from the more-level roads at the top of the hill. There is a lovely historic chapel and several benches located throughout the cemetery where you can rest and observe the birds. This is a favorite birding location for Danielle Belleny, aka the Cemetery Birder. Nearby birding can be found at Purgatory Creek Natural Area, Prospect Park, Aquarena Springs, or Schulle Canyon Natural Area.

Tombstone Tail: Turkey Vulture

This large scavenger can be seen soaring in slow, wobbly circles as it searches for carrion by using its keen sense of smell. Turkey Vultures are nature's janitors, cleaning up freshly deceased carcasses across much of the Americas. Only in extreme cases will they feed on live prey. Many live year-round in Texas, while others migrate through in large groups called kettles. I will never forget watching hundreds of them soar effortlessly over the Chamberlain Cemetery in Kingsville during the fall migration.

Lockhart: Lockhart Municipal Burial Park

State Highway 183 and Flores Street

After the Civil War, the town of Lockhart grew rapidly, as people left the war-torn states of the South in search of farmable lands and new opportunities. With few railroads and a demand for beef in the North, the cattle drives began around 1867 and lasted only until the 1880s. Lockhart was one of the central stops along the way, as the herds of Longhorn cattle crossed Plum Creek and marched north along the prairie toward Austin, Waco, Fort Worth, and finally into Missouri. A typical drive

Tombstone Tale

Hollow zinc or white bronze monuments were popular from the mid-1870s to 1914 and could be purchased from the Monumental Bronze Company of Bridgeport, Connecticut. A person could select the style from a catalog and choose the decorative panels for the sides. According to Tui Snider, author of *Understanding Cemetery Symbols: A Field Guide to Historic Graveyards*, the hollow monuments were popular hiding spots for illegal bottles of liquor during the Prohibition era.

took around seven months to complete and averaged about fifteen miles per day. The massive herds with their cowboy escorts often left the town damaged as they passed and certainly left it dusty.

Lockhart has stayed true to the beef and swine industry, as it is generally known as one of the barbecue powerhouses of Texas. The cemetery is across the street from the Kreuz Market, where you can dine without utensils, and whatever you do, don't ask for sauce. If you venture into the town square, there are more barbecue options and numerous historical markers that make for an interesting walking tour.

The cemetery sprawls over a small hill and several rolling acres that are flanked on two sides by the Lockhart City Park and Town Branch Creek. The mix of woodlands, grasslands, and a small pond offers good birding habitat year-round. When I visited in May, I was greeted by a domestic duck and a Black-bellied Whistling-Duck strolling down the dirt road together like a pair of old friends. They walked up to me to see if I had a treat for them, then waddled away after I informed them that I had not brought them anything. The Northern Mockingbirds were also out in force that morning as I meandered down the dirt roads and studied the gravestones and birds in the older section.

During the spring the large live oaks, post oaks, and cedar elms host migrants such as Northern Parulas and Black-throated Green and Yellow Warblers. Swarms of Cliff Swallows nest under the nearby highway overpass and hunt for insects in the airspace above the cemetery. The spring also brings additional insect eaters such as Great Crested and Scissor-tailed Flycatchers, Western Kingbirds, and Eastern Phoebes. As fall returns, so do the birds I call the "cool kids"—otherwise known as Cedar Waxwings, plus American Pipits, Ruby-crowned Kinglets, and the always-abundant Yellow-rumped Warblers. Black-crested and Tufted Titmice exist together, so look carefully for the difference between the two; they are known to hybridize together. Some of the year-round residents include Crested Caracaras, Eastern Bluebirds, American Robins, Lesser Goldfinches, and Red-winged Blackbirds. I think there is more hawk activity here than has been reported, and I look forward to returning in the fall to see what passes overhead.

The gravel roads are not suitable for people with limited mobility; however, much of the birding activity can be done from a car. Nearby birding can be found next door at the City Park or down the road at Lockhart State Park. The Cementerio Navarro Historico is located just east of Highway 183 on Mulberry Street and is worth a visit.

Tombstone Tail: Black-bellied Whistling-Duck

This odd-looking duck has long pink legs, a pink bill, rufous upperparts, and a black belly. These ducks can often be found perched on a fence post, deck, or log and were once called "Tree Ducks." They can be found in wetlands of South and Central Texas, suburban yards, golf courses, and agricultural fields, where they feed, mostly at night, on vegetation and grains. Since the 1980s, they have been expanding their range north of their traditional home of South Texas and along the coast. They sound as if they have swallowed a whistle and are trying to get it unstuck from their long goose-like necks.

Austin: Texas State Cemetery

909 Navasota Street

The Texas State Cemetery was established in Austin in 1851 to be the final resting place for governors and other state-level elected officials, veterans of war, and other important citizens. The site is located about a mile east of the Capitol and sits on twenty-two acres of rolling hills that were once owned by Andrew Jackson Hamilton. The first person to be buried on the hill was General Edward Burleson in 1851.

During and after the Civil War over two thousand Confederates and their wives were interred in the section set aside for them. Many of those burials came later as men from the Texas Confederate Home or the Confederate Women's Home passed away. An acre of land was set aside for veterans of the Union; however, those bodies were later moved to National Cemetery in San Antonio.

By the 1990s the cemetery had fallen into disrepair. Lieutenant Governor Bob Bullock called for a major cleanup of the cemetery, and the Texas legislature approved the funds to create a master plan. JVR & Associates and Texas Parks and Wildlife Department completed a Texas Cemetery Master Plan to "strategize long-term goals in dealing with natural, ceremonial, functional, and cultural issues at the cemetery" (11). Lake Flato Architects designed the monolithic stone Visitor Center along the perimeter on Navasota Street. It is modeled after the Alamo's Long Barracks and the Granary

Tombstone Tale

The tomb of Confederate general Albert Sidney Johnston is a study in Gothic architecture and symbolism. The statue and tomb were designed and sculpted in 1904 by Elizabet Ney, a German-born local sculptor. Ney poetically captures the death of the antebellum South encased in a beautiful yet inescapable cage.

at Mission San José. According to the current Texas State Cemetery Master Plan, "The 255-foot long Visitor Center forms a pedestrian portal into the cemetery and contains an exhibit gallery, offices, and a maintenance facility" (12).

The design also includes a water feature that resembles a Hill Country creek that flows over layers of limestone into several small pools. The sound of the water is calming and offers tranquility to the visitors as they enter. It also provides a good source of water for the birds. There are several nonnative species of plants along the Visitor Center and water feature, which I find disappointing. In my view, the State Cemetery should represent the best of Texas' cultural and natural heritage. That small flaw aside, the majestic live oak and pecan trees are a welcome refuge in the urban center for migrating and resident birds.

As you walk through the rolling hills of the cemetery, you might note that there are more than just elected officials and veterans buried here. Governor George W. Bush appointed the Texas State Cemetery Committee and tasked them with figuring out how to make the cemetery more inclusive and better represent the cultural diversity of the state. In my view, that representation still seems a little thin even after more than twenty years, but it is better than it was. It is certainly more inclusive of football and literary legends.

I was pleased when William (Bill) D. Wittliff, writer, photographer, and creative powerhouse, was approved to be interred at this location when he passed in 2019. Wittliff wrote the screenplays for *Raggedy Man*, *Red Headed Stranger*, *Legends of the Fall*, and *Lonesome Dove*. Additionally, he inspired and assisted young artists to follow their dreams and perfect their craft and share the value and power that art and storytelling have on our human experience. Thankfully, he saw that my brother, Mark Bristol, was a gifted artist, if not a gifted baseball player, when he coached Little League in west Austin. Mark credits Bill as one of the biggest influences on his career as a filmmaker, writer, and artist.

Folklorist and author James Frank Dobie and his wife, Bertha McKee Dobie, are also buried here. Bertha was an active garden club member and worked hard to preserve the Texas bluebells in the 1940s and 1950s. She was an avid birder and spent many a spring on the coast with her husband and her nephew Edgar Kincaid when they visited their friends Connie and Jack Hagar. Bertha was also a prolific writer who often published stories and observations and was an advocate for nature.

The birding here is best during the spring migration, when Black-throated Green, Yellow, Chestnut-sided, Nashville, Common Yellow-throated, and Wilson's Warblers can be found. During the spring and summer, it is also common to see Chimney Swifts, Purple Martins, and Common Nighthawks sweeping the skies for insects. There is a Purple Martin house located in one of the northern lawns. Year-round resident birds include Great-tailed Grackles, Blue Jays, House Finches, White-winged Doves, Black-crested Titmice, and lots of the state bird of Texas—Northern Mockingbirds. As fall and winter arrive, sometimes on the same day, look for the return of Yellow-rumped and Orange-crowned Warblers, Cedar Waxwings, Chipping Sparrows, and Ruby-crowned Kinglets. Monk Parakeets nest in the neighborhoods that surround the cemetery and can be seen flying overhead pretty much every day of the year; occasionally they stop to feed on the lush green lawn.

The Visitor Center offers a nice restroom and historic time line of the state and cemetery. There are also tours that start at the Visitor Center off Navasota Street. The paved paths are accessible, but anyone who is mobility impaired might require assistance, as some of the hills are steep and might not be easy to navigate alone. Nearby birding can be found at the State Capitol, Oakwood Cemetery, or Roy G. Guerrero Colorado River Metro Park. Evergreen Cemetery off East Twelfth Street offers some areas of good habitat and interesting birding.

Tombstone Tail: Northern Mockingbird

This medium-sized gray-and-white bird is the state bird of Texas. Males can sing up to fifteen different songs that mimic those of other birds and often can give a clue about what other birds live in the area. A male can learn up to two hundred songs and calls in his life and can decide which ones to string together each spring to attract a mate. Because of their musical ability, mockingbirds were often trapped and sold in the 1800s; as a result, they almost disappeared from the eastern part of North America. The Migratory Bird Treaty Act of 1918 protected them and all songbirds. They have made a strong comeback because they are well adapted to urban living.

Austin: Oakwood Cemetery

1601 Navasota Street

The city-run cemetery contains some amazing Austinites and state legends. Bill Harvey states in *Texas Cemeteries,* "Oakwood Cemetery exemplifies the history of Texas perhaps more than any other cemetery in the state, largely as a result of Austin's role in its exploration and governance. Oakwood also is a testament to the remarkable contribution that Texas' women have made to the state's history and heritage. Some of Texas' most prominent women are at peace in Oakwood" (34). Indeed, there are some impressive women: Ima Hogg, Annie Webb Blanton, Jane McCallum, Susanna Dickinson Hannig, and the Texas Cattle Queen, Elizabeth "Lizzie" Johnson Williams, to name a few.

When I visited for the first time to bird in mid-June, I expected to see throngs of White-winged Doves, Blue Jays, and Northern Mockingbirds. I was not expecting to be greeted by a pair of Black-bellied Whistling-Ducks sitting in the post oak tree. That is what I love about being in nature; you never know what delights await you.

One thing you might notice right away when visiting the oldest city cemetery in Austin is that it might appear somewhat unkempt or unmowed in some areas. Do not despair. Because the wildflowers and grasses are allowed to grow, the insects and birds have plenty to eat in all seasons. Flowers and grass growing on the graves is in stark contrast to the early days of Oakwood when many of the graves were scraped clean of vegetation. This Victorian-era practice gave visitors the sense that the gravesite was fresh, thus provoking the grief and emotions felt when the person was first buried. Other than the main road, the roads are unpaved, which gives a feeling of being in the country even though you are in the middle of a booming metropolis. The city trudges

Tombstone Tale

The angel is carrying the urn safely to eternity.

and churns just past the perimeter of the forty acres; however, it is remarkably peaceful inside the iron gates.

There is often a nice breeze that moves across the mix of grasses, flowers, and majestic trees set upon the hill. The oldest graves date back to 1839 when the cemetery was established and can be found in the "Old Grounds" south of Main Avenue. To the north of Main Avenue is the Historic "Colored Grounds." The cemetery reflects the segregation of the city and the country at the time it was established. Unlike many segregated cemeteries, this one does not fence off sections of cultural, racial, or religious diversity, with the exception of the two consecrated Beth Israel Jewish sections.

The grasses are abundant in the Historic "Colored Grounds" area near the chapel and attract Chipping, White-crowned, Song, and Vesper Sparrows during the fall and winter. I have spotted Blue-headed Vireos, Black-and-white Warblers, and American Pipits during October in this section. Winter brings the mobs of Cedar Waxwings and Yellow-rumped Warblers that move between the adjacent neighborhoods and the mix of live oak, cedar, pecan, and cedar elm trees in the cemetery. On a warm December afternoon, I witnessed a Peregrine Falcon dive-bomb a young Red-tailed Hawk. The falcon, known as Tower Girl, lives on top of the University of Texas Tower. She moved with such incredible speed that it was hard to keep her in the view finder of my binoculars. The hawk finally made it to the safety of a tree just outside the cemetery, and the falcon circled a few more times, then headed back north toward campus.

The large grove of live oaks at the corner of North Street and West Avenue brings in the migrants during the spring. Look for American Redstarts and Magnolia and Yellow Warblers to arrive in late April and early May alongside Ovenbirds, Chimney Swifts, and Common Nighthawks. There is an impressive Texas persimmon tree just inside the fence of the Beth Israel Cemetery #1 along the southwestern corner. Northern Mockingbirds, Northern Cardinals, and Blue Jays enjoy feasting on the fruit during the summer. From May to August the trees are filled with nesting urban birds, including House Finches, Carolina Wrens, European Starlings, Lesser Goldfinches, and Summer Tanagers.

Ruby-throated and Black-chinned Hummingbirds can be seen buzzing around the variety of flowers, including the red yuccas sprinkled throughout the northern sections. A drainage ditch that might have once been a creek also draws the birds in, especially during the drier spells.

The City of Austin maintains the property and offers tours to learn more about the famous and infamous interred at Oakwood. The City of Austin Parks Department also has an informative story map history on its website that was created in 2020. The main road in the older cemetery is paved, as are the roads in the additional forty-acre annex across the street. For people with limited mobility, I recommend the annex, which also has plenty of good habitat and birds. Nearby birding can be found at McKinney Falls State Park, Texas State Cemetery, and Lady Bird Lake.

Tombstone Tail: Monk Parakeet

This bright green bird is native to South America and was introduced in Austin in the 1970s after a failed pet trader released birds (or so the story goes). Monk Parakeets thrive in the Austin climate and build large colonial nests in the light structures of sports fields across the city. They are constantly chatting with each other as they feed or work on their large, multichambered nests. Some nests can contain living space for more than twenty birds. They are social birds that spend a good deal of time grooming each other or strolling through parks together looking for seeds or grubs. It's fun to bird with people new to Austin and be there when they see the parakeet for the first time.

Georgetown: Old Georgetown Cemetery
200 Scenic Drive

The first graves at this historic pioneer cemetery go back to the 1840s, when many of the first Anglo settlers to the region were buried here. There are only eighty-seven marked graves and an unknown number of unmarked graves in this small cemetery. There is no doubt that this location has seen a flood or two in its time, which has contributed to many of the tombstones being worn down or toppled over.

There are several historical markers at the entrance of the cemetery that share more about the settlers, cemetery, and park system. Once you have had your fill of early Georgetown history, venture down the paved path, first to enjoy the cemetery grounds and then to see the striking cliff above the Blue Hole swimming area. The giant live oak trees surrounding the cemetery and river host a parade of colorful spring migrants such as White-eyed and Blue-headed Vireos, Black-throated Green Warblers, Common Yellowthroats, and Yellow-breasted Chats. The summer is a good time to see Northern Rough-winged and Cliff Swallows, while Purple Martins and Common Nighthawks flash along the water's edge and across the cliffs. Down by the water, look for Great Blue and Green Herons, Snowy and Great Egrets, and Belted Kingfishers. Throughout

Tombstone Tale

The fringed veil draped over the headstone represents the thin shroud between the land of the living and that of the afterlife. The motif was popular during the Victorian era.

the winter the smaller birds such as Ruby-crowned Kinglets, Blue-gray Gnatcatchers, Cedar Waxwings, and Yellow-rumped Warblers dance about the trees gleaning insects and feasting on berries. Harris's, Song, and White-throated Sparrows and Dark-eyed Juncos also return in the winter and can be seen in the grassy areas of the cemetery and park. Every time I have visited I have seen Turkey and Black Vultures gliding through the endless sky. There are over one hundred species recorded for Blue Hole Park, which includes the cemetery.

There is a paved, accessible trail that connects the sidewalks along Scenic Drive to Blue Hole Park. Be aware that there is not designated parking off Scenic Drive, and it can get busy during the summer. Nearby birding locations can be found at Lake Georgetown, San Gabriel Park, Berry Springs Park and Preserve.

Tombstone Tail: Great Blue Heron

This stately, slate-blue wading bird can be found in wetlands and coastlines across the Americas. Great Blue Herons are the largest heron in North America and have a long, S-curved neck and spear-like beak that make it easy for them to snatch up fish, frogs, crawfish, snakes, or snails in shallow waters. They remove oils from their face by preening their specialized feathers or "comb" with an adapted claw on their middle toe. When it is time build a nest, the males present the females with individual sticks that she either accepts and weaves into the nest or tosses over the edge. They will build colonies or rookeries with other birds such as egrets and Roseate Spoonbills. A healthy bird can live more than twenty years.

Georgetown: International Order of Odd Fellows Cemetery

1117 East Seventh Street

I have been pleased with what I have come across in the few times I have visited this large city-run cemetery. The interesting history and gravestones are toward the front of the site just past the entrance gates. However, the better birding is all the way in the back and along the fence line and creek. If you want to get right to the birding, I recommend parking near the back fence of the cemetery by the gate that leads to the park.

The willow and hackberry trees along the creek are attractive to warblers and vireos during the spring migration. When I visited in April, I was delighted to find Painted Buntings, Western Kingbirds, Summer Tanagers, and Eastern Bluebirds, and I even spotted a Swainson's Hawk circling overhead. The bluebonnets were in bloom when I visited, and that alone was worth the trip. Nothing says Hill Country spring like the smell of bluebonnets and the sweet sound of an Eastern Bluebird under a bright blue sky. On that visit I also found Chipping, Lark, and White-throated Sparrows darting in and out of the grasses to the chain-link fence. The morning was so nice that I walked for several hours and, for a time, followed the lonely sound of the Greater Roadrunner until I finally spotted him darting out of the fence line to snatch up a lizard.

When I visited in the winter, I was pleased to find Yellow-rumped and Orange-crowned Warblers, Cedar Waxwings, Ruby-Crowned Kinglets, and Dark-eyed Juncos all dancing through the trees and underbrush of this location. I also spotted American Crows, Common Ravens, and a pair of Red-tailed Hawks on that day.

The majority of roads here are gravel, which makes for easy walking, but they are not the best for wheeled devices. Nearby birding can be found at Blue Hole Park, San Gabriel

Tombstone Tale

A putto, or winged cherub, is a Greco-Roman figure associated with the gods and the realm of heaven. This one seems to be waiting peacefully to blow his horn and announce the ascension of the departed.

Park, or Macedonia Cemetery. Berry Springs Park and Preserve is also nearby and is one of my favorite Central Texas birding spots. Technically, Berry Springs could be considered a cemetery birding location as there is a family burial plot located at the park.

Tombstone Tail: Cedar Waxwing

I refer to Cedar Waxwings as the "cool kids" because they often hang out in flocks or cliques and their black eye mask looks like they are wearing dark sunglasses. Indeed, they are cool in that they are one of only a few birds that can digest all parts of the fruits they eat, a trait that makes them an active seed spreader. Their populations are stable because they have adapted to eating the berries of some invasive plants as well as native ones. They winter as far south as Mexico and across most of the southern portion of the United States and will breed throughout the woodlands of Canada, with some living year-round across the northern states. When in Texas during the winter, they can often be seen in flocks of one hundred or greater. During the winter storm of 2021 there were reports of large numbers of dead Cedar Waxwings. I am interested to see how well their numbers recover.

Liberty Hill: Liberty Hill Cemetery
16101 Texas Highway 29

You know it's a good sign when you pull up to a cemetery and huddled under the live oaks are another pair of birders peering through their binoculars and pointing excitedly at the trees. The excited birders were watching a Blackburnian Warbler feed along the higher branches while a pair of Summer Tanagers passed by with nesting materials. With over one hundred species of birds being recorded here on eBird, this is a peaceful place to deploy some camp chairs and watch for migrants in the shade of the oak grove.

I spent a long and peaceful May morning walking around the sixteen-acre site as the COVID-19 stay-at-home order had just been lifted; nevertheless, Texas and the world were still deep in the throes of the pandemic. Walking the cemetery in the time of a global pandemic gave me an even deeper empathy for the souls who suffered waves of other diseases that passed through.

When the first settlers wandered northwest from Austin in the 1840s, they were taking a huge risk, as the Comanche still fiercely guarded the lands along the San Gabriel watersheds. A few daring families crossed the river and staked their claims on

Tombstone Tale

The Order of the Eastern Star is a body of the Freemasons and is most associated with the women's auxiliary. Traditionally, a woman had to be a sister, wife, widow, or daughter of a Mason to join the order.

the rugged hills between the two forks of the San Gabriel River. Their family names—Bryson, Poole, Smith, and Spencer—can be found throughout the cemetery and town. The Bryson family established the cemetery and operated the stagecoach stop just across the highway.

As I walked among the headstones, I noticed one that belongs to a Nancy Russell, who was born in 1777 and died in 1857. She was born into an emerging country and died in an emerging state. The headstone captured my attention as it is unusual to find the grave of woman born in the 1770s this far west. Not far from her headstone is an obelisk dedicated to Lillian Rivers, which features arrowheads and interesting geodes. Perhaps one of the most interesting markers is that of Benita Gonzalez, which looks like a stylized marble skateboard on a stack of books.

The cemetery has great bird habitat both within the boundaries of the yard and along the perimeter. Not far beyond the fence along the back are several stock ponds and the South Fork of the San Gabriel River. The wetlands support Great Blue Herons, Great and Snowy Egrets, and Black-bellied Whistling-Ducks, which can be seen flying over from time to time. During the fall, the Sandhill Cranes have been spotted from here as they fly south. The fall also brings the return of American Kestrels, Orange-crowned and Yellow-rumped Warblers, Dark-eyed Juncos, and five different types of sparrows. I suspect there are more sparrows that visit the location during the fall and winter.

During the spring migration, warblers and vireos can be found in the live oaks that grace the grounds, while Summer Tanagers and Painted Buntings will nest and stay for the summer. This peaceful location is a good place to listen to and look for the Chuck-will's-widow and Yellow-billed Cuckoos from May to July. This is the heart of the endangered Golden-cheeked Warbler habitat, so I would not be surprised if one occurs here from time to time. I plan on returning in March to listen for its distinctive song.

On the western side is a section of unmowed grasslands that supports sparrows in the winter and Blue Grosbeaks, Dickcissels, and Lark Sparrows during the spring and summer. As I strained to take a decent photo of the Dickcissel, I witnessed a Common Raven being harassed by two American Crows. Williamson County is on the eastern edge of the Common Raven's range; however, it does seem to consistently show up on the bird checklist for the cemetery and nearby locations.

The paved roads are a little rough but okay for people using a wheeled device to aid their mobility. Additional birding can be found at the Balcones Canyonlands National Wildlife Refuge, Sawyer Park, or one of my favorite places, Devine Lake Park in Leander.

Tombstone Tail: Golden-cheeked Warbler

Every Golden-cheeked Warbler is a native-born Texan. These warblers nest exclusively in the oak-juniper forested canyons of Central Texas. The endangered birds have suffered massive habitat loss in both their breeding range of Central Texas and their winter range in southern Mexico and Central America. Conservation efforts began in Central Texas in the 1970s with a larger push to set aside lands in the 1990s as the human populations of Hays, Travis, and Williamson Counties boomed again. These warblers arrive in Texas in March, one of the first warblers to start the spring migration. During March and April, males can be heard singing their distinctive ballad that sounds like the song "La Cucaracha." This species is under constant attack as various land development groups try to remove this bird from the US Fish and Wildlife Endangered Species list.

Lampasas: Oak Hill Cemetery

1010 West Avenue East

Long before the first European settlers arrived in the area, the Tonkawa, Apache, and Comanche frequented Sulphur Springs, which flowed from the deep layers of limestone. The grasslands, oak forests, and clear rivers also brought bison into the region, which made it rich hunting grounds for the first people. Today, the bison are gone, but hunting and fishing still remain two of the economic engines in the county.

The mineral-filled springs became famous in the 1880s, and health spas sprang up to entice guests to heal ailments such as digestion issues, arthritis, skin irritations, infertility, and even nervous disorders. The Hannah Springs Company built a Bath House and Opera House and marketed the town as an oasis of health and culture. The Atchison, Topeka and Santa Fe Railway built the famous two-hundred-room, two-story Park Hotel near Hancock Springs. Of all the many grand hotels, only the Star Hotel still exists in the town.

Tombstone Tale

The dove often represents the Holy Spirit rising, and the olive branch is associated with peace

Even as the spas and resorts developed, life was not without hardships. Prior to 1882 when the railroad was extended to Lampasas, the drovers and cowboys herded millions of cattle through the area to stop over at the river and springs. Gunfights were common, and the edge of the frontier was attractive to a wide range of morally flexible and corrupt persons.

Fire, flood, and drought also plagued the county. With wool, cotton, and cattle as the mainstays of industry, the seven-year drought of the 1950s hit the region hard. Once the beautiful rain clouds finally accumulated on the horizon, they unleashed over twelve inches of rain in one event to cause the worst flooding ever in the region, and over six feet of water filled the buildings along the town square.

All this hardship led to the need for a city cemetery. In 1872, Hartwell Fountain gave ten acres to the city for use as a cemetery. Now known as Oak Hill Cemetery, the original ten acres has expanded to include over sixty acres of rolling limestone hills adjacent to a medium-sized soil-conservation pond. The pond attracts waterfowl year-round, with the most activity occurring during the winter. From October to April, look for Gadwalls, Redheads, American Wigeons, Northern Pintails, and Ring-necked and Wood Ducks to be present on the lake. Greater Yellowlegs and Great Egrets feed gracefully along the edges of the wetland. The fall and winter also bring in Northern Flickers, Eastern Bluebirds, Cedar Waxwings, and Chipping Sparrows that feed in the oaks and grasses along the hills. Lark Sparrows are more common during the summer; however, some will stay in the area year-round.

With the arrival of spring, look for Western Kingbirds, Scissor-tailed Flycatchers, and Cave and Barn Swallows to be feeding throughout the cemetery. Along the edges of the cemetery where the brush and trees are dense, I found Bell's and White-eyed Vireos in April. Summer Tanagers and Painted Buntings can also be heard singing during the spring and will nest in the area. The year-round birds are consistent with those found across much of the central part of the Edwards Plateau: Northern Cardinals, Northern Mockingbirds, White-winged Doves, Blue Jays, Black-crested Titmice, and Bewick's and Carolina Wrens. Greater Roadrunners can be found throughout the cemetery as they hunt for lizards, snakes, and insects. When I visited in April, a pair was cooing softly to each other in the cool spring morning. With over 110 species recorded at this location, the birding here is solid for most of the year.

Most of the streets are paved and suitable for wheeled mobility devices. Some of the inclines might be steep, but they are easily avoided to still offer a rewarding birding experience. The Highland Lakes Birding and Wildflower Society often takes birding field trips to this location and is to thank for its recording of many of the more than one hundred birds sighted here. Nearby birding can be found at Cooper Springs Nature Trail and Park, Hancock Springs Park, or Colorado Bend State Park.

Tombstone Tail: Green-winged Teal

This dapper dabbling duck is the smallest of the dabblers in North America. What it lacks in size it makes up for in quantity, with flocks numbering into the thousands during the winter. This is also the second-most-hunted duck, just after the Mallard. Regulated bag limits and hunting seasons have helped keep its populations steady. The males have a rich cinnamon-colored head with an emerald-green crescent that swoops down the back of their neck. Females are generally mottled-brown with one cluster of emerald-green feathers on their wings. Males also have a patch of green on their wings that is less visible when they are in the water. Healthy teals can live up to twenty years.

Brownwood: Greenleaf Cemetery

2615 US 377

I did not think I was going to find many birds here when I first entered the gates off US 377 on a clear, cool March morning. Once I ventured to the older section among the mature live oak and pecan trees, I was proven wrong. A Northern Mockingbird was busy announcing the arrival of spring from the top of one of the historical markers located in this section. In the trees above the markers were Black-crested Titmice, Carolina Chickadees, Eastern Bluebirds, House Finches, and American Goldfinches. Along the fence line I observed several American Robins, and I stopped to take their picture when a male Northern Cardinal showed up to say, *look-at-me*.

The mix of oaks, pecans, and grasses supports a variety of birds during the spring and fall migrations. Watch for Dickcissels to be feeding in the grasslands, while Barn Swallows and Purple Martins sweep between the headstones. Red-eyed Vireos pass quickly through the area, while White-eyed Vireos linger for the summer along with Painted Buntings and Lark Sparrows. As fall and winter return, watch for Spotted Towhees; Song, Field, Chipping, and White-crowned Sparrows; along with Yellow-rumped and Orange-crowned Warblers.

The cemetery is much larger than the original five acres that were given in 1868 by Greenleaf Fisk. I could not find information on the current acreage, but I walked one and a half miles on my first visit and still did not see all the sections. The roads here are paved and accessible for people with limited mobility. As I walked, I was shocked and pleased to find the grave of Robert E. Howard, who was the creator of Conan the Barbarian and a celebrated poet. Also buried at Greenleaf is Mollie Armstrong, the first female optometrist in Texas.

The cemetery has a long and interesting history that captures a snapshot of the town's evolution. An interesting fact I learned from the Brown County History Center

Tombstone Tale

A thistle, a symbol of Scotland, often adorns the headstones of people of Scottish heritage.

was that in 1918 the Spanish flu was so deadly in the area that the cemetery saw an average of four burials per day. Crews worked days and nights to dig the graves and set the headstones.

If you don't get your fill of birding and history at Greenleaf, I recommend visiting the Santa Anna Cemetery in Santa Anna and the Coleman City Cemetery in Coleman. There is also good birding at Lake Brownwood State Park and Riverside Park, both located in Brownwood.

Tombstone Tail: Red-eyed Vireo

This olive-green and white vireo sports a distinct black cap and red eyes. These vireos winter in the Amazon Basin and return to Texas and parts of North America to breed where mixed forests with abundant undergrowth occur. The males are prolific singers and spend a great deal of their time announcing the boundaries of their territory from the tops of trees. Males have been known to sing over twenty thousand times in a day. Males and females will aggressively defend their nests, especially against cowbirds. Caterpillars make up 50 percent of their diet, with mosquitos, flies, moths, and other insects along with berries and seeds making up the rest. Their populations are strong; however, since they prefer the interior of dense forests, habitat loss and urban encroachment impact their survival.

Hamilton: Independent Order of Odd Fellows Cemetery Complex

567 North Rice Street

The small town of Hamilton sits tucked away along the banks of Pecan Creek and at the intersection of Highways 281 and 36. It has been the county seat of Hamilton County since 1856, with the first families settling in the area in 1854. Despite being a fairly small town, it has an interesting history that the citizens celebrate and honor with various historical markers and murals. One such citizen is Ann Whitney (1828–67).

Ann Whitney was a young teacher in Massachusetts who answered an advertisement for a schoolteacher position in the newly settled town of Hamilton. She did not know then that she would become the heroine of Hamilton County. She made the ultimate sacrifice of her life to protect the schoolchildren in her care from an attack by Native Americans. She barred the door with her body as she was being shot with arrows to allow the children time to escape out the back window. Thanks to her, the children lived and recounted her valor over the years. In addition to the historical marker at her grave, she is memorialized by the Ann Whitney Elementary School.

Tombstone Tale

The hand pointing up simply means gone to heaven or gone home.

The cemetery is a complex of the Independent Order of Odd Fellows (IOOF), Graves Gentry, and Old Hamilton Cemeteries. As soon as I parked along Bell Street, I was instantly drawn in by the quaintness of the location. The curbed family plots, old stone walls, iron lychgates, and wildflowers make for a picture-perfect rural cemetery.

The birding here is not off the charts, but I have been pleased the few times I have visited. This is not a spring-migrant trap for warblers, but there are a good number of flycatchers that arrive in April and stick around until September. The lovely Lark Sparrows, Painted Buntings, and Barn Swallows also return in the spring and stay through the summer. In the fall, Rufous-crowned, White-crowned, Savannah, and Chipping Sparrows all return along with Dark-eyed Juncos and Pine Siskins. The winter also sees the return of Ruby-crowned and Golden-crowned Kinglets. American Robins, Eastern Bluebirds, and House Finches hang out year-round, alongside Downy, Ladder-backed, and Red-bellied Woodpeckers. Northern Flickers can be found here during the winter and early spring. It is also common to see three types of wrens at this location with Bewick's, House, and Carolina Wrens all living in the area.

This is a historic cemetery with several terraces that are not suitable for people with limited mobility. The cemetery is also close to Shrunk and Pecan Creek Parks; both have a Texas Parks and Wildlife Birding Trails sign and offer additional good places to bird. City Lake Park is also just down the road, which is another good birding location with plenty of waterfowl in the winter.

Tombstone Tail: Lark Sparrow

This medium-sized sparrow has a distinct rust, buff, and black mask; streaky upperparts; and a buff belly. These sparrows can be found year-round across most of Central and East Texas where open grasslands are abundant. Their numbers increase during spring and summer as larger numbers migrate from Mexico as far north as British Columbia. Look for them to be strolling along in grasslands or flying in and out of thickets as they search for seeds and insects. A group of sparrows is called a crew or flutter.

Meridian: Meridian City Cemetery

410 South Hill Street

Meridian is the county seat of Bosque County, which sits on the northern edge of the Edwards Plateau and Cross Timbers region. When the town was being surveyed by Texas Revolution war hero George B. Erath, he included the grounds for the cemetery in the original plan. Set upon a hill overlooking the town, the cemetery is a lovely place for the departed to spend eternity listening to the breeze ease through the oak and cedar groves.

The large trees offer cooling shade in the warmer months that makes this cemetery easy to visit in just about any season. My husband and I enjoy camping at Meridian State Park, and I try to come visit the cemetery when we are in town. Admittedly, the

Tombstone Tale

A mortar and pestle most often represent someone who was a pharmacist or a doctor.

best birding in the area is out at the state park, especially when the Golden-cheeked Warblers are nesting in the spring. That said, I am always impressed with the number of birds I find at the cemetery.

When I visited in December, it seemed that every tree had a flock of something in it. There were flocks of Northern Cardinals, House Finches, Cedar Waxwings, American Robins, Chipping Sparrows, Dark-eyed Juncos, and Yellow-rumped Warblers. There was even a murder of American Crows squawking in the distance as they circled the courthouse. In the spring, I dropped by and watched a pair of Painted Buntings build their nest and listened to the enchanting song of the Summer Tanager. The hilltop vantage makes this a good place to see migrating geese or hawks during the fall.

Meridian has been a farming and ranching community since it was founded and remains so today. Several notable people have come from Meridian, including famed folklorist and song writer John Lomax. There are less notable people, such as J. J. and Ida Lumpkin, who did not have to be famous to enhance the lives of the townspeople. The Lumpkins are credited with donating the first library building and books to the town, thus increasing literacy in children and inspiring the imaginations of all generations through reading.

The shaded graveled roads offer easy walking but are not ideal for people with limited mobility. I will admit I ate my lunch and birded from the car at this location one cold, rainy afternoon and observed plenty of birds. The pecan groves at the city park along the river offer additional birding in town. Meridian State Park is just south of town and has excellent birding in all seasons.

Tombstone Tail: Eastern Screech-Owl

This little owl can be found across the United States and northern Mexico, east of the Rocky Mountains. It nests in small cavities and will take up residence in nesting boxes in yards and parks. When the female is incubating the eggs and sitting with the brood, she is totally dependent on the male to bring food. The male stays close in the nook of a tree or another cavity where he can keep watch over the nest. This little owl is a master of camouflage, as its feathers closely resemble the pattern of tree bark. Pairs will mate for life and return to a good nesting spot year after year.

Eastern Kingbird in spring migration - Georgetown

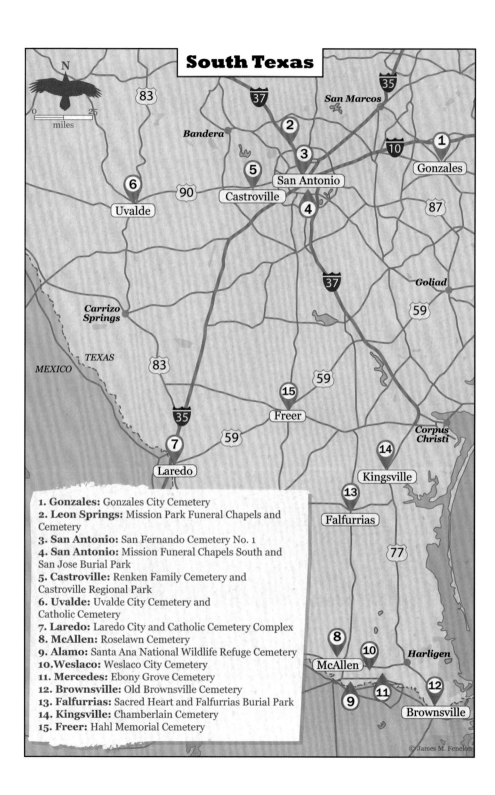

South Texas

N

0 — 25
miles

83

37

35

San Marcos

2

Bandera

10

1

Gonzales

3

5

6

90

San Antonio

Castroville

87

Uvalde

4

Carrizo
Springs

Goliad

37

59

TEXAS

MEXICO

83

59

15

Freer

Corpus
Christi

35

59

14

7

Kingsville

Laredo

13

Falfurrias

8

77

10

Harligen

McAllen

9

11

12

Brownsville

1. **Gonzales:** Gonzales City Cemetery
2. **Leon Springs:** Mission Park Funeral Chapels and Cemetery
3. **San Antonio:** San Fernando Cemetery No. 1
4. **San Antonio:** Mission Funeral Chapels South and San Jose Burial Park
5. **Castroville:** Renken Family Cemetery and Castroville Regional Park
6. **Uvalde:** Uvalde City Cemetery and Catholic Cemetery
7. **Laredo:** Laredo City and Catholic Cemetery Complex
8. **McAllen:** Roselawn Cemetery
9. **Alamo:** Santa Ana National Wildlife Refuge Cemetery
10. **Weslaco:** Weslaco City Cemetery
11. **Mercedes:** Ebony Grove Cemetery
12. **Brownsville:** Old Brownsville Cemetery
13. **Falfurrias:** Sacred Heart and Falfurrias Burial Park
14. **Kingsville:** Chamberlain Cemetery
15. **Freer:** Hahl Memorial Cemetery

©James M. Fenelon

South Texas

South Texas includes around 20.5 million acres of land that roughly starts around San Antonio and encompasses everything to the south with the exception of the Coastal Bend region, which hugs the coastline. As an ecoregion, it mostly contains the South Texas Plains with a mix of the Gulf Coast Prairies and Marshes. The first Spanish explorers reported stirrup-high grasslands punctuated by brush stands and subtropical woodlands, especially along the rivers. A remnant of the subtropical sabal palm forest can still be found along the Rio Grande at the Sabal Palm Audubon Center south of Brownsville.

The grasslands became world famous as a place for raising cattle and cultivating cotton. In the Rio Grande Valley, considered one of the most productive agricultural regions in the country, the fertile soils with irrigation sustain citrus trees and vegetables of every sort. Grazing and farming changed the landscape, and as domesticated animals increased, so did the intensity of the scrub brush. The King and Kenedy Ranches once sprawled over millions of acres in the region and are still formidable islands of habitat for thousands of species of plants and animals.

Overhunting of White-winged Dove and white-tailed deer sounded the alarm for conservation lands to be set aside to protect these important species and their habitat. A system of national wildlife refuges, state parks, and state wildlife management areas, along with a variety of local nature centers and private landowners, help protect these South Texas species.

There is a vast area between the Nueces River and Rio Grande that is still more populated by cattle than people. However, along the Lower Rio Grande Valley, there is intense human activity, as the metro area now has the eighth-largest population in the United States. The Valley also offers some of the best birding in the world and is host to nine World Birding Centers where visitors can enjoy the natural wonders of the region.

Gonzales: Gonzales City Cemetery
1200 North College Street

Set on the banks of the San Marcos and Guadalupe Rivers, the town of Gonzales has a rich and significant history. In 1835, fewer than one hundred people lived in Gonzales, but it was still considered a major town in DeWitt's Colony. The settlers, living in constant fear of attacks from Native Americans, had a small cannon, a gift from the Mexican government, to help ward off raiding parties. It was the cannon that blasted Gonzales into the history books when John H. Moore rallied his fellow Texans to dare commander Francisco de Castañeda and one hundred Mexican dragoons to "come and take it." The Battle of Gonzales was the first skirmish of the Texas Revolution and emboldened the Texans with the notion that they could defeat the mighty Mexican army and free themselves from Mexico.

The rest, as they say, is history. The town has multiple historical markers and a museum that I recommend visiting to learn more about the people and history of the community. There are also several interesting public and private cemeteries located in and around the historic town; however, the old City Cemetery has the best birding due to the variety of trees mixed with native grasses and shrubs. I have visited several times and always seem to find something new. The cemetery was founded in 1838 when many of the early settlers' graves were moved from the town's center to this

Tombstone Tale

The French word *botonee* means "button." The botonee cross has a cluster of buttons or balls at the three points. The metal botonee crosses were popular among Catholic Germans and French settlers.

location. The mix of Mexican, German, French, English, and eastern European names on the headstones tell the story of Texas.

The large, old trees are attractive to Red-bellied, Downy, Ladder-backed, and occasionally Golden-fronted Woodpeckers throughout the year. Other year-round residents include American Crows, Mourning and White-winged Doves, Northern Mockingbirds, Tufted Titmice, Eastern Bluebirds, Northern Cardinals, and Killdeers—lots of Killdeers.

During the spring and summer, the warblers migrate through but do not pause long. If the winds are right, they will fly right past Gonzales as they move north from the coast. With that said, Nashville Warblers and Common Yellowthroats do frequent the area along with other songbirds such as Summer Tanagers and Indigo and Painted Buntings. The flycatchers stick around longer, with many arriving in late March and staying until September. Chimney Swifts, Purple Martins, and Barn Swallows can also be seen feeding in the open spaces of the newer burial grounds during the spring and summer.

Look for American Pipits and Chipping, Savannah, Song, and Lincoln's Sparrows to be feeding in the grasslands during the fall and winter. Winter is also a good time to watch the trees in the older part of the cemetery for Cedar Waxwings, American Goldfinches, and Yellow-rumped, Pine, and Orange-crowned Warblers. Carolina and House Wrens, House Finches, and House Sparrows can frequently be found along the fence line.

As in many historic cemeteries the central looping road is a gravel mix that makes for easy walking but is not suitable for wheelchairs or wheeled walkers. The road is tight in the cemetery, so it is best to park along North College Street and walk in through the main gate. Nearby birding can be found at Palmetto State Park, Independence Park along the Guadalupe River, or the cemetery complex off Holmes Street.

Tombstone Tail: Chipping Sparrow

This busy sparrow can be found in cemeteries across Texas, especially if there is a mix of native grasslands and mature trees. The distinctive rust-colored cap makes these sparrows easy to identify once they sit still long enough to focus on. They constantly make a chip sound as they forage for food. During migrations, they take to the trees to forage for insects to fuel them up for their journey. Chipping Sparrows winter in Mexico and Texas and summer as far north as Alaska, with some birds living year-round in Central and East Texas.

San Antonio: Mission Funeral Chapels and Cemetery and San José Burial Park

8235 Mission Road

This is an interesting complex of cemeteries south of downtown San Antonio between Missions San José and San Juan. The Mission Funeral Chapels and Cemetery, along with San Jose Burial Park, create a fair amount of habitat for the birds. Both have wetlands, mature trees, and plenty of watered grass. Mission Park is the better birding park, especially down by New Espada Lake, which shares a shore with Espada Park and the Mission Trails system that follows the San Antonio River. This is an active burial park, so please be considerate and give grieving families plenty of space.

On a perfect fall day in November my husband and I spotted thirty species of birds in two hours. The mature live oak, red oak, cypress, hackberry, pecan, palm, and willow trees stand watch over the graves and provide food and lodging for migrating and resident birds. We parked along the palm tree–lined driveway that enters from Mission Road near the row of mausoleums. Along the ridge the trees were bustling with resident birds such as Northern Mockingbirds, Northern Cardinals, Carolina Chickadees, and Blue Jays, while a Red-tailed Hawk soared overhead.

Down the hill by New Espada Lake is where the real action happens in this immaculately kept cemetery. The wetlands provide habitat for Black-bellied Whistling-Ducks, Neotropic Cormorants, and Pie-billed Grebes, while the willow trees host warblers during the spring. There is a resident Belted Kingfisher that frequents the

Tombstone Tale

The Egyptian revival style was popular in the 1920s. The sphinx has a lion's body and face or head of a man and can often be found guarding the entrance to a tomb or mausoleum. The vulture's wings surrounding the sun disc represent the Egyptian mythological god Ra, who rules the sun, earth, and the underworld.

small lake and does not mind stopping for a quick photo opportunity as long as you do not get too close.

William H. Chambers purchased the rolling hills above the San Antonio River as a wedding gift for his wife, Clara Mahone Chambers. In 1907, they opened the first perpetual-care cemetery in Bexar County. The cemetery is now owned and operated by Mission Park Funeral Chapels and Cemeteries, which also maintains the historic San Jose Burial Park. I have to admit I very much enjoyed sitting by the lake at the San Jose site to watch the ducks and marvel at the cypress trees in their rich rusty fall color.

Both cemeteries offer first-rate birding for all mobility types. The paved roads are well maintained and easy to navigate. Nearby birding can be found at Espada Park, San Antonio Missions National Historical Park, and Mitchell Lake Audubon Center. The Audubon Center offers excellent education programs and guided bird walks to learn more about the fascinating species of the region. Please note that the Audubon Center hours change for each season, so check its website before visiting.

Tombstone Tail: Belted Kingfisher

This is the most common kingfisher in Texas; however, it is often easier to hear its distinct rattle call than to see one. These kingfishers have keen vision and can see you coming long before you see them; they also use that vision to peer into clear water to spy a tasty fish. Their large beak and head are adapted to plunge into the water at high speeds to snatch up a fish. Like owls, they regurgitate the bones of their prey in pellets. They are one of the few birds in which the females are more brightly colored than the males, even if that is only by one rust-colored breast patch. They build their nests in burrows along the banks of streams, rivers, or lakes, and pairs are in constant communication with each other during nesting season.

San Antonio: San Fernando Cemetery No. 1
1100 South Colorado

This historic Catholic cemetery is located near the confluence of Alazan and Apache Creeks in the Avenida Guadalupe neighborhood of southwest San Antonio. Burials began here in the 1840s, and it is the final resting place of many famous Texans, including José Antonio Navarro, who was one of three Mexicans and one of two native-born Texan signers of the Texas Declaration of Independence.

The Santa Rosa Hospital, later the Children's Hospital of San Antonio, was established in 1869 by the Sisters of Charity of the Incarnate Word, and soon thereafter they started offering services to children. One of San Antonio's oldest cemeteries was located next to the hospital. When the hospital expanded in 1920 and the cemetery was razed, it was reported that all three thousand bodies were moved to San Fernando Cemetery No. 1 in just twenty-four hours. There was deep skepticism from the beginning that all the remains had actually made it. Sadly, many of the burial records housed at the San Fernando Cathedral perished in a flood during 1921.

Tombstone Tale

Many statues have been erected that characterize the seven virtues. Faith is often represented by an angel or virgin holding or leaning on a cross. The flower wreath in her hand represents beauty and victory over death.

In 2016 those fears were further confirmed when remains were found by a construction crew working at the Children's Hospital as it expanded again. Construction on the hospital's prayer garden came to a halt after the discovery. At first it was thought that just a few bodies had been left behind after the move. However, after several months of excavation and cataloging it was announced that they had remains for around seventy people. The descendants of many of the first families of San Antonio came together to question if the remains of their ancestors had actually been moved in the 1920s or if just the headstones had been relocated.

Descendants of the Native Americans, Canary Islanders, Spaniards, Mexicans, Tejanos, German, Italian, and French early settlers still live in the area and were alarmed by the discovery. More insult to injury was added when the family members learned these seventy persons would be reinterred at Sunset Memorial Park. Why not San Fernando Cemetery or another Catholic cemetery? Because Texas law states that bodies found under these circumstances have to be reinterred at a perpetual-care facility, which Sunset Memorial is and San Fernando Cemetery is not.

The history of this site is almost more exciting than the birding. However, I was very pleased to come across Pyrrhuloxias, Loggerhead Shrikes, and Ruby-crowned Kinglets all feeding in the same bush in section 12 when I visited in January. I was also excited to see a Great Egret lumber past as it traveled from one creek to the next. Apache Creek is visible from the cemetery and hosts egrets and herons along the waterway, while the grasses along the banks are home to wintering sparrows and Lesser and American Goldfinches. The Apache Creek Trail runs along the creek and is part of the network of trails that connect using the green infrastructure of the arroyos. The spring and summer bring the return of Great Crested and Scissor-tailed Flycatchers and Western Kingbirds, along with Chimney Swifts and Barn Swallows. The pretty little Inca Doves can be found here year-round along with White-winged and Eurasian Collared Doves.

The gravel roads might not be suitable for people with limited mobility. However, the mature oaks and mesquites offer shade along the roads, which makes for enjoyable walking. Birding nearby and in the city can be found at Confluence Park, Elmendorf Lake Park, and the San Antonio Botanical Gardens. I have also found excellent birding in Brackenridge Park between the Witte Museum and San Antonio Zoo.

Tombstone Tail: Pyrrhuloxia

This red-and-gray bird looks like a cardinal with an extra-large beak and crest. Its big beak allows it to be an opportunistic eater in the desert-scrub ecoregions of Arizona, New Mexico, Texas, and Mexico. Like most desert birds, Pyrrhuloxias acquire most of the water they need from the fruits and insects they consume. During the winter they form large flocks of up to one thousand birds that disperse in the spring as they partner up for breeding season. The Pyrrhuloxia's cheerful song is much like a Northern Cardinal's, and during the spring the males are quite vocal.

Leon Springs: Mission Park Funeral Chapels and Cemetery

20900 Interstate 10 West

This considerable cemetery rests along the banks of Leon Creek and is flanked by Raymond Russell Park and the Dominion Country Club and Golf Course, creating a decent-sized swath of habitat. This is still an active burial park, so please exercise respect and reverence when visiting. It is a large location, so plan to take your time to wander down the paved, looping roads, and if you get tired, there are plenty of benches to take a moment to relax and reflect.

The riparian area and mix of beautiful live oaks and grasses are attractive to migrating Black-throated Green, Yellow, Nashville, and Tennessee Warblers. I have also found Painted Buntings and Summer Tanagers singing and building their nests during the spring. One Summer Tanager was tugging at the string of a deflated balloon to use as nesting material; it eventually gave up and moved on to gather a long strand of grass instead.

Tombstone Tale

An *exedra* is an ancient Greek burial fixture that serves as a place to sit and reflect. It is often a curved bench made of marble and features the name or names of the family members interred in the plot or mausoleum it graces.

During the fall, Northern Flickers, Blue-headed Vireos, and Hermit Thrushes all return, along with Cedar Waxwings and Yellow-rumped Warblers. The fall and winter also bring in Chipping, Lincoln's, Savannah, Rufous-crowned, and White-throated Sparrows, along with Spotted Towhees and American Goldfinches. When I visited in the winter, I witnessed a Great Egret hunting in the creek, and I stirred up a mess of ducks that I did not identify. Here I have also watched Golden-fronted Woodpeckers scoot along the trees in search of insects.

The paved, looping streets offer accessible birding for people using a wheeled mobility device and for people with small children in strollers. The cemetery is located close to the Friedrich Wilderness Park and Camp Bullis Military Reserve, which are prime Golden-cheeked Warbler and Black-capped Vireo habitat. I would not be surprised if one popped up at this location from time to time. There have been almost two hundred species of birds recorded at the Friedrich Wilderness Park, which is located just across the highway.

Tombstone Tail: Great Egret

This elegant, large white wading bird can be found year-round in Texas' wetlands and along the coast. As I noted in Parking Lot Birding, "During breeding season males develop a neon-green patch between their beak and eye, and they develop long plumes along their back that are used to dazzle the females. Human females also became enamored with these plumes during the Victorian era and used them to decorate their hats" (23). Thanks to the Migratory Bird Treaty Act of 1918 and changes in the millinery trade, their populations have recovered and are stable after being hunted almost to extinction.

Castroville: Renken Family Cemetery and Castroville Regional Park

816 Alsace Avenue

This is a great example of a small family burial plot that was so common throughout Texas before larger cemeteries were established in local towns. There are actually two family plots in close proximity; the Renken graves are located in the park, and the Ihnken family cemetery is just across the street. When Henry Renken's wife died in 1876, he chose this place to bury her instead of the established St. Louis Cemetery around the corner. I can only think that this piece of land had some meaning to the two, as it was donated back to Henry after he had sold the property just two years previously to the Ihnken family. Renken was by no means poor and certainly had other lands to choose from; however, this is the place he wanted for his beloved Lissette, who had crossed the ocean with him from their homeland in Germany.

Tombstone Tale

Crosses are more common in Catholic cemeteries but can be found even in a nondenominational graveyard. The Cross of Suffering has pointed ends to represent the suffering of Christ. (The photo of the crosses comes from the St. Louis Cemetery.)

Lissette was the first wife of Henry Renken, and even though he remarried, he chose to be buried next to her and was later joined by their daughter. Renken was mayor of Castroville, and the symbol on his headstone indicates he was a Mason and community leader until his death in 1885.

In 1842, Henri Castro entered into a contract with the newly established Texas government to settle a colony along the Medina River and populate it primarily with German and French citizens from the Alsace region. Between 1843 and 1847, Castro was successful in bringing twenty-seven shiploads of 485 families and 457 single men from Europe to the region. Eventually Castro brought over six thousand people to Texas to settle the 1.6-million-acre land grant of which he was the empresario. Each wave of immigrants brought their own culture, language, food, and unique Alsatian style of architecture that can be seen throughout the town. The town still boasts itself as the "Little Alsace of Texas."

The 126-acre Castroville Regional Park is situated along the Medina River and has 223 species of birds recorded on eBird. I would say that there are no bad birding days at this park unless there is some extreme Texas-strength weather event. The birding is good in every season, mostly because there are so many year-round birds that live in the woods along the crystal-clear river or in the grasslands near the graves. There are viewing platforms along the river, which make it easy to spot Great Blue and Green Herons, Great and Snowy Egrets, and Belted and Green Kingfishers, with an occasional visit from a Ringed Kingfisher. The wren population is also healthy here, with Carolina, Bewick's, Cactus, House, and Winter Wrens all spending time in the park.

During the spring migration and into the summer a colorful array of birds passes through, such as Yellow, Black-and-white, and Nashville Warblers; Northern Parulas; Summer Tanagers; and Indigo and Painted Buntings. There are a surprising number of Audubon's, Bullock's, Hooded, and Scott's Orioles that arrive in spring and linger into the summer. The wetlands and open fields make a perfect place for the Barn, Cave, Cliff, and Northern Rough-winged Swallows to feed alongside other insect eaters such as Chimney Swifts, Purple Martins, and Vermilion Flycatchers. The fall and winter continue to be active with Verdins, Hermit Thrushes, American Robins, Eastern Meadowlarks, and thirteen types of sparrows. During the winter it is also common to see Crested Caracaras, Red-shouldered and Red-tailed Hawks, and Ospreys.

Portions of this park are accessible to wheeled mobility devices, while other parts of the paved roads might be a little rough. There is a decomposed granite walking trail, and for the more adventurous, there is a longer trail that takes visitors up on the bluff above the park. Nearby birding can be found at the St. Louis and Zion Lutheran Cemetery complex on the northwestern edge of the park. Both are worth a visit both to bird and to see one of the most unique graveyards in Texas.

Tombstone Tail: Audubon's Oriole

This black and lemon-yellow bird was once called the Black-headed Oriole, which seems like a better name. Both the males and females have a black head, wings, and tail, with bright yellow body and underparts. Castroville is in the northern range of these birds, which live only in Mexico and Texas. Since the 1920s the species has been in decline, especially in Texas, due to habitat loss and nest invasion from the Bronzed Cowbird. They are a treat to see and hear, as their song is as bold and beautiful as their colors.

Uvalde: Uvalde City and Catholic Cemeteries
1210 West Main Street

I was pleasantly surprised by how good the birding was at this location when my mother and I drove through the gates and parked near Vice President John Nance Garner's (1868–1967) grave. Garner and his wife, Mariette, were responsible for establishing Garner State Park in the 1930s. As the thirty-second vice President, Garner pushed to enact the New Deal and create the Civilian Conservation Corps (CCC) along with President Franklin D. Roosevelt. There is a nice museum in town to learn more about "Cactus Jack" (Garner's nickname) and his equally dynamic wife.

When we arrived, we were greeted by a very handsome Greater Roadrunner. He was so busy displaying for his lady friend that he was totally uninterested in us. In the same area we spotted Pyrrhuloxias, White-crowned Sparrows, Eastern Meadowlarks, and the always-present Northern Mockingbirds.

The cemetery is well maintained and filled with Confederate and Union graves as this part of the country opened up after the Civil War and, more important, after the Comanche and Lipan Apache were defeated. Veterans of both sides of the conflict settled and died here as they moved west looking for land and opportunity.

A Vermilion Flycatcher posed on an old iron fence in the amber light of the warm February afternoon when we visited. The brilliant red flycatcher was not to be outdone by the Loggerhead Shrike, which impaled its sunset meal on the thorn of a mesquite

Tombstone Tale

During the Victorian era into the mid-1900s the flower box was a popular style. The box sometimes looks more like a bathtub than a box. The purpose was to provide a place for family members to plant flowers and leave gifts to the departed. Many are now filled in with gravel or left fallow instead of being maintained as intended.

tree as I watched. A few trees down, two Golden-fronted Woodpeckers worked along the trunk of a large hackberry tree. The pair constantly chattered to each other and threw a verbal fit when a Yellow-bellied Sapsucker arrived. We were busy looking at our smartphones to verify that the bird was in fact a sapsucker when a high-pitched screech got us to raise our heads. An American Kestrel was in hot pursuit of a Red-tailed Hawk, and they looked like a pair of jet fighters sweeping through the open spaces between the large trees. Finally, the hawk gained enough altitude to cause the daring kestrel to retreat. We also observed Curve-billed Thrashers, Blue-headed Vireos, Ruby-crowned Kinglets, Cactus Wrens, and Killdeers as we meandered through the grounds. All of this action happened in less than an hour.

During the fall and winter Eastern and Western Meadowlarks can both be found in the area as can Lincoln's, Song, Vesper, White-crowned, Lark, and Black-throated Sparrows. Occasionally a Cassin's Sparrow passes through. Look for Blue Grosbeaks, Painted Buntings, Summer Tanagers, and Bullock's, Hooded, and Orchard Orioles during the spring and summer. Spring brings insect specialists into the area, such as Ash-throated, Brown-crested, and Great Crested Flycatchers; Black, Eastern, and Say's Phoebes; and Couch's and Western Kingbirds. If you like wrens as much as I do, then this is a great place to search for Bewick's, Cactus, Carolina, and House Wrens with an occasional visit from a Winter Wren.

The roads are not paved at this location or across the street at the Hillcrest Cemetery, which makes it difficult for people with limited mobility. With that said, most of the habitat where the birds exist can be seen from a car if visitors wish to use their car as a mobile bird blind. Nearby birding can be found at the Cook's Slough Nature Center, where more than 280 species have been recorded. Garner State Park is also a wonderful place to bird; however, it can get a bit crowded on the weekends during the spring migration, so make sure you reserve your day pass or campsite well in advance. The Seminole Indian Scout Cemetery between Uvalde and Brackettville is a noteworthy point of interest if your travels take you farther west.

Tombstone Tail: Greater Roadrunner

This fleet-footed bird can outrun a human but, contrary to popular belief, cannot outrun a coyote. Coyotes often prey on the birds, as do bobcats; roadrunners can evade them with short flights or by leaping into trees. Like many birds of the Southwest, they can extract most of the water they need from the lizards, snakes, toads, moths, and even other birds that they feed on. They also eat venomous snakes such as rattlesnakes. A pair will hunt a rattler with one distracting the snake while the other sneaks up behind it and pins its head to the ground, when both dive in to peck the snake to death. In the past few decades they have expanded their range east to include parts of Louisiana and Missouri. Measuring around two feet in length from beak to tail, they are impressive birds.

Laredo: Laredo City and Catholic Cemetery Complex

3600 McPherson Road

Laredo has a long and complicated history that is all reflected in the family, religious, and fraternal plots that grace the large cemetery complex. The City Cemetery was established in 1892, over 130 years after Tomás Sánchez de la Barrera y Garza brought the first settlers into the area with the hopes of establishing a town. The early Spanish settlers found the lack of rain and arid land difficult to farm except along the life-giving river. However, Spain was counting on settlers to establish a city to thwart the western expansion of the French and bring religion to the Indigenous people. In those early years, the settlers saw little of either the French or Indigenous people.

Tombstone Tale

The Knights of Pythias is a benevolent society formed in 1864 and is based on the Greek legend of Damon and Pythias. Traditionally a secret fraternal order steeped in ritual, it is now a more open charitable organization.

The Carrizo, Borrado, and Lipan did not live in the area; however, they did pass through en route to trade with neighboring people. Once the citizens of Laredo had something to offer, Native Americans would come to the banks of the river to trade. By 1775 the Spanish government had established a military garrison, and soon the population grew to over seven hundred people, including one hundred Carrizo, who were part of the larger Coahuiltecan group who lived in South Texas.

After the Texas Revolution the city of Laredo was akin to and supported by Mexico more than Texas. After all, Texas currency had little value and the borderlands were a long way from the new capital in Austin. In 1838 a group of ranchers gathered to form the Republic of the Rio Grande and proclaimed Laredo the capital. They wanted to be independent from Texas and Mexico. Several skirmishes ensued, but in the end the republic failed. By 1846 a garrison was established under the command of former president of the Republic of Texas, Mirabeau B. Lamar.

The 1880s saw the arrival of three railroads that connected the city with commerce in Texas, the United States, and Mexico. At the same time coal was discovered north of the city, and the railroads were right there to deliver that product to points north, south, east, and west. The railroad industry was hard and dangerous work, with over 70 percent of its workforce maimed or disabled during their employment. The Order of Railway Conductors was formed in 1868, and shortly thereafter an order was established in Laredo. It offered death and disability insurance to all eligible white male employees of the industry. Their section of the city cemetery can be found near the main gate.

The cemetery is filled with members of various benevolent societies, including Woodmen of the World, Freemasons, Master Workmen of Laredo, Society de Obreros, Independent Order of Odd Fellows, Sociedad Mutualista Benito Juárez, Knights of Pythias, Elks, and Improved Order of Red Men. Most of the societies offered death insurance of some kind to help cover or offset the expense of a funeral and headstone. Some offered life insurance as a means to support a widow and her children. For the most part, the policies were offered only to men until the 1960s. The societies also provided their members with a way to collectively give back to the community through various charity events, civic improvements, and mission-driven advocacy.

The older section of the Catholic Cemetery is by far the most interesting in regard to both history and birds. One of the most notable and fascinating persons buried in this section is José de los Santos Benavides (1823–91). If you are interested in early Texas history along the border, pick up a copy of *Tejano Tiger* by Jerry Thompson to learn more about Santos Benavides and Laredo. Even though this is the best section to bird, it is not to say that it is not worth exploring all of the grounds.

The year-round birds might be the most dynamic group at this location, with Green Jays, Great Kiskadees, Couch's Kingbirds, Olive Sparrows, Pyrrhuloxias, and even an occasional Audubon's Oriole all being present. The Green and Monk Parakeets roost in a large colony not far from the cemetery and can be seen flying by on most days. Look along the edges of the Catholic Cemetery for Long-billed Thrashers and Cactus Wrens and into the trees for Golden-fronted and Ladder-backed Woodpeckers. Five species of doves—Eurasian Collared, Inca, White-tipped, White-winged, and Mourning—call the city home, and all can be found at the cemetery.

During the spring and summer, look for Barn Swallows and Chimney Swifts to arrive alongside Purple Martins and Lesser Nighthawks. When my mother and I visited in early May, we were pleased to find a zipper of Scissor-tailed Flycatchers and a few Western Kingbirds. We also watched a Northern Harrier struggle against the strong afternoon winds as it hunted along the open spaces of the City Cemetery. When fall turns to winter, look for the return of Clay-colored Thrushes, American Robins, Verdins, Vermilion Flycatchers, and Ruby-crowned Kinglets.

Enough of the roads here are paved to offer people operating a wheelchair or walker a solid opportunity to bird. There are many trees; however, the location can get hot, which makes the best time to visit either early morning or evening. Additional birding can be found at Lake Casa Blanca State Park, North Central Park, or Slaughter Park. Laredo hosts a wonderful birding festival in February each year that is worth checking out to discover more about this interesting region.

Tombstone Tail: Green Jay

This vibrant green, yellow, blue, and black bird is common in the Rio Grande Valley, with a northern range that includes Laredo. These jays are opportunistic eaters and will forage on fruits, seeds, insects, and even small reptiles. If they are determined to get at an insect, they will use a stick as a tool to pry bark loose or reach into a tree cavity. Like other jays they are talkers and will mimic other birds, including raptors, to scare away a bird that might be dining on something they want. Often you might see Green Jays in sets of three or more because the offspring will stay with their parents for at least a year. A group of jays is called a party.

McAllen: Roselawn Cemetery

1201 South Main Street

You won't find any shorebirds or waterfowl at this twenty-two-acre cemetery, but you will find over 120 species of other birds throughout the seasons. Established in 1908 as McAllen Cemetery, it remains the foremost burial park of the community. The name later changed to Roselawn after a beautification project planted rows of rose bushes. Some of the roses can still be found throughout the grounds and are attractive to Ruby-throated, Black-chinned, and Buff-bellied Hummingbirds that reside or pass through the area.

The grounds are nicely laid out with mature trees that shade the paved streets, which makes walking or wheeling the multiple loops pleasant even on a hot day. In the northeastern section there are some particularly large trees and a couple of birdbaths where I have observed Black-and-white and Yellow-rumped Warblers, Green Jays, White-eyed and Blue-headed Vireos, and Chipping Sparrows. The Great Kiskadees were chatting and chasing each other when I visited in early April. During the spring, look for Least and Brown-crested Flycatchers, Purple Martins, Barn Swallows, and Chimney Swifts to sail past as they feed on flying insects. Swainson's Thrushes and Ovenbirds can be seen scratching along the ground with Inca and White-tipped Doves and Common Ground-Doves. As winter returns, so do the Black-throated Gray,

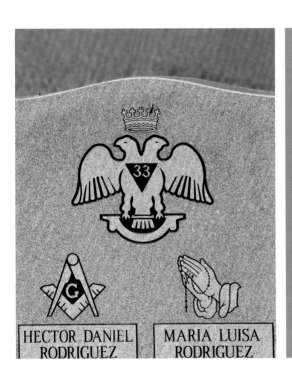

HECTOR DANIEL RODRIGUEZ | MARIA LUISA RODRIGUEZ

Tombstone Tale

The Freemason's symbol is the compass over the carpenter's square with the letter "G" in the middle. The letter stands for the Greek word *Gnosis*, which means "knowledge." The double-headed eagle is an ancient symbol that represents the duality of man. The number 33 means that this person reached the highest level in the Mason's order, a 33rd degree Mason.

Black-throated Green, and Wilson's Warblers; Plumbeous Vireos; and Greater Pewees. A Gray Hawk has been sighted here on numerous occasions.

Nearby birding can be found at any of the nine World Birding Centers, including Quinta Mazatlan Nature Center, Old Hidalgo Pumphouse, and Bentsen–Rio Grande Valley State Park. The McAllen Nature Center offers thirty-three acres to explore, including a short ADA trail and bird blind.

Tombstone Tail: Wilson's Warbler

This bright yellow bird might be little, but boy can it fly. These warblers winter in the Rio Grande Valley into Central America and breed in northern Canada with a widespread migration pattern. Males are lemon-yellow with a jaunty black cap; females do not have the cap. Their populations are in steep decline according to Cornell Lab of Ornithology, who cite habitat loss from humans and fires and nest parasitism from Brown-headed Cowbirds as the largest threats. Look for them feeding lower in the forest and scrub country and moving with lightning-fast speed.

Alamo: Santa Ana National Wildlife Refuge Cementario Viejo / Old Cemetery

3325 Green Jay Road

This renowned birding location just so happens to have a 150-year-old cemetery on it as well. The 2,088-acre Santa Ana National Wildlife Refuge was established in 1943 to protect the habitat for migratory and resident birds. Today, the Spanish moss–draped ebony forest hosts over four hundred species of birds and three hundred species of butterflies, which is half of all the types of butterflies found in North America.

The Cementario Viejo (Old Cemetery) is located a little over a mile and half south of the Visitor Center on Wildlife Drive. It is one of my favorite walks in the refuge. As you meander through the forest, be sure to stop at the canopy walk to look for hawks circling overhead. The refuge is famous for being home to Hook-billed and White-tailed Kites, which can be found in the park most of the year. In the fall and winter of 2021, a Bat Falcon was spotted at the park and sent many a birder from across the country racing to the Rio Grande Valley to search for it. Bat Falcons are rare in the United States, as they typically live in Central and South America. That is the beauty of birding in the Valley—birds that are not common to the United States will slip north of the Rio Grande to offer us birders a rare treat.

I cannot even begin to list all the amazing birds that exist or visit this location. Green Jays and Golden-fronted Woodpeckers can be seen and heard throughout the refuge. The Altamira Oriole is another resident worth noting. During nesting season, the female Altamiras weave pear-shaped hanging nests that can often be found on electrical wires or the branches of mature trees. Spring brings the return of the cuckoos, with four of these special birds occurring at the park—Groove-billed Anis, Greater Roadrunners, and Yellow-billed and the less common Black-billed Cuckoos. With so many species of birds living in or visiting the forest, river, and lakes of the refuge, it is hard not to see something new each time you visit.

The Cementario Viejo only has about thirty graves, many of them unmarked. The most notable grave belongs to Cristoval Leal (1833–76) and is an aboveground crypt. The cemetery stands as a reminder that the refuge was once a working ranch that supported a number of families. It also represents the small, family cemeteries utilized in the region prior to the development of townships and establishment of municipal cemeteries. There is a historical marker at the cemetery, and the refuge offers guided tours that share more about the history of the park while birding.

When you do visit this location, plan on making a day of it, and be sure to pack some water and a snack if you plan on walking to the cemetery or along the fourteen miles of trails. There is also a tram that can take you to the cemetery and other birding points in the park. Nearby birding can be found at the Old Hildalgo Pumphouse or Quinta Mazatlan World Birding Center.

Tombstone Tail: Common Pauraque

This bird is a master of camouflage, as the pattern on its feathers mimics the sticks and leaves of the open woodland and scrub thickets it inhabits. Pauraques are nightjars, which means they hunt flying insects from dusk to dawn and sleep on the ground during the day. During breeding season a pair will scratch out a shallow indentation on the ground as a nest. They can be found only in the scrub and ebony forests of the Rio Grande Valley in the United States and are abundant from Mexico to northern Argentina. Their flight can seem erratic, like that of a bat, as they chase insects. Like other night-flying birds, they can be blinded or disoriented by bright lights.

Weslaco: Weslaco City Cemetery

Intersection of East Illinois and East Tenth Streets

The cemetery is about ten acres and shares a fence line with the Frontera Audubon Center, where more than 280 species of birds have been recorded. When I arrived on a cloudy day in November, I walked along the fence and peered into the tangle of thornscrub to watch Pyrrhuloxias, Northern Cardinals, Inca Doves, and Curve-billed Thrashers pick through the leaf litter for insects. Down by the drainage channel there were several small wading birds, including a Solitary Sandpiper who didn't mind me taking his picture and watching him for a spell. The tall grasses across the drainage channel offered decent hunting grounds for Vermilion Flycatchers and Couch's King-

Tombstone Tale

Altars come in many forms, from large marble fixtures to simple wooden boxes. The purpose of the Catholic altars are to house a statue of Jesus, Mary, Our Lady of the Guadalupe, or a preferred saint. It is a place for family members to make offerings and leave grave gifts when they visit.

birds. I even witnessed a Northern Harrier swoop down on a squirrel that had ventured a little too far from the mesquite tree. During the spring and summer, watch for Olive-sided, Yellow-bellied, Acadian, Willow, Least, and Great Crested Flycatchers to visit the grasslands while Philadelphia, Warbling, and Red-eyed Vireos feed in the trees.

When I returned the following October, I was treated to over twenty-three species, including a committee of more than forty Turkey and Black Vultures that were drying their wings in the morning sun. I also watched a Clay-colored Thrush dart in and out of a low bush searching for insects. I will admit that it took me a while to identify the Northern Parula since it was not in its spring breeding colors. That is one of the things I love about birding in various seasons; many of the males change colors, which makes it important to consider their habits, range, and habitats to accurately identify them.

Interred at Weslaco City Cemetery is a distant relative of mine and one of the town's founders, Edmond "Ed" Cooper Couch. Ed Couch, and a number of his relatives, purchased the land from the W. E. Stewart Land Company (WESLACO) in 1919. They laid out the town and quickly started selling lots for fifty to four hundred dollars. Ed had learned how to be a savvy marketer, entrepreneur, and banker from his older brother, George Ruben Couch of Haskell, and quickly applied his skills in the wilds of South Texas. He and his partners advertised heavily in the Midwest and northern states with the promise of sunny warm days all year long.

In 1929, Ed ran for county judge as a member of the Good Government League. The league was dedicated to cleaning up the government, which had become incredibly corrupt in the Valley, especially during Prohibition. Ed's son-in-law, Claude Kelley, continued to live with the Couches after his wife, Edrie Couch Kelley, died in 1927. Claude returned to the Couches' home on the evening of March 29, 1929, and later that night he was bludgeoned with a hatchet while sleeping in the room normally occupied by Ed and Allie Couch. Claude lived in agony until he passed away in June and never regained his ability to speak.

An all-out search was conducted to find the killers. The Texas Rangers were called in as suspicion began to build that this was politically motivated. Three men were finally arrested and confessed that Ed Couch's political rival, a member of the Baker family, had hired them to murder Ed, but they had accidentally killed Claude instead. The murder and trial filled the pages of newspapers across Texas between 1929 and 1933. Ed Couch went on to become county judge and later founded the town of Edcouch. He worked to bring the railroad to the Valley, install flood-control methods, and improve the roads so farmers could get their products to the rail hubs more efficiently. He and his wife, Allie, were deeply invested in the community and even donated land for a city park in Weslaco; the land was later sold by the city and is now occupied by the Villa de Cortez Hotel.

A portion of the roads are paved, and the rest are tightly compacted gravel that is suitable for wheeled mobility devices. They are also shaded in many places with hackberry, mesquite, and palm trees that make it pleasant to walk. Nearby birding can be found next door at the Frontera Audubon Center or Estero Llano Grande State Park and World Birding Center.

Tombstone Tail: Plain Chachalaca

The Cornell Lab of Ornithology describes this chicken-sized bird as having the "grace of a bulldozer," and I wholeheartedly agree. Chachalacas can be heard and seen throughout the Rio Grande Valley into Central America. It is common to find these social birds in groups touring the feeding stations of parks or hanging around fruit-bearing trees. They actually spend a lot of time in trees feeding, roosting, and grooming each other or themselves. In Texas they are considered a game bird and hunted on occasion.

Mercedes: Ebony Grove Cemetery

301 Jose Cantu Road

I only had about an hour to spare when I visited this nine-acre cemetery, but I liked it immediately. The habitat is great, and I look forward to more people reporting their observations from this location. The grounds are flanked on three sides by the Arroyo Colorado, which snakes across the Rio Grande Valley for ninety miles to create some of the best wetlands and riparian habitat for birds and other wildlife in the region. Satellite images of the boundaries of the cemetery show that it forms the shape of a shield, which is also distinctive.

Perhaps the most unique feature is the impressive stand of ebony trees mixed with live oaks, hackberries, and mesquites. The best way to enjoy this space is to park near the entrance and meander along the dirt road that curves around the edge. From there you can see the birds enjoying the canopy of the open forest and grasses or catch them as they dart in and out of the thicket alongside the fence. While walking the edges, look for year-round residents such as Long-billed and Curve-billed Thrashers, White-eyed Vireos, and Olive Sparrows. This is a good place to observe wintering birds such as Lincoln's Sparrows; Gray Catbirds; Black-and-white, Orange-crowned, Wilson's, and Yellow-rumped Warblers; and Blue-headed Vireos feeding in the trees from October to April. There is an abundance of large trees with holes made from the Golden-fronted

Tombstone Tale

Saint Francis of Assisi is best known as the Italian Catholic friar who established the Franciscan Order around AD 1200. He is the patron saint of animals and nature and is often depicted wearing a simple robe and surrounded by animals or holding birds.

Woodpeckers, and I feel certain an Eastern Screech-Owl can be found in the area. Keep an eye on the sky as you saunter around, as you might catch a glimpse of migrating hawks in late summer or early fall or see a squadron of American White Pelicans move along the arroyo. With over ninety species of birds observed here, this can be a tranquil space to bird in the bustling Rio Grande Valley.

The roads here are dirt and gravel and might not be suitable for people with limited mobility. Nearby birding can be found in Weslaco at the Estero Llano Grande State Park or in La Feria at the La Feria Nature Center.

Tombstone Tail: Groove-billed Ani

This iridescent black bird is a South Texas specialty, with most living year-round in the thorny brush country and in dry semitropical areas of Texas, Mexico, and Central America. Anis are a member of the cuckoo family, which means they have two toes that face forward and two that face backward. They are not a graceful or elegant bird and often appear disheveled and clumsy as they crash through the brush hunting lizards and insects. Despite being somewhat brutish in appearance, they have a pretty tijo sound that often gives away their location. They tend to hang out in small groups of one to five birds, so keep an eye out for others if you are lucky enough to see one.

Brownsville: Old Brownsville Cemetery
Intersection of East Sixth and East Monroe Streets

To walk through the thick stone-and-iron entrance of the Old Brownsville Cemetery is to be transported back in time. The cobblestone road and the mausoleums give it an Old World feeling even beyond its more than 160 years of existence. The cemetery was officially established in 1868; however, there are headstones that indicate the space was in use from the early 1850s.

The historical marker located by the main gate accurately states that the cemetery reflects the many cultures, wars, personal conflicts, and diseases of the town. The headstones, monuments, hand-painted crosses, crypts, and names reveal the waves

Tombstone Tale

In ancient Greek and Roman cultures the dead were often buried along the roads leading to their town. Prominent citizens built large mausoleums to house their families and tell their stories. The tradition continued into France and Spain and eventually into the Americas as they were being colonized. Even in modern cemeteries the mausoleum structures are generally located near the central road.

of people who came to the region seeking a place to make their fortunes, raise their families, spread their faith, or escape their troubles back home. There are additional historical markers throughout the cemetery that offer interesting insights into the men and women who helped build the region.

Like many old cemeteries, this one reflects the cultural and economic segregation that existed and changed as new waves of immigrants arrived or new wealth was made. Members of the Rio Grande Masons Lodge No. 81, which comprised many of the city founders and much of the wealth of the town, reside in their own area. The less fortunate were restricted to Potter's Field in the lower grounds near the *resaca*. However, in the 1960s the Potter's Field graves were moved up the hill after Hurricane Beulah hit the area and coffins floated into the waterway. Some of the other sections include Sociedad Benito, Sociedad Miguel Hidalgo Parcel, Knights of Columbus, International Order of Odd Fellows, and Sociedad Concordia.

The Woodmen of the World seem to be equally distributed around the grounds, and their headstones are inscribed in English or Spanish depending on the person. On the northwest side behind a large brick wall is the Hebrew Cemetery, which is not open to the public but has nice trees that the birds enjoy.

While exploring this location, it's best to stay on the road or on the cobblestone paths since the headstones are packed in tight after family plots filled over the decades. There are a good variety of large trees to draw the birds in, and there is a portion of the Old Town Resaca that borders the northern edge of the cemetery that supports ducks and shorebirds as well as Anhingas and Double-crested and Neotropic Cormorants. Visitors can make their way down to the *resaca* by following the path closest to the entrance wall or on the opposite end near Potter's Field.

After I had my fill of South Texas history, I let my eyes and ears focus on the birds that live and pass through the location. As the crisp November day drew to a close, flocks of Red-crowned Parrots, Green Parakeets, Great-tailed Grackles, and Black-bellied Whistling-Ducks began to arrive and settle into their roosts for the evening. It was a visual and aural spectacle I will never forget. I also encountered a dandy of a Great Kiskadee who wanted me to take its picture from every angle, which I obliged. On our visit we heard a Belted Kingfisher but did not see it; Ringed and Green Kingfishers have also been spotted at this location. This is a good place to look for Black Phoebes, Vermilion Flycatchers, or Brown-crested Flycatchers that visit during the summer.

The cobbled street and tight, uneven paths are not accessible to people using a mobility device. Nearby birding can be found at Gladys Porter Zoo, Sabal Palms Sanctuary, and Resaca de la Palma State Park and World Birding Center. Resaca de la Palma is closed on Mondays and Tuesdays, so plan accordingly if you intend to visit the state park. The more I get to know that park, the more I like it, as it offers some really excellent parking lot birding.

Tombstone Tail: Great Kiskadee

Cornell Lab of Ornithology states that these birds "hunt like a flycatcher, fish like a kingfisher, and forage like a jay." They are omnivores that will eat fruits, insects, and small rodents and even dive into shallow waters to retrieve a fish. Both males and females sport a black mask, yellow body, and rust-colored wings. Their distinct *kis-ka-dee* call often gives away their location. I personally think they are saying *look-at-me*. They are considered to be one of the most widely distributed flycatchers in the Americas that do not migrate. In the United States they can be found only in South Texas, with the highest concentration in the Rio Grande Valley.

Falfurrias: Sacred Heart and Falfurrias Burial Park

509 West Travis Street

When I drove through the gates of this large cemetery, I was struck by how dark it was. The canopy of trees shaded out the intense South Texas sun, creating a dramatic experience I was not expecting. The two cemeteries blend together into a large, peaceful place to bird.

Falfurrias sits in the heart of the South Texas ranching country and is not lacking for habitat for migrating and year-round feathered friends. The cemetery offers hefty hackberry and live oak trees that are nature's grocery store for the birds. Both types of trees can support large numbers of insects that the birds feed on. While I was strolling around the grounds, I noticed several families were watering their plots. The watered areas help increase the insect populations, thus creating even more food for the birds.

Tombstone Tale

Wooden crosses are commonly used as a placeholder until a headstone can be installed. However, often the wooden marker is the only option for a family. These crosses do not stand the test of time in wet climates but can last several decades in a drier location.

Two of the plots had sprinklers, and the Northern Cardinals and Olive Sparrows were bathing in the mist.

There are over 160 species reported at this location, as the habitat supports year-round birds such as Great Kiskadees, Green Jays, Couch's Kingbirds, and Clay-colored Thrushes. All of the doves that Texas has to offer also occur here, with White-tipped, White-winged, Common Ground, Inca, Mourning, and Eurasian Collared Doves all milling around the grounds and perching on the headstones. During the spring and summer the trees and shrubs are certainly attractive to Summer Tanagers and Painted Buntings, which nest in the region. Hooded and Orchard Orioles, Blue Grosbeaks, and Buff-bellied Hummingbirds also add a splash of color to the cemetery in the spring. There are reports of Tropical and Northern Parulas here as well.

During the fall, look for the return of Yellow-rumped, Yellow-throated, and Orange-crowned Warblers; Blue-headed Vireos; Blue-gray Gnatcatchers; American Kestrels; and Lincoln's Sparrows. Fall and winter also see the return of Red-naped and Yellow-bellied Sapsuckers to join the local Golden-fronted and Ladder-backed Wood-peckers in the tangle of trees. When I visited in late October, I was treated to a zipper of male Scissor-tailed Flycatchers that were migrating en masse ahead of a cold front. They perched on the wires, fences, telephone poles, and just about every upright object that rimmed the cemetery.

The gravel and dirt roads are not suitable for wheeled mobility devices but do make for easy walking in the shade of the thick forest. For nearby birding, check out the rest stop south of town on Highway 281, which exists in an amazing motte of live oaks. Or shuffle on down "Hawk Alley" on Highway 285 during the fall to see White-tailed, Harris's, Red-shouldered, and a bevy of other hawks and raptors.

Tombstone Tail: White-tipped Dove

This dove looks like a heftier version of a White-winged Dove minus the white wing bar. The white tips refer to the tipped feathers on the tail, which are visible only when it fans its tail or flies. These doves are also more solitary than their white-winged counterparts. In the United States they can be found only in the southern reaches of South Texas. In Central and South America, they are widely spread, reaching as far as southern Brazil. While their populations are strong, habitat loss in Texas and Mexico continues to be a threat.

Kingsville: Chamberlain Cemetery

735 West Caesar Avenue

The first large monument visitors see when they enter the cemetery is that of the King family, which is fitting since it is located in Kingsville next to the King Ranch on land given by Henrietta Chamberlain King. Henrietta was deeply devoted to her Presbyterian faith, a quality her father, a Presbyterian minister, had instilled in her. Because of her devotion to her faith and father, the cemetery was given in his name instead of receiving the King brand like everything else in the town. The entire King family has a long and interesting history that is far too long to squeeze into one book, let alone a paragraph. I recommend taking the time to visit the King Ranch Museum to learn more.

There are a respectable variety of mature trees, a few birdbaths are scattered around, and the cemetery is bordered on all sides by additional habitat to support the more than 140 species of birds at this location. It also resides squarely in the migration flight path for thousands of passing Sandhill Cranes, Turkey Vultures, Snow Geese, and hawks. When my mother and I visited in November, we were treated to a river

Tombstone Tale

Books have many meanings on headstones. An open book often means the person was taken too young and had more life to live. A closed book indicates that the person lived a full life with all the chapters completed.

of Black and Turkey Vultures along with Sandhill Cranes passing by as they rode the thermals in front of a wicked norther. Back down on the ground I watched a few Lesser Goldfinches and Lark Sparrows bathe in the standing water the sprinkler had left behind along the road. Along the northeast fence line is a drainage ditch that was busy with Green Jays, Northern Cardinals, House Wrens, Chipping Sparrows, and Golden-fronted Woodpeckers. The Golden-fronted Woodpeckers seem to spend as much time on the ground here as they did in the trees. It is also reported that Northern Bobwhites and Wild Turkeys pass through the fields just beyond the fence line and on occasion wander through the graveyard.

The cemetery sprawls over forty acres and is joined by the Santa Gertrudis Memorial Cemetery. They are not really joined, but they are next to each other. A holdover from the days of separate, but not always equal. There is good tree cover, native grasses, and even some brush piles along the fence line that separate the two cemeteries, which make for good bird habitat for Curve-billed and Long-billed Thrashers. Harris's and White-tailed Hawks are often seen hunting in the surrounding fields or perched in the large trees. The field belonging to the school across West Caesar Avenue is a good place to see resident Killdeers and migrating Long-billed Curlews, Greater Yellowlegs, and an assortment of other shorebirds, especially when there is shallow standing water.

The roads at this location are paved and offer easy walking and wheeling for all mobility types. If you get a chance to take a birding tour of the King Ranch, I highly recommend it. There are over three hundred species of birds that have been recorded at the ranch, and that number seems to climb each year. Dick Kleberg Park also offers decent birding in town.

Tombstone Tail: Crested Caracara

This raptor is neither an eagle nor a hawk but a large falcon. However, it acts more like a carrion-eating vulture than a fast-moving falcon. Caracaras can often be seen walking or even running, sometimes in pairs, along the ground like chickens or roadrunners while searching for smaller prey. Traditionally, these birds existed mostly in South Texas and are not known to migrate, but they are expanding their range, and we now have a pair in our neighborhood in North Austin. A healthy bird can live up to twenty years.

Freer: Hahl Memorial Cemetery
Hahl Cemetery Road

Freer is referred to as the buckle in the oil belt of Texas. Originally called Government Wells for the water well that the US Calvary dug around 1876, it later took on the name of one of the founding families. Early settlers tried to make a go of ranching the scrub country and hardpan caliche, but without good water the land just could not support much livestock or people. But the salty water gave a few oil wildcatters the idea that under all that scrub and rock there might be a massive salt dome.

The first big oil boom arrived in 1920 in Freer and then hit again in 1932. Once the oil boom came to town, so did the gamblers, drifters, drunks, prostitutes, and oil men. In 1935, *Life* magazine published an article on the community and called Freer "the last of the tough frontier towns." It remains an oil and gas town today, and most major oil companies hold leases and pipelines across Duval County. Hunting is also a staple

Tombstone Tale

While store-bought or chiseled marble headstones are nice, there is something heartwarming about a handcrafted grave marker. It can range from solemn to whimsical in an effort to reflect the departed and what stands out in the memories and thoughts of those they left behind.

economic engine for the region; white-tailed deer, Northern Bobwhites, and, sadly, some exotic species can also be found here too.

There is not much to the cemetery, but I have visited several times as I traveled to and from my friend's family ranch just northeast of Freer. It's a great place to stretch your legs and look for South Texas birds. With the vast majority of the county being privately owned, the cemetery makes for a nice place to peer into the scrub and observe the local birds. I also enjoy walking in the cemetery and looking at the multitude of handmade headstones, including several that feature oil derricks and pumpjacks. The sign posted as you enter the location states that graves must be hand-dug or make arrangements with the funeral home. That is not a common sign, as most burials can only be managed through a funeral home and certainly not dug by hand.

Some of the year-round birds include Northern Bobwhites, Long-billed and Curve-billed Thrashers, Green Jays, Great Kiskadees, Cactus Wrens, and Pyrrhuloxias. This is also a place where you can find five species of doves, including Inca, White-tipped, White-winged, Mourning, and Eurasian Collared Doves. During the spring migration Audubon's, Orchard, and Bullock's Orioles pass through, while the Great Crested, Brown-crested, Scissor-tailed, and Vermilion Flycatchers all stick around in the summer. During the fall, check the fence posts and telephone poles for Harris's and White-tailed Hawks and Merlins.

The hard caliche roads might be suitable for someone walking with a cane or walker, but probably not for a wheelchair. There is not much shade along the roads, so keep that in mind when visiting on a warm day. Nearby birding can be found at the Freer Wastewater Treatment Ponds, Benavides Wastewater Treatment Ponds, Choke Canyon State Park, or Lake Corpus Christi State Park. It's worth a trip into town to see the rattlesnake roadside attraction for a photo op. In South Texas "nearby" is a relative term, as most everything is a little farther apart than in other parts of the state that are more populated with people and towns.

Tombstone Tail: Couch's Kingbird

The Couch's Kingbird and the Tropical Kingbird are difficult to tell apart; however, Couch's has a slightly more greenish tone to its grayish upper parts, and it has a slightly shorter bill. It was actually considered a subspecies of the Tropical until 1980. Couch's can be found year-round in eastern Mexico and South Texas, with reports of it venturing as far north as Austin. It prefers lightly wooded areas where it can perch and launch after insects.

Inca Doves at Hillcrest Memorial Park in Edinburg, Texas

Coastal Bend

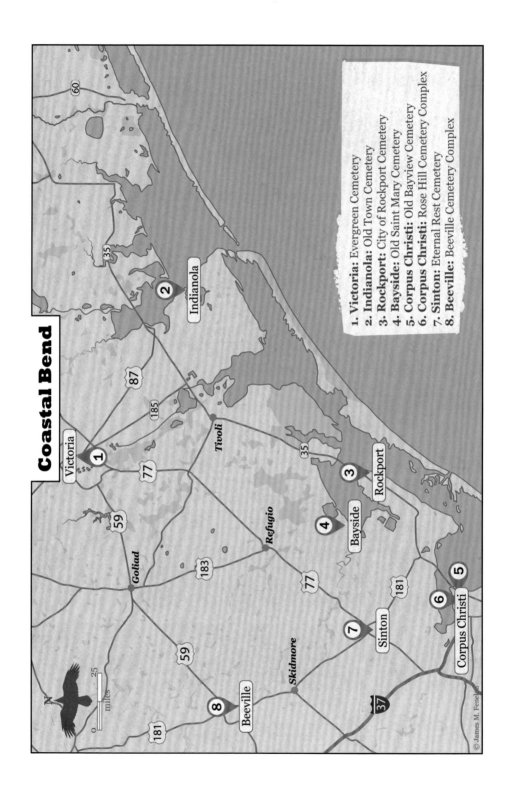

1. **Victoria:** Evergreen Cemetery
2. **Indianola:** Old Town Cemetery
3. **Rockport:** City of Rockport Cemetery
4. **Bayside:** Old Saint Mary Cemetery
5. **Corpus Christi:** Old Bayview Cemetery
6. **Corpus Christi:** Rose Hill Cemetery Complex
7. **Sinton:** Eternal Rest Cemetery
8. **Beeville:** Beeville Cemetery Complex

© James M. Fenelon

Coastal Bend

The Coastal Bend region is part of the Gulf Coast Prairies and Marshes and South Texas Plains where the Gulf of Mexico bends inland. The region is characterized by barrier islands, estuaries, rivers, coastal oak forests, and scrub country. In essence it is a birding paradise year-round.

The San Antonio River empties its fresh water into San Antonio Bay, where the endangered Whooping Cranes come to winter and dine on blue crab. With only a few hundred Whoopers left in the wild, it is a thrill to see these large white birds wading through the marshes. Sandhill Cranes also winter in the region and will often feed in the same areas as the Whoopers. The towns of Rockport and Fulton are famous for their giant oak trees that appear to be constantly bending in the sea breeze. The second-largest live oak in Texas is located at Goose Island State Park and has with-stood countless hurricanes and storms in its one thousand years of existence. The oak forests also support millions of migratory birds and butterflies that travel along the Mississippi and Central Flyways each spring and fall.

Mustang, Padre, and several smaller islands shield the inland from hurricanes and storms and also supply humans and birds miles of white sandy beaches. Padre Island National Seashore protects much of the barrier island, which is also the nesting site for endangered and threatened sea turtles and nesting and wintering habitat for dozens of species of coastal birds. Mustang Island State Park protects the dunes and habitat on Mustang Island between Corpus Christi and Port Aransas. Both locations give a glimpse into what the islands might have looked like when the first Anglos came ashore to explore the wilds of Tejas.

Victoria: Evergreen Cemetery
1899 North Vine Street

The town of Victoria has a long and interesting history that starts with the Karankawa, who often camped along the banks of the Guadalupe River as they followed their well-worn trails through the region. These first peoples were hit hard with European diseases brought over by the Spanish explorers. Thus, they were quite diminished by the time the colonization wave came to the land of Tejas.

In 1824, Martín De León and his wife were given permission by the provincial delegation of San Fernando de Béxar to settle forty families between the Guadalupe and Lavaca Rivers, where they founded the town Nuestra Señora Guadalupe de Jesús Victoria. De León's Colony consisted mostly of his own family and relations, other Mexican families, and a few Anglos. Each settler received a town lot plus one league (4,228 acres) of grazing land and one labor (177 acres) of arable land. After founding the town, he quickly set up a leadership council of ten, who were entrusted with the colonists' welfare and the growth of the community. Even though the De León family supported the Texas Revolution, they fell victim to discrimination and lost most of their vast ranchlands, cattle, horses, and worldly possessions when they were forced to flee to Louisiana. Martín De León and many of the family members are buried at Evergreen, which features several historical markers that tell the impressive tale of this pioneering family.

The first graveyard in Victoria was located where Memorial Square now stands. At the time, many families preferred to bury their relatives on family plots at their estates, so the city aldermen enacted an ordinance requiring deceased citizens to be buried at a cemetery. As the town grew, so did the need for a public cemetery; in 1849 Evergreen Cemetery was established. Additional lands were given throughout the years,

Tombstone Tale

The Viking ship being guided by the angel of death represents the departed's final journey to the afterlife. This Viking motif was one of the panels people could choose for their prefabricated white bronze monument.

and it now covers thirty acres of rolling tree-covered hills adjacent to the Athey Nature Area, Memorial Park Cemetery, and two Catholic cemeteries.

As you walk the grounds, it is easy to ascertain the growth of the city as waves of Mexicans, Germans, Bohemians, Italians, Jews, French, and Scots arrived to build new lives in the New World. The graves also tell the story of the waves of sickness such as yellow fever, cholera, smallpox, and the Spanish flu that swept through the community. Under one of the large live oak groves is a cluster of tall, slender headstones that feature oval-shaped photos of family members from 1910 to 1920. Several of them have haunting eyes that seem to stare back at you from the silent depths of the past.

The mix of mature trees and open space makes Evergreen a pleasant place to watch for warblers and vireos during the spring migration. Starting in late March and early April, the waves of migrants arrive with Black-throated Green, Yellow, Worm-eating, Magnolia, Blackburnian, Chestnut-sided, Tennessee, and Nashville Warblers. Joining the warblers are White-eyed, Red-eyed, and Yellow-throated Vireos that all pass through in a few weeks. Spring also means the return of the Mississippi Kites that nest in the area. Watch the trees for perching Couch's and Western Kingbirds and Great Crested, Alder, Acadian, and Willow Flycatchers.

This place can also be a study in blackbirds with Great-tailed Grackles and Brown-headed and Bronzed Cowbirds living here year-round, while Orchard and Baltimore Orioles arrive in the spring, and Common Grackles return in the fall and winter. If you visit in the fall, watch the skies for passing flocks of Snow Geese, Sandhill Cranes, American White Pelicans, or Wood Storks. Fall also means the return of the sparrows, American Robins, Hermit Thrushes, and Pine Warblers.

The mix of paved and gravel roads at this cemetery complex offers easy walking, but the roads are not suitable for wheelchairs or people using a wheeled walker, as the only paved road is quite steep. The birding here is best from September to May, as the summer months can be hot, buggy, and not as active with birds. Nearby birding can be found at Athey Natural Area, Riverside Park, and the grounds of the Texas Zoo.

Tombstone Tail: Black-throated Green Warbler

This medium-sized warbler has a brilliant yellow face, olive-green upperparts, white underparts, and white-and-black wing bars, and males have a distinct black throat. During the spring these warblers migrate from South America, Mexico, and the Caribbean through Central and East Texas to the pine mixed forests of the northern United States and Canada. Watch for them in the spring migration to be high in the canopy gleaning insects. When they reach their breeding range, males become prolific singers, with one bird documented as singing 460 times in one hour. Their populations are stable; however, loss of habitat in both their winter and summer ranges is an issue.

Indianola: Old Town Cemetery
Zimmerman Road

This small, lonely cemetery is about all that is left of the once-thriving port city of Indianola, originally Indian Point, that was founded in 1846. Though the cemetery itself is not very big, it is surrounded by more than seventy acres of preserves owned and managed by the Texas Ornithological Society. Magic Ridge Preserve is a mix of marshlands and Tamaulipan scrub that supports nearly three hundred species of migratory or resident birds. One of the best places to see these birds is from the low ridge that the cemetery graces.

When standing on the cemetery's hallowed ground, it is almost unfathomable to think of a bustling town of nearly five thousand people. For thousands, Indianola was their point of entry into the United States and their introduction to Texas.

Tombstone Tale

Irises represent hope and rebirth or the sorrow of the Virgin Mary. They can either be planted at the cemetery or are part of a headstone.

The port and townsite were chosen by Prince Carl of Solms-Braunfels, who is credited with bringing the first wave of German immigrants to Texas. His idea was to have a remote port city where the Germans could enter the state and then travel to their colonies of New Braunfels and Fredericksburg with as little contact with other non-German populations as possible. The German nobles that brought the first waves of Germans to Texas wanted them to retain all their customs and language instead of integrating with other settlers. Immigrants were recruited and sponsored by the Adelsverein, a society founded and funded by a collection of German nobles who had aspirations of creating a new Germany on Texas soil through mass immigration. The endeavor was not long lived as the nobles ran out of funding. In 1846, the town leaders changed the name from Karlshafen to Indianola.

From 1846 to 1875, the port was second only to Galveston. In 1875, a large hurricane swept into Matagorda Bay and killed between 150 and 300 people and destroyed a large part of the town. From 1875 to 1886, the town continued to be an important port but was already in decline. Then in 1886, a massive category 4 hurricane hit the town and destroyed or damaged almost every structure. The citizens fared better during this storm, having been warned by sailors who had spotted the storm brewing in the Gulf of Mexico. After the hurricane the county seat was moved to Port Lavaca, and the town of Indianola faded into history when no one wanted to rebuild after two devastating storms. Much of the town that was once so vibrant is now covered by the bay. In addition to the historical markers at the cemetery there are clusters of them along the bay drive that give more information about the community.

Today the birds enjoy the bay, marshes, and scrub country of the ridge just as they did long before the area was settled. The mix of scrub brush supports a few South Texas specialty birds that hang out from time to time. Groove-billed Anis, Couch's Kingbirds, and even Great Kiskadees have been reported in the area. The real magic of the ridge is the wealth of shorebirds, colonial wading birds, and waterfowl. Wilson's and Semipalmated Plovers, Wilson's Phalaropes, White-rumped Sandpipers, and Dunlins can be found feeding in the shallows of the ponds. Some of the colonial wading birds include Great and Snowy Egrets; Great Blue, Little Blue, and Tricolored Herons; Wood Storks; and Roseate Spoonbills. Songbirds, including Painted and Indigo Buntings, Blue and Rose-breasted Grosbeaks, and Scarlet and Summer Tanagers, all arrive on the sea breezes of spring.

The wetlands are also a favored wintering place for Snow and Greater White-fronted Geese, Redheads, Buffleheads, Blue-winged and Green-winged Teals, and American White Pelicans. In September and October, the area is a gathering place for Ruby-throated Hummingbirds and other migrants as they fuel up for their leap of faith across the open waters of the Gulf of Mexico. With almost three hundred species of birds recorded at this location, there really isn't a bad birding day here—unless there is a hurricane brewing in the Gulf.

When visiting this remote location, I hope you will take the time to read the historical marker about Angelina Belle Peyton Eberly (1798–1860), who was buried at this location. She is credited for stopping Sam Houston's men from removing the state archives from the town of Austin, thus keeping Austin as the capital city.

The drive to the cemetery is a great car-birding opportunity for people with limited mobility. However, the cemetery is walk-in only and does not have an accessible path. The closest restroom to this location is at Indianola Beach Park, but it is not always unlocked, so plan accordingly. Nearby birding can be found at Powderhorn Wildlife Management Area and the Boggy Bayou Nature Park in Port O'Connor.

Tombstone Tail: Tricolored Heron

Formerly known as the Louisiana Heron, this medium-sized wading bird can be found in marshes and wetlands along coastlines from South America to the United States. These herons hunt alone for fish and crustaceans as they dance about in shallow waters and nest in large colonies alongside other wading birds. They are easy to mistake for a Little Blue Heron or Reddish Egret; however, their white bellies distinguish them. Most Tricolors will stay year-round along the Texas coast, although they will travel medium distances during migration. Healthy birds can live up to seventeen years.

Rockport: City of Rockport Cemetery
Tule Park Drive

The best time to visit this tranquil cemetery by the bay is in March or April when the wildflowers are in full bloom. The Rockport Cemetery Association intentionally does not mow from December to late May to allow the wildflowers to grow and seed. When I visited in mid-March, the headstones stood out boldly from a carpet of color. My eyes were not the only things enjoying the flowers; the first hummingbirds and butterflies to arrive for the spring migrations were dancing from one nectar producer to the next.

The mix of native flowers, grasses, shrubs, and twisted coastal oaks makes this an ideal birding spot. I also like it because the paved roads that form several loops make this location accessible for people with limited mobility. During the spring migration, look to the oak trees to find Black-throated Green, Black-and-white, Prothonotary, Yellow, Canada, and Common Yellowthroat Warblers; Summer Tanagers; and Baltimore Orioles. The native grasses and trees support a good number of insects that are enjoyed by Acadian, Least, Yellow-bellied, and Scissor-tailed Flycatchers in the spring and summer. There are several Vermilion Flycatchers that live year-round at

Tombstone Tale

The US War Department set the standards for military-issued markers in 1873. The white marble headstones stand twelve inches tall, ten inches wide, and four inches thick. In 1906, Congress approved a special marker for Confederate soldiers that had a more pointed top and displayed the Southern Cross of Honor. The Union Army had a shield sunken into the stone. After World Wars I and II more modifications followed that later included the in-ground headstones that are popular in heavily mowed perpetual-care cemeteries.

this location and can be found perching on headstones and fences. During the spring and fall migration the Buff-bellied, Ruby-throated, and Black-chinned Hummingbirds are present with an occasional visit from a Rufous Hummingbird. During September, the cities of Rockport and Fulton host the Hummingbird Festival, which celebrates the hummers gathering along the coast to make their leap of faith across the Gulf of Mexico or head down the coastline to winter in Central and South America.

Because of the proximity to Little Bay, the Rookery, and Tule Park there is always something interesting flying overhead. During the spring Great Blue Herons and Great Egrets, along with other herons and egrets, can be seen passing by with nesting materials as they head to and from the Rookery just south of the cemetery. Laughing Gulls, pelicans, terns, and other shorebirds are also in constant motion as they circle the area. The late fall and winter bring in the Chipping, Field, Vesper, White-crowned, Seaside, and Savannah Sparrows, along with Eastern Meadowlarks. Keep an eye to the sky during the winter for White-tailed and Red-tailed Hawks and Ospreys.

There are a lot of great places to bird along the coast, but I find this place to be really special no matter what time of year I visit. I also enjoy stopping to pay my respects to one of my nature heroes, Connie Hagar (1886–1973). Connie recorded the birds along the Texas coast for decades and helped establish Rockport as an important stop for birds and birders. She is memorialized in Rockport at the Connie Hagar Sanctuary along Little Bay and at the Connie and Jack Hagar Cottage Sanctuary. Both locations offer excellent birding and interpretive panels to learn more about this remarkable woman. Karen Harden McCracken does an excellent job capturing Connie's story in *The Life History of a Texas Birdwatcher: Connie Hagar of Rockport*. Connie often visited cemeteries to look for birds and native flowers. Her story inspired me to write this book.

Tombstone Tail: Brown Pelican

When you visit the Texas Gulf Coast, you are never far from a squadron of Brown Pelicans gliding by. These birds seem common now; however, they had almost disappeared by the 1960s mostly due to the ill effects of the pesticide DDT. The pesticide weakened the shells of their eggs, causing them to crack when the large parents rested on them during incubation. Year after year, clutch after clutch was lost. Once DDT was banned, the large fish-eating birds recovered, and now healthy birds can live up to forty years. The US Fish and Wildlife Department delisted the pelicans from the endangered species list in 1985; however, they are still vulnerable to oil and chemical spills.

Bayside: Old Saint Mary Cemetery
FM 136 to Bayside Cemetery Road, Refugio County

The coastal town of St. Mary's was founded around 1857 by Joseph F. Smith. The town enjoyed modest prosperity until 1886, when the same storm that destroyed Indianola and other coastal communities also destroyed St. Mary's. The ten acres of land that the cemetery resides on were donated in 1857, and the first-known burial took place around 1860. Some of the live oaks look as though they might have already been large, stately trees at the time the first graves were dug. The mature trees mixed with the

Tombstone Tale

The Daughters of Rebekah were originally a female auxiliary group for the Independent Order of Odd Fellows. Their emblem is laced with meaning. The dove implies peace, the lily stands for purity, and the moon and stars represent the never-failing order of God and nature. Tucked behind the dove is a beehive that exemplifies the power of collective industry. (This photo was taken in Victoria because the emblem I found at Bayside was quite damaged).

grasslands of the coastal plains and nearby bay make this an interesting place to look for birds from October to May.

Over 143 species of birds have been recorded on eBird at this location. Eleven species of warblers have been documented here, including two of my favorites—the Bay-breasted and the Blackburnian; both typically pass through in late April and early May. Other springtime visitors include the Great Crested and Scissor-tailed Flycatchers, Eastern and Western Kingbirds, Painted and Indigo Buntings, and Dickcissels. During the fall and winter, look for Roseate Spoonbills, White Ibis, American White Pelicans, and Wood Storks to pass overhead as they move from Copano and Mission Bays to the wetlands farther inland. On most days you will find a Loggerhead Shrike perched on the wire near the entrance.

The gravel road makes for easy walking but might not be suitable for people using a wheeled mobility device. There are plenty of places in the area to bird, including Black Point Bay just south of Bayside or the Fennessey Ranch just a few miles north of the cemetery. The Fennessey Ranch is a private ranch that offers bird trips by appointment or in connection with Mission-Aransas National Estuarine Research Reserve at the University of Texas Marine Science Institute in Port Aransas.

Tombstone Tail: Roseate Spoonbill

The brilliant pink or rose color of this large wading bird comes from the small crustaceans it eats that feed on algae. These now-abundant spoonbills were once hunted to near extinction because their wings were popular for fans and their feathers were used in Victorian-era hats. Thanks to conservation efforts starting in the 1890s, especially along the Texas coast, the birds have made a strong recovery. Older birds lose the feathers on top of their head, which gives them a bald look. The large spoon bill, red eyes, bright pink feathers, long legs, and bald head certainly give this bird a comical look when viewed up close. Healthy birds can live up to fifteen years.

Corpus Christi: Old Bayview Cemetery

1150 Ramirez Street

Set upon a hill overlooking the city and the Corpus Christi and Nueces Bays, this cemetery tells the tales of hardship and triumph in early-Texas life along the coast. It is the oldest federal military cemetery in the state and was established after the land was donated by Colonel H. L. Kinney in 1845. Kinney made the donation after the steamer ship *Dayton* blew up while transporting troops to and from St. Joseph Island and Corpus Christi.

Veterans of four different wars are buried here—War of 1812, Texas War for Independence, Indian Campaigns, and Civil War. One of the African American Buffalo Soldiers who served in the Civil War, George Owens, is also buried here. As the city grew, the cemetery became the community cemetery instead of one reserved for military. Unlike other burial grounds of the time it was never separated by race or religion.

There are plenty of historical markers to read as you walk along under the shade of the mesquite trees. One that caught my attention was that of Eli T. Merriman, one

INFANTRY   ARTILLERY   DRAGOONS

FOR ADDITIONAL INFORMATION ON THESE MEN
VISIT THE CORPUS CHRISTI PUBLIC LIBRARY

SPONSORED BY   DEDICATED
DESCENDANTS OF MEXICAN WAR VETERANS   SEPTEMBER
WILLIAM J. BOZIC JR   19,
ROSA G. GONZALES   2004

Tombstone Tale

The Descendants of Mexican War Veterans erected a memorial to those who served. The monument displays several of the symbols used on individual veteran's headstones.

of only three doctors in Corpus Christi when a yellow fever epidemic broke out in 1867. He and his wife turned their home into a hospital to treat victims of the disease. Merriman died after contracting the illness and was buried on the hill overlooking the bays.

The birding here is not off the charts but certainly worth exploring. The most common year-round birds are Great Kiskadees, Couch's Kingbirds, Loggerhead Shrikes, Northern Mockingbirds, and Golden-fronted Woodpeckers. The tree canopy can host spring migrants such as Philadelphia and Red-eyed Vireos; Orchard and Baltimore Orioles; Yellow-breasted Chats; and Black-throated Green, Blue-winged, Yellow, Magnolia, and Chestnut-sided Warblers. During the spring, the Laughing Gulls are joined by Franklin's Gulls as they migrate through and are often seen floating over the bluff on the south breeze. When I visited in March, I was greeted by a pair of Pyrrhuloxias feeding in the grass just past the gate off Ramirez Street. The walk-in gate is the only way to enter this location.

While walking the grounds, you might notice many broken headstones and monuments. My mother made the comment that the broken headstones reflected the broken lives that so many of the interred suffered. Indeed, there are some sad stories of men and women who died too young or in the prime of their lives. It is easy to get lost in the suffering; I try to remind myself how incredibly lucky we are to live in modern times with new advancements happening every day in the medical world, better diet, improved housing, clean water and air, and all the little things that we sometimes take for granted.

There is not a central road or paved path here that make it accessible to people with limited mobility. Nearby birding can be found at Blucher Park, Rosehill Memorial Park, or Hans and Pat Sutter Wildlife Refuge. The South Texas Botanical Gardens and Nature Center has accessible trails and offers a myriad of excellent programs and classes.

Tombstone Tail: Blue-winged Warbler

This bright yellow and blue-gray warbler has a black streak or mask across the eyes and is considered a shrubland specialist. Look for these warblers to be dangling, often upside down, from a branch or leaves as they forage for insects. They migrate through Texas on their way from Central America to central and eastern forests and fields of the United States. They are on the Partners in Flight Red Watch List as a bird of concern because of declining populations due to habitat loss, hybridization with Golden-winged Warblers, and nest parasitization by Brown-headed Cowbirds.

Corpus Christi: Rose Hill Cemetery Complex
2731 Comanche Street

I was first introduced to this amazing birding location in May 2019 and was instantly impressed. In fact, it was this location that transformed me into a believer that cemeteries are a valuable piece of the conservation puzzle, and with over two hundred species recorded here, it won't take you long to become dazzled by this place.

On the day my husband and I visited in May, we sighted thirty-three species of birds, including the rare Hermit Warbler. Admittedly, we would have never seen the Hermit Warbler without the help of two friendly birders who drove across the cemetery to pick us up to come see what they had spotted. As word got out about this rare bird, more local birders arrived, including the editor of the *Corpus Christi Caller-Times*, David Sikes. It was an experience that I will never forget. I will also never forget how respectful the other birders were as they took great care to stay on the paved drives and parked their cars on the outer perimeter to avoid impeding those visiting

Tombstone Tale

Symbols and messages are not limited to the distant past. Modern headstones can also capture a person's life passions and purpose. With new laser etching the sky's the limit on what can be included on a modern monument.

the graves of their loved ones. One of the many things I really enjoy about birding is meeting nice people who are willing to share what they are seeing and respect the space they are visiting.

I visited in March 2020 and again was dazzled by the abundance of birds. On that trip my mother and I sighted several Black-throated Green Warblers that had just arrived on the south winds. That same morning, we spotted four other wintering warblers: Yellow-throated, Orange-crowned, Black-and-white, and Yellow-rumped. In total, over thirty species of warblers have been recorded at this location.

Why is the birding so great here? The secret is the large canopy of live oak trees towering over the lush, watered lawns. The trees and the watered lawns incubate insects that the hungry migrating songbirds gobble up. There are a good number of interesting year-round resident birds that are also worth noting: Great Kiskadees, Golden-fronted Woodpeckers, Couch's Kingbirds, and the festive yellow and black Lesser Goldfinches.

During September Yellow-billed Cuckoos; Buff-bellied and Ruby-throated Hummingbirds; and Olive-sided, Least, Acadian, and Yellow-bellied Flycatchers all spend a few weeks feeding here before moving farther south. Around the same time, keep your eyes to the skies as Broad-winged Hawks sail past on their route along the coastline through Mexico and deeper into Central America. The White-eyed and Blue-headed Vireos winter at this location along with Chipping Sparrows and a handful of Baltimore Orioles.

The paved streets that meander through the canopy of oaks are accessible to people of all mobility types or birding with small children. Nearby birding can be found at South Texas Botanical Gardens or Oso Bay Wetlands Preserve. Hazel Bazemore Park in Calallen is also one of my favorite parks to visit during the spring and fall hawk migration.

Tombstone Tail: Chestnut-sided Warbler

This white, gray, and black warbler with a distinct chestnut stripe on its side moves from Central America into Texas as it migrates quickly through the state. This is a slender warbler that spends much of its time gleaning insects from the ends of thin branches. Males will sing to the females during breeding season; listen for their *please-please-pleased-to-meetcha* song during the spring. These long-distant migrants are in decline because of habitat loss in both the wintering and breeding areas. Because they prefer to return to the same place year after year, it is disruptive when their habitat is logged or cleared for development. Toxic home and agriculture pesticides also pose a threat to all insect-eating birds.

Sinton: Eternal Rest Cemetery

9129 US Highway 77 Business

This is a busy cemetery, so please exercise respect when visiting, especially on the weekends. I also recommend parking near the entrance because the gravel roads are tight in some areas. The streets create two big loops to meander along and watch for White-winged, Common Ground, White-tipped, and Mourning Doves perching in the trees or on headstones or strolling along the ground. When I visited in January, I was impressed with the number of Eastern Bluebirds and Northern Mockingbirds also perching on the headstones. While I was walking the cemetery with my mother, a woman showed up to put out bird seed along the road and in a feeder near the back fence. The seed was descended on by a conclave of Northern Cardinals, with a few Pyrrhuloxias joining the group.

The cemetery is rimmed by Chiltipin Creek on two sides; however, the creek is not visible from the cemetery because of a large flood-prevention berm. The thicket along the berm is a good place to look for Blue-gray Gnatcatchers, Yellow-rumped Warblers,

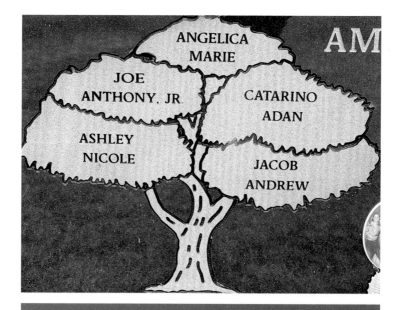

Tombstone Tale

The family tree is a way to share relations and memorialize the family connections. It has become more popular in recent years, especially on a shared family plot.

and Ruby-crowned Kinglets in the winter and early spring. The grasslands on the opposite side of the cemetery can host Vesper, Savannah, Chipping, and Lincoln's Sparrows. During the spring, look along the fence line where the native flowers bloom to find Ruby-throated, Black-chinned, and Buff-bellied Hummingbirds. Spring also brings the return of Barn and Cliff Swallows, Purple Martins, Chimney Swifts, and Common Nighthawks. A few of the local birds include Green Jays, Great Kiskadees, Crested Caracaras, and Northern Harriers. Because of the cemetery's proximity to the creek and wetlands at Welder Park, it is common to see passing flocks of Northern Shovelers, Gadwalls, Black-bellied Whistling-Ducks, and White Ibis.

The land for the cemetery was donated by Bessie Welder in 1960. The Welders were (and still are) a ranching family with a deep conservation ethic who gave the land for Welder Park just north of the cemetery. They also donated the lands for the Rob and Bessie Welder Park located north of town off Highway 181. Additionally, they founded the Rob and Bessie Welder Wildlife Foundation off Highway 77. Visitation to the Welder Wildlife Foundation is by appointment only, so plan accordingly. All of the Welder parks offer interesting places to bird in the Sinton area. As a side note, Katie Owens Welder served on the first State Parks Board in 1924 to help establish the state park system in Texas.

The gravel roads are not suitable for a wheelchair but offer easy walking with limited shade along the central road. In addition to the parks just mentioned, nearby birding can be found at the Sinton Cemetery or Evergreen Cemetery in Odem. Both offer good habitat that is similar to that at Eternal Rest Cemetery, minus the proximity to the creek and wetlands.

Tombstone Tail: Eastern Meadowlark

When an Eastern Meadowlark is perched on a fence or headstone, it is easy to see the bright yellow breast with the distinct black V shape. However, when meadowlarks are in the grass searching for insects, they are well camouflaged and difficult to see. During breeding season males often perch to sing. These ground-nesting birds are in sharp decline because of overgrazing on public and private lands, early and frequent mowing during nesting season, and the overuse of pesticides. Humans can help these birds recover by setting aside more grasslands and reducing the use of pesticides.

Beeville: Beeville Cemetery Complex

East Hefferman Street

This is a large cemetery complex comprising three separate burial grounds that were, and still are to an extent, separated by religion and race. Saint Rose, Saint Joseph, and Glenwood form the complex, which contains several mature live oak groves, cedar trees, palms, and a good amount of scrub along the fence lines in addition to the grasslands of the yard.

When I arrived and pulled through the gates at Saint Rose, the historic African American cemetery, I was greeted by a Wild Turkey that scampered off into the scrub brush. In that same area along the fence I saw Indigo and Painted Buntings, Blue and Rose-breasted Grosbeaks, Baltimore Orioles, and Yellow-rumped Warblers all feeding on the mulberry tree in mid-April. As I walked along the grounds, I watched Mississippi Kites fly over in a great kettle followed by a flock of Franklin's Gulls. Both times that I visited in the spring of 2021, I saw an Audubon's Oriole in the large oak trees near the far end of Saint Joseph Cemetery. On my first visit in April I was pleased to find twenty-five species fluttering about in just under an hour. When I returned with my family for a second visit, we saw thirty-one species, including the dazzling Scarlet Tanager.

Saint Rose received burials prior to the official dedication. Among the first known individuals interred here was a former enslaved person, Nancy Williams, who died in 1901. The land was officially deeded for the purpose of an African American cemetery in 1921. There are historical markers at the entrances of each of the cemeteries that are worth reading.

Each cemetery has several gravel roads to meander down. The roads are compacted and might be suitable for some mobility devices depending on the comfort level of the

Tombstone Tale

The angel represents the connection to the heavenly realm. It can often represent the eternal youth, beauty, and purity desired in eternity.

individual. It is easy to see most of the bird habitat from a vehicle if visitors wish to use their car as a bird blind. Nearby birding can be found at the Veterans Memorial Park in Beeville or in Sinton at the Rob and Bessie Welder Park.

Tombstone Tail: Scarlet Tanager

This bird is appropriately named; the males have a rich, scarlet-red body with jet-black wings and tail feathers. The females are a slightly dull, lemon-yellow color with darker yellow wings and tail feathers. They winter in the tropical forests of northwestern South America and summer in the east-central part of the United States and follow a spring and fall migration that takes them through central and eastern parts of Texas. They eat fruits, berries, and insects, with a strong affinity for gypsy moth caterpillars. Their nests are a favorite target of the Brown-headed Cowbird, and both parents will aggressively defend the nest if they spy a female cowbird lurking around. A group of tanagers is called a season, and a healthy bird can live up to eleven years.

Wildflowers in bloom in March—Rockport City Cemetery

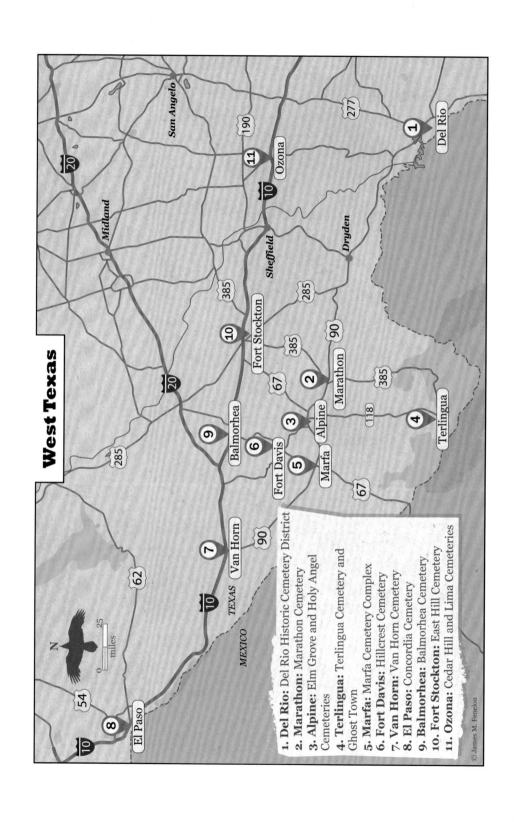

West Texas

1. **Del Rio:** Del Rio Historic Cemetery District
2. **Marathon:** Marathon Cemetery
3. **Alpine:** Elm Grove and Holy Angel Cemeteries
4. **Terlingua:** Terlingua Cemetery and Ghost Town
5. **Marfa:** Marfa Cemetery Complex
6. **Fort Davis:** Hillcrest Cemetery
7. **Van Horn:** Van Horn Cemetery
8. **El Paso:** Concordia Cemetery
9. **Balmorhea:** Balmorhea Cemetery
10. **Fort Stockton:** East Hill Cemetery
11. **Ozona:** Cedar Hill and Lima Cemeteries

© James M. Fenelon

West Texas

West Texas is defined by wide-open spaces that ramble right up to the mountains or right down to the Pecos River or Rio Grande. It is the only place in Texas where the desert and the mountains exist in the same vista. The variety of elevations and ecosystems supports some of the most diverse plant life in the state, with Texas Parks and Wildlife reporting over 260 species of grasses and 447 species of woody plants. Those plants do not culminate in rich, dense forests; instead, they are scattered throughout the immense region and cluster in canyons or near water sources. The diversity of vegetation supports large game such as mule and white-tailed deer, mountain lions, desert bighorn sheep, pronghorn antelope, and javelinas. A few black bears have come back into the region at the higher elevations and seem to be limited to Big Bend National Park and surrounding wildlife management lands. The vegetation and water also support some of the most unique birds in Texas.

This was the stronghold of the nomadic Apache, who moved along the watersheds and had a deep understanding and respect for the vastness, dangers, and delights afforded by the land and wildlife. The big grasslands were also enticing to cattle ranchers, who started to arrive in the 1850s. Massive ranches were established, water wells were dug, and soon the grasslands were supporting large herds of cattle, sheep, and goats. However, once the droughts returned in 1905, thousands of domestic animals starved to death and forever changed the rangeland management of the region. Ranching, oil and gas, and water are the big economic drivers of the area, with nature tourism now breaking into the top-five list. With over fifteen species of hummingbirds occurring in the Fort Davis area during the fall migrations and over 450 species of birds being recorded at Big Bend National Park, it is no wonder that this region is on many a birder's bucket list.

Del Rio: Del Rio Historic Cemetery District

West Second and St. Peter Streets

It is always a positive sign to be welcomed to the cemetery by two Cooper's Hawks engaged in a high-speed mating chase in and out of the towering Italian cypress trees. This burial complex contains four historic cemeteries: Westlawn (formerly known as the public cemetery), Sacred Heart Catholic, St. Joseph's, and the Masonic Cemetery. Within each cemetery further separation occurs and is a tangible reminder of the ethnic, religious, and fraternal enclaves that have existed in Del Rio since it was founded. The Del Rio Cemeteries District is listed on the National Register of Historic Places.

As Westlawn developed, it added a space for African Americans, Babyland, Potter's Field, Stranger's Rest, and eventually a section for the International Order of Odd Fellows. Sacred Heart was traditionally divided into three sections for Italians, Mexicans, and all other Catholics. Del Rio had a large influx of Italian migrants into the region in the late 1880s; some arrived as workers on the railroad, and others pursued farming,

Tombstone Tale

Our Lady of Guadalupe embodies the unique spirit of Mexico, and the symbols that surround her blend the Aztec and Catholic influences. Her flowing robes are often colored blue with gold stars to represent both the sky and her status as royalty, while the cross on her necklace reflects the devotion to the Catholic Church. She is depicted as standing on the crescent moon and an angel flying from the sacred Aztec grounds. Since the 1880s she has been known as the "Patroness of the Americas" and the "Queen of Mexico." As a guardian of the departed, her image is often housed in an altar where grave gifts can be left.

ranching, and even mining. Since Westlawn is now open to all citizens, a fact that was not always so, surnames from all cultures can be found throughout the grounds. The markers remain as reminders of the hotel and business owners, ranchers, bull riders, telegraph operators, Indian scouts, Boy and Girl Scouts, county judges, law enforcement, and schoolteachers who helped build Del Rio into the city it is today. Since Del Rio was not very developed before the American Civil War, the headstones do not date back much past the 1890s, with the majority being less than fifty years old. The dates might not be as impressive, but the variety of homemade and handcrafted markers are worth noting.

When I visited, I parked in Westlawn and explored each of the grounds from there. The cemeteries are known for the towering Italian and Arizona cypress trees that line the roads. Neither is native to Texas, but they do offer great cover and perching spots for the birds. The birds at this location add a splash of color to the sun-bleached desert soils, grasses, and tombstones. During the winter months, the Pyrrhuloxias gather in large flocks and can be found feeding in the grasses throughout the complex. They are a year-round bird; however, seeing the large wintering flocks is a delightful experience. Other winter birds include Yellow-rumped Warblers and Yellow-bellied Sapsuckers. In sticking with the yellow theme, look for Yellow-headed Blackbirds, Yellow-breasted Chats, Western Kingbirds, and Yellow Warblers during the spring migration or hanging around through the summer. The year-round birds are worth the trip regardless of the season: Bewick's and Cactus Wrens, Great Kiskadees, Lesser Goldfinches, and Golden-fronted Woodpeckers. The two darlings of the cemetery were the Vermilion Flycatcher and the Verdin. While I like the flashy Vermilion Flycatcher, I have to admit my favorite bird in West Texas is the Cactus Wren, which is abundant at this location. I never get tired of seeing these wrens taking a dust bath.

Only a portion of the roads here are paved and suitable for wheeled mobility devices. Nearby birding can be found along the San Felipe Riverwalk and Lion's Park, Cienegas Terrace ponds, and the San Felipe Cemetery on the southeastern edge of town.

Tombstone Tail: Vermilion Flycatcher

I love the genus name of this bird, Pyrocephalus, which means "fire headed." It's hard to miss the fiery, jewel-like color of the male Vermilion Flycatcher as it perches in low branches across West and South Texas into Mexico. The females are said to be drab; however, I find their orange and gray colors to be equally attractive. While courting, the males will sometimes present females with feasts such as butterflies or larger insects. Cemeteries are a good place to find these birds, as they enjoy watered lawns where insects are prolific and there are plenty of places to perch.

Marathon: Marathon Cemetery

Cemetery Road and Avenue D

There is a stark beauty to Marathon and the Big Bend region that I like more and more each time I visit. The town of Marathon finally acquired a post office in 1883, and the paperwork noted that they had a whopping population of 130 people. Various land-exploitation schemes came and went over the years, as eager entrepreneurs tried to establish a rubber-making plant, oil fields, wax-making business, and even a large beekeeping community. However, the land is stubborn and does not want to give up its wilds easily in this part of the world. Even the original military outpost at nearby Fort Pena Colorado Park finally faded into history, but not before one last surge of

Tombstone Tale

Planting evergreen trees at graveyards is a tradition rooted in Greek and pagan cultures and is a symbol of everlasting life. During the 1700s the tradition gained favor again, as a cult of melancholy began to form. It was thought that trees evoke deep emotions, especially when juxtaposed with the solemnness of death. German immigrants were fond of the tradition and incorporated it in rural cemeteries across Texas.

military initiative in 1911, when the US military strengthened its presence along the border during the Mexican Revolution. Captain Douglas MacArthur and Lieutenant George Patton were both stationed for a short time at this lonely outpost.

In 1927, Alfred Gage, a man with a vision, arrived and built the iconic Gage Hotel. He left his home in Vermont as a young man with the plan to be a rancher in Texas. He accomplished his goal by amassing more than five hundred thousand acres of ranchlands in the area. In the mid-1920s Gage decided to build a hotel, something the town lacked after fires devastated several of the buildings downtown. The hotel doubled as his ranching headquarters and soon became a destination for writers and artists coming to marvel at the land and be inspired by the ever-changing light. The hotel continues to be an oasis for travelers to this day.

The small cemetery was established in 1902 on the low hill to the south of town and was originally divided into Anglo and Mexican sections that are still apparent today. While it is still an active cemetery, I would not exactly call it busy. It is beautiful in its own way, with a mix of stone monuments, metal markers, and wooden crosses. The decorations are almost as interesting as the birds and seem to be instantly old as they bleach in the sun, even if they were placed there only days before. The next time I visit, I plan on taking a camp chair to sit in the shade, watch the birds, and listen to the quiet conversation of nature as it whispers softly on the breeze.

It is an ideal spot to look for the Zone-tailed and Gray Hawks that pass through in April and for other raptors during the rest of the year. The cemetery has something few other places in town can offer—tall trees. Those trees are a welcome sight to spring and fall migrants such as the beautiful Scott's and Orchard Orioles. While several varieties of hummingbirds arrive in the spring, the best time to see the Rufous or Calliope Hummingbirds is in August and September.

The first time I visited this location was on one of our Great Texas Birding Classic competitions. I was with my mother and husband, and we were greeted at the stone gates by a covey of Scaled Quail. I do not recall how many other species we spied that evening, but there are more than eighty types of birds recorded on the eBird website for this location. Less than a mile away at the Gage Gardens, nearly two hundred species have been recorded. The garden has a pond, a fountain, and bird feeders that, naturally, makes it more attractive to the birds.

This is a good place to look for Vermilion Flycatchers, Say's Phoebes, and Cassin's and Western Kingbirds. The grasslands near the entrance harbor both Eastern and Western Meadowlarks and Blue Grosbeaks. Both Lark Sparrows and Lark Buntings have also been sighted in that area. During the winter and early spring, keep an eye out for Black-throated, Vesper, Chipping, Grasshopper, and White-crowned Sparrows. There are reports of Eastern, Western, and Mountain Bluebirds being sighted here in November and December. A local birder told me that it is common to see a Barn Owl at the cemetery; however, I have not been lucky enough to find one.

The unpaved and uneven hardpan road is not suitable for wheelchairs. I also recommend visiting in the morning or evening, as there is little shade along the central road. Nearby birding can be found at the Gage Gardens, Fort Pena Colorado Park, and of course, the mighty Big Bend National Park. If you get a chance, check out the cemetery in Terlingua between Big Bend National Park and Big Bend Ranch State Park. It is worth the journey.

Tombstone Tail: Scott's Oriole

The male and female Scott's Oriole are both a vivid yellow, with the females being less vibrant and lacking the dramatic black hood that the males feature. They are dependent on yucca plants for their nesting fibers, nectar, and the insects that live on them. Their beautiful song is as bright and bold as their lemon color and a favorite sound of the Southwest. They can be found in Texas in the Trans-Pecos region with a few nesting as far east as Junction.

Alpine: Elm Grove and Holy Angel Cemeteries
605 West Uvalde Avenue

Elm Grove and Holy Angel Cemeteries reflect the segregation of Anglos and Hispanics that often still exists today. Holy Angel Cemetery was once known as the "Alpine Mexican Cemetery." The birds move easily between both locations regardless of the name or the wall that reminds us that humans are still overcoming their tribal tendencies. The acreage enclosed by both cemeteries has one of the larger collection of trees in town. When I visited during late summer, three of the trees were topped with Harris's Hawks that were being relentlessly attacked by Northern Mockingbirds.

On that same visit my mother and I spotted twenty-one species of birds at five in the afternoon. The only reason we were out at that time of day in August was that a

Tombstone Tale

Daughters of the Republic of Texas (DRT) was formed in 1891 in Galveston by Betty Ballinger and Hally Bryan to connect the descendants of the pioneering families and soldiers of the Republic of Texas. One of the first major projects of the DRT was to secure the San Jacinto Battleground in the 1890s. As a result, they established the first state park in Texas. Today they operate a museum and are a repository for thousands of archived materials.

pleasant afternoon storm bubbled up and cloudbursts of rain cooled the air along with the summer breeze. The summer in my hometown of Austin had been dry since early June, and the smell of rain mixed with the dried grass was heavenly.

A few birds of note from that visit were the dashing black-and-white Lark Bunting, a male and female Blue Grosbeak, and two Vermilion Flycatcher parents showing their fledgling how to snatch a meal from the ground. Along the fence line we watched a chime of Cactus Wrens feeding below the cholla cactus that housed a cluster of their nests.

There are over one hundred species of birds recorded on eBird for this location, and I think that number might be higher with a little more investigation. Because some of the family plots are watered, the insect population supports Cassin's and Western Kingbirds, Barn Swallows, and Lark Sparrows during the summer. Loggerhead Shrikes, Say's Phoebes, Pyrrhuloxias, and Acorn Woodpeckers are some of the local birds that also enjoy the large trees and abundant insect population. During the spring this is a good place to find Scott's, Orchard, Hooded, and Baltimore Orioles. When I visited in early April 2022, there were dozens of Yellow-rumped (Audubon's) Warblers bathing in the sprinklers and feeding in the grasses. This version of the Yellow-rumps has a yellow crown and yellow throat patch in addition to its yellow rump. On that visit I also finally correctly identified, on my own, the Clay-colored Sparrow that I often misidentify as a Lark or Field Sparrow. During the winter, watch for Red Crossbills and Cassin's Finches to join the resident Lesser and House Finches.

One of the more interesting people buried here is Crystal Hope Holland Spanell (1886–1916). Her family owned the Holland Hotel in downtown Alpine, and she was reported to be one of the most beautiful women in Texas during her short lifetime. Sadly, she had a jealous husband who was not able to control his emotions. On the evening of July 20, 1916, he suspected his wife was having an affair with one of their friends. He requested the three of them take a drive and then gunned down Crystal and the friend in cold blood just down the street from the hotel. Despite having multiple witnesses, Spanell was found not guilty of the murders. In those days it was common to blame the victim, especially if she was a lovely woman who *made* her husband fly into jealous rages. It is reported that people from all over the region came to her funeral and the cemetery on the day she was laid to rest.

Like most West Texas cemeteries this one has hard-packed gravel roads that are not ideal for wheeled devices but can be manageable depending on a person's comfort. This location is well suited to do a little car birding if the roads seem too rough. Nearby birding can be found at Kokernot Park and Chihuahuan Desert Research Institute. I am also a big fan of the bird blinds at Davis Mountains State Park.

Tombstone Tail: Harris's Hawk

Look for this large chocolate-brown, chestnut-red, and white hawk with bright yellow legs to be perched on high points in parts of the arid Southwest and Mexico. These hawks are more common in the scrub country of South Texas; however, they can also be found in the Trans-Pecos region. They are social raptors and will hunt cooperatively with members of their family group. If food is plentiful, a female might have multiple clutches in one year. Young hawks can often be seen playing with insects or sticks to practice pouncing and cooperative hunting skills. Their populations are stable; however, habitat loss due to oil and gas exploration and development does pose a threat to these desert and scrub-country specialists.

Terlingua: Terlingua Cemetery and Ghost Town
Terlingua Ghost Town Road

When most people think about Terlingua, they have visions of people gathered around vats of bubbling hot chili at the famous Chili Cookoff. Or maybe they see themselves waiting in the hot, dusty parking lot for the river guide bus to haul them away for a raft trip down the mighty Rio Grande. Others might remember it fondly as a place where they picked up a few provisions before marching off on a long hike at Big Bend National Park or Big Bend Ranch State Park.

Our modern visions of the remote desert town might be pleasant enough; however, for the early settlers it was one step above hell on earth. In the mid-1880s, mercury,

Tombstone Tale

The origins of the tradition of Dia de los Muertos (Day of the Dead) started in pre-Columbian Mexico as a time to honor the dead. The tradition has continued and spans two days: Dia de los Inocentes (November 1) honors the children, and Dia de los Muertos (November 2) honors the adults. As part of the celebration candles are lit and placed on graves along with photos, gifts, letters, poetry, food, and drinks. It is also a time to clean the cemetery and headstones as a family or community and share stories.

otherwise known as quicksilver, was discovered in the area. Early settlers noticed that Native Americans were using a red dye to create their pictographs. The dye was made from a red pigment from the mineral cinnabar, from which quicksilver is extracted. The Chisos Mine was established in 1902, and the town slowly swelled to over a thousand people. (I'm still not sure how they had enough water for all of them.) The mine sprawled out over miles and had seventeen levels of underventilated hell.

Aboveground, Terlingua was a true company town complete with the owner's big house, known as the Perry Mansion, that sat high on the hill, a general store, mail service three times a week, and a company doctor. What they really needed was a company dentist, who might have been able to help them prevent their teeth from dissolving. Smelting mercury released toxic fumes into the air, which caused a condition known as "salivation." The poison in the fumes stimulated the saliva glands, which were filled with toxins, and the teeth loosened and fell out.

The cemetery was established in 1903. Many of the early graves are unmarked or marked with a rock pile or cross but lack the name of the interred. Most of the early people in the cemetery died in mine-related accidents or from mercury poisoning, while many died in the Spanish flu outbreak of 1917–18.

The cemetery is one of the most-photographed graveyards in Texas, and when you visit, I'm sure you will understand why. While walking among the wooden crosses, altars, rock piles, and headstones, it is easy to be immersed in the hardship, suffering, and stark loneliness of the land and the people who tried to tame it or at least soften it enough to call it home.

Birds also might not be the first thing that pops in one's mind when thinking of this desert community. With over one hundred species recorded at the cemetery and adjacent ghost town, it is a good spot to find some avian desert dwellers. A few of the notable year-round birds are Scaled Quail, Say's Phoebes, Verdins, Black-throated Sparrows, Curve-billed Thrashers, and Cactus and Canyon Wrens. During the spring the Barn, Cliff, and Cave Swallows return along with Ash-throated Flycatchers and Western Kingbirds. Three of the flashier spring migrants are the Wilson's Warblers, Scott's Orioles, and Blue Grosbeaks. The late-summer to early-fall hummingbird migration typically takes the birds to a higher elevation; however, there are reports of Black-chinned, Anna's, and Rufous Hummingbirds passing through. During the winter, look for White-crowned Sparrows, Vespers, Black Phoebes, Yellow-headed Blackbirds, and Yellow-rumped Warblers.

When I visited one morning in August, I spotted fourteen species in about an hour as I walked through the cemetery and around the ghost town. Admittedly, I saw the most birds in the small park area across from the Starlight Theater along the ravine overlooking the cemetery. The small greenspace was also filled with jackrabbits. If you visit in the summer, be sure to go early in the morning, take plenty of water, and watch for snakes. Actually, that advice is true for most of the year. The entire area is not suitable for wheeled devices, as it is rocky and unpaved.

The best place to see the hummingbirds during the August and September migration is at the Christmas Mountain Oasis. The oasis is privately owned and operated by a woman and her army of volunteers and requires a reservation and a four-wheel-drive vehicle. Neither the reservation nor the four-wheel-drive vehicle is optional.

Tombstone Tail: Black-tailed Gnatcatcher

According to the Cornell Lab of Ornithology this tiny songbird weighs about as much as a nickel. Like its relative the Blue-gray Gnatcatcher, it moves with a frantic energy as it searches for insects on mesquite- and cactus-lined arroyos of its preferred desert habitat. Unlike the Blue-gray, the Black-tailed Gnatcatcher cannot survive in a densely human-populated area or a landscape dominated by nonnative plants. It extracts most of the water it needs from the insects it consumes. The males are handsome little birds with a black cap and tail, gray body, and white eye ring. Females are similar but lack the black cap.

Marfa: Marfa Cemetery Complex
211 West San Antonio Street

This is a fairly large cemetery complex considering the town has always been sparsely populated. The complex contains the Cementerio de la Merced and Catholic and Marfa City Cemeteries. I will keep the description of this location short in the spirit of the minimalist art and lifestyle movement that has made Marfa a popular vacation spot for artists and art lovers from around the world.

There are enough trees, native grasses, and adjacent fields to support resident and migrant birds. From October to March, look for Baird's, Brewer's, Black-throated, Grasshopper, Vesper, and White-crowned Sparrows feeding on the seeds of the wispy native grasses of the Marfa Plateau. Keep an eye on the field past the Catholic Cemetery toward the railroad track for Northern Harriers to float along the top of the

Tombstone Tale

Grave goods are slightly different from grave decorations in that grave goods are usually something that once belonged to the departed. Sometimes they are placed in the coffin; other times they are left at the gravesite or worked into the marker. For many families it is a way to celebrate the life and memory of that person.

grasses while looking for mice and other small game. If you are lucky, and I hope you are, you might catch a glimpse of the Chestnut-collared Longspur here. Some of the resident birds include Say's Phoebes, Dark-eyed Juncos, Killdeers, Eastern Meadow-larks, and the talkative Chihuahuan Ravens. Spring brings the return of Common Nighthawks, Barn Swallows, and one of my favorite Trans-Pecos migrant birds, the Scott's Oriole. The few blooming flowers attract Black-chinned Hummingbirds from April to August.

All three cemeteries have family plots with curbing, and each of the interred faces the rising sun as it climbs up over the mountains to the east. I woke up early to greet the sun in this special place, and I must admit, some of the graves along the eastern boundary of Cementerio de la Merced have front-row seats to the eternal brilliance of nature every morning. Both Merced and the Catholic Cemetery have individual graves in between the family plots and layers of offerings and memorabilia. One particular gravesite featured a mannequin in a full-length fancy party dress with fairy wings standing over a well-decorated Christmas tree that matched the dress. I've seen a lot of graveside goods, decorations, and offerings, but that was a first for me.

I reveled in the solitude and peacefulness of this space when I visited, and I will always remember the changing light as the sun set in the evening and rose again the next morning. The rough roads are not suitable for wheeled mobility devices but of-fer a safe, contained space to bird in the middle of the vast openness of West Texas. Nearby birding can be found at the Chinati Foundation, Dixon Water Foundation, Marfa settling ponds, and Marfa Lights viewing platform.

Tombstone Tail: White-crowned Sparrow

Males of this species feature a distinct black-and-white crown on their head, which sets them apart from other sparrows. Females have a rust-and-gray-striped head. They winter all across North America and will migrate to the Arctic Circle, Canada, and Alaska to breed. They have been known to travel up to three hundred miles a night as they migrate. Their beautiful song really sets them apart and is one of the most-studied vocalizations of all animal behavior. Males learn the song from their natal neighborhood and will start repeating it in the first few months of life. Each region has a distinct song, and it is a joy to hear across Texas. Look for them along fence lines and cemetery edges.

Van Horn: Van Horn Cemetery
West Ninth Street

For many, the town of Van Horn is the gateway to Guadalupe Mountains National Park to the north or Big Bend National Park to the south. The clear springs located along the base of the nearby mountains were a welcome sight to nomadic tribes, early explorers, and Anglo pioneers. In the 1860s the San Antonio to El Paso Overland Mail route passed through. The mail and stage routes laid the foundation for later highways and eventually Interstate 10. The town is filled with hotels and motels that tell the tale of the town's value as a resting place along the long journey through the lonely western part of Texas.

The grounds are laid out in a grid that has dirt roads and a pleasant pavilion in the center. What makes this a special birding location are the large, watered pine trees, adjacent arroyo, and native grasses. With more than 130 species of birds recorded at this location, suffice it to say that birding is good in all seasons. Both Gambel's and Scaled Quail can be found at this site year-round alongside Say's Phoebes and Pyrrhuloxias. Bullock's and Scott's Orioles arrive here in late spring and summer alongside Western Tanagers. This is a good place to look for Black-chinned, Rufous, and Broad-tailed

Tombstone Tale

The urn is often considered a vessel for the departed, while the veil can represent protection or the barrier between the living and the dead. The closed book generally means a full life that was lived with all the chapters completed and that has reached the end.

Hummingbirds during August and early September and to find Western and Cassin's Kingbirds chattering away as they breed and raise their young from April to September.

Fall brings the return of sparrows, including both Canyon and Green-tailed Towhees as well as Brewer's and Cassin's Sparrows. The Red Crossbill is reported here frequently on eBird. Late fall and winter are also good times to see Blue-gray and Black-tailed Gnatcatchers and Red-breasted Nuthatches.

It is hard to even say there are nearby places to bird since Van Horn is 120 miles from Fort Stockton to the east, 120 miles from El Paso to the west, or 80 miles from Fort Davis to the south.

Tombstone Tail: Western Kingbird

The sexes of this large, yellow-bellied flycatcher are similar. They have an all-purpose bill, which allows them to eat a variety of food from insects to berries. When chasing an insect, they launch from their perch to catch the prey while in flight. Cemeteries with open grasslands, shrubs, and plenty of places to perch make excellent habitat for these flycatchers. They breed across the western part of North America and winter in Central America, with some staying in Florida year-round.

El Paso: Concordia Cemetery

3700 East Yandell

When the cemetery was established in 1856, it was located three miles outside town. Today, this historic fifty-two-acre burial ground sits in the heart of the booming metropolis of El Paso. The 166-year-old cemetery reflects the many cultures, clubs, and individuals that built the city and surrounding communities. Lying peacefully in the walled grounds are Catholic priests, Mormons, Freemasons, Woodmen of the World, gunslingers such as John Wesley Hardin, Texas Rangers, and Buffalo Soldiers. This location is one of the few cemeteries in Texas that has a separate walled and gated section for Chinese, many of whom came to El Paso while building the railroad. The B'Nai Zion and Mt. Sinai Jewish Cemeteries are also part of the complex but are main-

Tombstone Tale

The letters "IHS" stand for *iota, eta,* and *sigma* from the Greek alphabet. The abbreviation represents the first three letters of the name Jesus and is often paired with a cross.

tained separately. The two Jewish sections are watered and feature most of the larger trees in the complex.

When I arrived on a cool morning in February, I was greeted by two Curve-billed Thrashers looking for insects in the shade of the historical marker. A Northern Flicker caught my attention near the Chinese cemetery, and I watched it walk among the tombstones and pick through the dried grass for several minutes before it flew off to meet its partner in a small tree near the center of the complex. The trees, sage, cactus, and other plants here are sparse but abundant enough to support a good variety of birds. According to the Concordia Heritage Association, 250 desert willows were planted at this location in 2012 by members of the local Lions Clubs. I would enjoy seeing those in bloom during the late summer when the Black-chinned, Rufous, and Broad-tailed Hummingbirds are in the area.

There are plenty of Rock Pigeons and Eurasian Collared, White-winged, Inca, and Mourning Doves to keep the Cooper's Hawks busy year-round. Some of the other year-round residents include Lesser Goldfinches, House Finches, Verdins, Cactus Wrens, Northern Mockingbirds, and Greater Roadrunners. During the fall and winter, keep an eye out for Ruby-crowned Kinglets, Say's Phoebes, Chipping Sparrows, and Dark-eyed Juncos. This would also be a good place to look for Dusky and Cordilleran Flycatchers, Summer and Western Tanagers, and Western Kingbirds during late spring to late summer.

Because of the lack of shade, I would not recommend visiting this location in the middle of the day once the temperatures start to rise. The best time to visit is early morning or just before dusk. The roads here are a hard-packed gravel that might be suitable for some wheeled mobility devices depending on the comfort level of the individual. For additional birding, check out Evergreen Cemetery just south of Interstate 10. Evergreen is watered and features several large pine trees. Ascarate Park has wetlands that support over 245 species of birds throughout the year. Franklin Mountains State Park is also a cool place to visit and bird when in the area.

Tombstone Tail: Curve-billed Thrasher

This thrasher is a desert and scrub-country specialist that lives in the desert Southwest of the United States and northern Mexico. Like most desert dwellers, thrashers are active in the early mornings and evenings but seek shade in the midday sun. Their drab coloring offers them camouflage, while their curved bill and orange eyes are their defining features. Pairs mate for life and can often be found running or hopping along the ground together as they search for insects, fruits, and seeds. The pair build their nests about three to five feet off the ground in cactus or scrub and defend their five- to ten-acre territory fiercely. Their populations are strong; however, habitat loss in the Arizona Sonoran Desert is a threat.

Fort Davis: Hillcrest Cemetery

Cemetery Road

It was hard for me to bird here, as all I wanted to do was sit and listen to the breeze pass through the pines and look out on the golden grasslands and rocky hills. I have to admit I did not see many birds the first morning, as I was totally entranced by the light and the vistas. On the second visit I had better focus and was pleased with the number of birds inside the perimeter of the peaceful cemetery and out in the grasslands beyond the boundary. With almost one hundred species recorded here, there is plenty of good birding year-round.

The grasslands and scrub harbor Scaled Quail and Greater Roadrunners that frequently come into the cemetery. There are various types of sparrows that visit year-round, with most occurring in the winter, such as Brewer's, Field, White-crowned, and Vesper Sparrows. The Black-chinned Hummingbird is often spotted here, with less frequent sightings of other types of hummingbirds during the spring and summer. Perhaps someone or a local organization might consider planting a pollinator garden with native plants near the entrance where the water faucet is located to attract a greater variety of hummers. The spring and summer bring in Lesser and Common Nighthawks, Ash-throated Flycatchers, Cassin's and Western Kingbirds, and Lark Sparrows. Some of the year-round favorites are the Eastern and Western Meadowlarks, Vermilion Flycatchers, House Finches, and Acorn Woodpeckers.

Fort Davis offers a good account of the military presence in the region; however, it seems it could do a little more to tell the story of the Apache and Comanche that once called this region home. The cool, dry air and stunning vistas have made Fort Davis an alluring vacation spot for decades, especially for Texans escaping hot, humid summers. People like Madge Lindsey and the Trans-Pecos Birding Conservation help

Tombstone Tale

The rose reflects the passion of our heart in the land of the living. In death and on a headstone, it can reflect the perfection of heaven. Roses are often shown with three leaves that reflect the Holy Trinity of the Father, Son, and Holy Ghost.

put on the Davis Mountains Hummingbird Celebration each year and bring needed awareness of the amazing birding this special place has to offer. The celebration takes place each year toward the end of August when the hummingbirds return to the "sky islands" before continuing south for the winter.

The dirt roads of this location are not suitable for people with limited mobility; however, I do recommend visiting the accessible bird blind at Davis Mountains State Park. The state park offers two excellent bird blinds and plenty of hiking trails and vistas to observe the native plants, animals, and birds of the region. The Chihuahuan Desert Research Institute has really excellent trails to walk and bird, plus an accessible bird blind. The grounds of the Fort Davis National Historic Site also yield some interesting birds, especially close to the cluster of cottonwoods near the entrance or along the Hospital Canyon Trail.

Tombstone Tail: Acorn Woodpecker

This bird might look a little clownish with its black-and-white face and scarlet-red cap; however, it is not clowning around when it comes to food collection and storage. These woodpeckers will store thousands of acorns and seeds in the holes of a pantry or granary tree; some might store up to fifty thousand acorns. They have complex social systems that include their young staying with them to help raise new chicks and defend their territory. Their social life is so complex that researchers have been studying the birds' behavior in one of the longest-running avian studies in North America. They cross into the United States only in the Big Bend and Trans-Pecos regions.

Balmorhea: Balmorhea Cemetery

Cemetery Road

At first glance this might seem like a pretty lonely place, as the wind tosses the tumbleweeds and dust carelessly about. However, the cemetery has something that few other places in the area have—trees. There are not many trees, but the ones that do exist are filled with birds as they seek shelter from the wind and shade from the sun. The grasses just beyond the fence offer cover and food for a plethora of seedeaters. A splash of color lifts the otherwise insipid landscape in the spring when the ocotillo cactus and purple sage bloom.

The cemetery is configured in a traditional grid pattern with Protestants and Catholics separated for the most part. It's a true Texas cemetery, with handcrafted headstones standing next to Woodmen of the World monuments or personalized granite arrowheads. Both the Catholic and Protestant sections have graves that are simply covered by a pile of rocks with little more to memorialize the life that once animated the body now

Tombstone Tale

This is one of the most unique altar tombs that I have come across. An altar tomb is typically a slightly raised box tomb with some sort of elaborate fixture on top. This features a cathedral where offerings and decorations can be left.

resting below. Some of the oldest graves date back to the 1880s; however, there might be older burials that did not have a headstone or marker.

If you ask me, the year-round residents consist of a pretty cool lineup of birds. Among the sage bushes and ocotillo cactus it's common to find Scaled Quail, Greater Roadrunners, Curve-billed Thrashers, and Pyrrhuloxias all scratching the ground for a meal. Say's Phoebes and Loggerhead Shrikes can be found perching on the headstones as they launch off to snatch a bug. Two of my favorite residents are the busy little Cactus and Rock Wrens. I never tire of the raspy call of the Cactus Wren; it sounds like pure Texas to me.

Not much happens here during the spring migration other than the arrival of a few passerines such as Scott's and Bullock's Orioles, Painted Buntings, Western Kingbirds, and Black-chinned Hummingbirds. As late hot summer rolls into early hot fall, a number of wintering birds begin to arrive and will stay until late March or even April. Because of the grasslands within and surrounding the cemetery, there are a number of sparrows that thrive here. Look for Cassin's, Chipping, Brewer's, Black-throated, White-crowned, Sagebrush, Vesper, and Lincoln's Sparrows throughout the grounds. The winter also brings Yellow-rumped Warblers, Black-tailed Gnatcatchers, Greentailed Towhees, Sage and Crissal Thrashers, and large flocks of Lark Buntings. Keep an ear out for the beautiful song of the Sage Thrashers in early spring before they migrate to points north to breed.

While researching this cemetery, I came across a tombstone of someone with a tale worth telling. Esther Elaine Carlson Moody (1941–2019) was born in Cayote, Texas, in 1941 to Curtis and Evelyn Carlson. Elaine graduated from Pecos High School in 1959 and married Claude Moody in 1969. Elaine went on to bring beauty to the Pecos-Balmorhea region for forty-five years as a beautician.

Having lived in a small town, I can say with authority that a beautician skilled enough to make it more than forty years is one talented woman and is also the keeper of many gossiped secrets. People tell their hair stylist information they would not dare tell their priest, pastor, or even the local bartender. Even though Elaine was not an elected official or commander of great wealth, she would have been an influencer nonetheless. I like to think about how many girls she made feel beautiful and special as they twirled off to homecoming or prom. How many women she emboldened by giving them the perfect hairstyle to secure a job, give a speech, get a date, or take control of her life. Hair has power, especially in Texas, and the crafter of the hair holds an almost mystical command in a community. Elaine might not have known the full weight of her power, but I have no doubt her clients did.

Just down the road from the town of Balmorhea is one of the world's best swimming holes. Balmorhea State Park encompasses San Solomon Springs, which pours fifteen million gallons of water through the 1.3-acre swimming pool each day. The state park and Balmorhea Lake, just north of the park, offer excellent birding throughout the year. If you visit Balmorhea Lake, be sure to check in at the bait shop to obtain a permit to enter the park and then drive to the dam located closest to town to view the wetlands. I will never forget watching the Western Grebes perform their water-ballet courtships on a cool morning in mid-April on the shallow waters of the lake. More than three hundred species of birds have been recorded at the lake, with most occurring in the wetlands and surrounding grasslands.

The compact dirt roads at the cemetery make for easy walking and might be suitable for some wheeled mobility devices. The open sightlines make this an easy cemetery for car birding.

Tombstone Tail: Cactus Wren

The distinct, raspy song of this wren is often used in movies to indicate that the scene is set in the Southwest. When these busy little birds are not singing, they are constructing their own nests, destroying another bird's nests, or hopping along the ground after bugs. They build their nests in the branches of cacti and shelter in them year-round, not just in breeding season. Like several other desert birds, they can acquire all the water they need from the insects and berries they consume. These birds are in sharp decline due to habitat loss and removal of cacti.

Fort Stockton: East Hill Cemetery

Old Cemetery Road

There are several cemeteries in Fort Stockton, but the best birding is by far at East Hill. When we visited in August, we were greeted by over a dozen coveys of Scaled Quail, each with over ten birds per grouping. My mother and I enjoyed watching them scamper about from one shadow of a headstone or bush to the next. The proud papa always hung back to make sure all the chicks made it safely to the next feeding point or protective shady spot.

On that same visit, my mother spotted a Lark Bunting, a life list bird for both of us. The black-and-white bird perched on several headstones before disappearing into the shade of the poplar tree. Because of the abundance of tall trees, a few watered

Tombstone Tale

In 1902, Sears, Roebuck and Company introduced the *Tombstones and Monuments* catalog. Its entrance into the headstone business meant that people of modest means could honor their loved ones with an attractive, ready-made monument. The catalog recommended verses and sayings, motifs, and lettering styles that could be replicated easily. Typically, it would take the company four to six weeks to letter the marker and ship it, via train, to the purchaser. Montgomery Ward entered the market in 1920.

plots, and several shrubs, the habitat is ripe for supporting a good number of desert birds. There are also miles of scrub and undeveloped land that sprawl beyond the boundaries of the cemetery, which create even more habitat for the birds and wildlife. During the spring and summer, look for Olive-sided, Ash-throated, Scissor-tailed, and Vermilion Flycatchers to be hunting insects alongside Say's Phoebes, Western Kingbirds, and Barn Swallows. As fall returns, so do the smaller birds, such as Ruby-crowned Kinglets, Orange-crowned and Yellow-rumped Warblers, and Red-breasted Nuthatches.

As we walked the compact dirt roads along the edge of the cemetery, where it rambles off into the scrub brush, we saw an enormous hawk circling. It took us a moment to identify the Ferruginous Hawk with the bright white underparts and dark outlined wing tips, as it seemed out of season for the hawk. Then we remembered we were at the tip of the fall migration, which might have started a few days early for some birds. Typically, the Ferruginous is more common in the late fall and winter along with Cooper's Hawks and American Kestrels. A Prairie Falcon has also been observed here in November.

The compacted dirt roads might be okay for some wheeled mobility devices, but it is also a good place to do a little car birding. I am eager to visit this location again in the fall or spring to learn about what lives here in those seasons. Nearby birding can be found at James Rooney Memorial Park, Fort Stockton wastewater treatment plant, and Imperial Reservoir between Fort Stockton and Grandfalls. There are more than 220 species of birds recorded at the Imperials Reservoir.

I will also note this is the final resting place of Jane Dunn Sibley (1924–2019). Jane was a patron of the arts in Austin and is credited with being one of the principal drivers for establishing Seminole Canyon State Park. Jane and her husband grew up in Fort Stockton and split their time between it and Austin after they married. The couple helped restore and donated some of the properties contained in the Fort Stockton Historic District. To learn more about this interesting woman, check out *Jane's Window: My Spirited Life in West Texas and Austin* by Jane Sibley and Jim Comer.

Tombstone Tail: House Finch

The male House Finch draws its rich red color from pigment in the food it consumes. The brighter the male's colors, the better his chances of successfully mating with a female. These finches are highly social birds that can often be found feeding together or with other finches in large flocks. Their traditional range included the western United States and Mexico until they were introduced to the eastern part of North America in the 1940s. A pair might have one to six broods in a breeding season and can live up to eleven years, which contributes to their populations remaining strong.

Ozona: Cedar Hill and Lima Cemeteries
168 South Highway 163

If you are traveling in West Texas on Interstate 10, this is the perfect place to get out to stretch your legs and do a little birding. Set in a little valley off Highway 163, there is plenty of habitat for the birds inside the large combined space of these two cemeteries and along the brushy slopes beyond the boundary. The main road of Cedar Hill is lined with large, welcoming trees. In fact, there is a good mix of mature trees throughout the site that hosts approximately 120 species of birds during the year.

It is apparent that the Cedar Hill and Lima Cemeteries were originally segregated; indeed, they are still separated physically by a wet-weather draw. Cedar Hill is a study in rectangles and squares. There are large square family plots laid out in a grid pattern filled with headstones that are variations of the rectangle; Mr. Stuart stands out with a white marble trapezoid. The older graves in the back have a little more variety, and there is plenty of variety across the wet-weather draw in the Lima Cemetery. There are also several bird feeders in Lima. Ample benches are located throughout both cemeteries where you can sit, enjoy the birds, and reflect while relaxing in the shaded embrace of the magnificent trees.

Tombstone Tale

Stacked graves are a style of marker that is more common in areas where the ground is difficult to dig. The cut limestone reflects the local materials, with the capstone resting on three pillars, perhaps representing the Trinity.

Some of the year-round favorites are the Greater Roadrunners, Woodhouse's Scrub-Jays, Canyon Towhees, Verdins, and the always brilliant Northern Cardinals. Loggerhead Shrikes can also be found in the region year-round but are more common during the winter. The spring migration brings Nashville and Yellow Warblers, Orchard Orioles, and Indigo Buntings. Because of the cedar breaks and good habitat along the hills, the threatened Black-capped Vireo has been recorded at this location along with White-eyed, Bell's, and Warbling Vireos. Keep an eye to the sky to watch for Zone-tailed and Red-tailed Hawks.

Each family plot has its own water hose and sprinkler. The water stimulates the insect growth, which in turn supports insect eaters such as Western Kingbirds and Brown-crested and Scissor-tailed Flycatchers during the summer, while the lovely Vermilion Flycatchers can be found feeding here year-round. The large live oaks are ideal nesting habitat for Summer Tanagers. Their pretty song can be heard throughout the grounds in late spring and early summer. As summer passes, the fall migration can be exciting here; even though the birds are not in their breeding colors, they are still fun to see. Winter visitors include Ruby and Golden-crowned Kinglets, Western Bluebirds, Hermit Thrushes, Cedar Waxwings, and of course, the ever-present Yellow-rumped Warblers.

Crockett County was named for Texas Revolution hero Davy Crockett, and Ozona is the only town in the county. The Apache, Comanche, and Kiowa all inhabited the region, and archeological findings place some residents of the "Basket-makers" era in the area as early as three thousand years ago. In 1536, the Spanish explorer Cabeza de Vaca stumbled across the rocky landscape, followed by Coronado, the Franciscan monks, and then 355 years later, E. M. Powell showed up, drilled a water well, and put Ozona on the map. Ozona is appropriately named for the fresh air.

Ozona and its clear well water were welcome sights along the Ozona-Comstock stagecoach line. The route linked Ozona to the seven-hundred-mile stage route between San Antonio and El Paso, a hot, dusty, bumpy stagecoach ride that took twenty-seven days to complete the distance and cost approximately one hundred dollars per person. Just think, if you sent a letter via the stage from San Antonio to El Paso, it would take more than twenty days to arrive and another twenty for your response to return. Or, the letter might be lost in transit as the stage came under attack by robbers—a common and unpleasant occurrence. Today we communicate via cell service in just seconds, or a person can travel between San Antonio and El Paso, via Ozona, in just under eight hours on Interstate 10. Ozona has an interesting history that is worth exploring at the cemetery and in town.

There are paved roads at this location that make it suitable for people with limited mobility. The shaded streets create a pleasant space to walk even on a warm day. Nearby birding can be found at the Crockett County Interpretive Trail, Sonora Cemetery, or the Twisted Flower Ranch, a private lodge that offers birding tours.

Tombstone Tail: Verdin

The male Verdin has a lemon-yellow head with a light gray body and a red spot on his shoulder, while the female is all buff. Verdins can be found darting in and out of the thorn and scrub brush of the desert Southwest and Mexico, where they glean insects and spiders and drink nectar from flowers when available. Like other desert birds, they get most of the water they need from the food they consume. They build nests to roost in and raise their chicks. The roosting nests help them stay warm in the winter. I agree with Gary Clark's statement in *Book of Texas Birds*, where he calls the Verdin "one of the prettiest little birds of the Big Bend region" (326). Sadly, the Partners in Flight and Cornell Lab of Ornithology both report Verdins to be in steep decline due to habitat loss.

Scaled Quail at East Hill Cemetery- Fort Stockton

Rolling Plains & High Plains

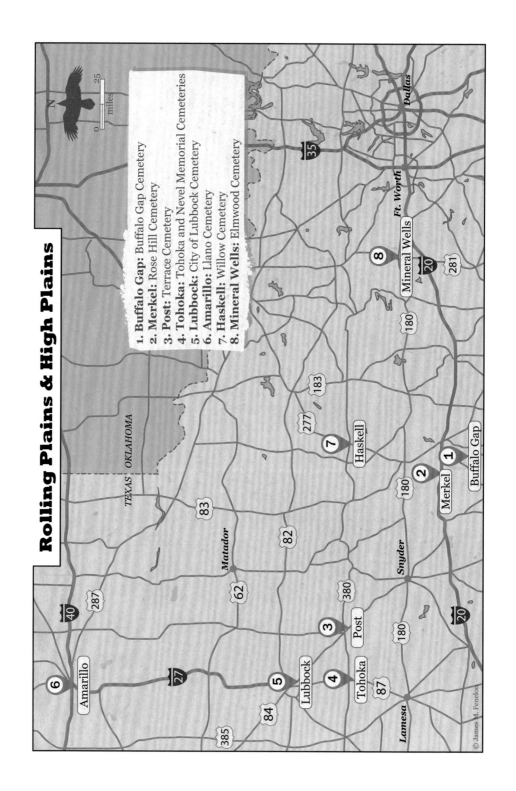

1. **Buffalo Gap:** Buffalo Gap Cemetery
2. **Merkel:** Rose Hill Cemetery
3. **Post:** Terrace Cemetery
4. **Tohoka:** Tohoka and Nevel Memorial Cemeteries
5. **Lubbock:** City of Lubbock Cemetery
6. **Amarillo:** Llano Cemetery
7. **Haskell:** Willow Cemetery
8. **Mineral Wells:** Elmwood Cemetery

© James M. Fenelon

Rolling Plains and High Plains

The more I learn about the ecoregions of the Rolling Plains and the High Plains, the more I like them. What really sealed the deal for me was when I visited between Christmas and New Year's and stood quietly on the edge of the playa lake at the Muleshoe Wildlife Refuge to watch thousands of Sandhill Cranes come in to roost. The cranes and large flocks of geese return to the region from November to March just as they have done for centuries.

As I stated in *Parking Lot Birding*,

> The area was once dominated by shortgrass prairies, but after water was discovered under the Caprock in the Ogallala Aquifer, the region became dominated by agricultural lands.
>
> Another liquid commodity lurks beneath the thin soil: oil. The region struck it rich with oil in the 1920s and has continued to be one of the most productive oil fields in the world. When visiting the area, make sure you scan the pumpjacks for hawks and vultures. If the jacks aren't pumping, the hawks will often perch on them to scan for a tasty meal of prairie dog, jackrabbit, or lizard. (203)

The Rolling Plains, compared to the High Plains, are more, well, rolling. They have rough canyons carved by the Brazos, Colorado, and Red Rivers along with other creeks and smaller rivers susceptible to flash flooding. This region was once known for its mixed-grass prairies, but most of that has been replaced by agriculture or mesquite tree savannas. Both regions were once the heart of the Comanche and Kiowa lands and supported large herds of American bison and Mustangs. Even though the herds of bison and Mustangs are gone, the birds still flock to the region as they follow their ancestral migration patterns.

Buffalo Gap: Buffalo Gap Cemetery
3241 FM 89

Long before Anglo settlers ventured into Texas, various Native Americans gathered in the area of the Callahan Divide to harvest American bison as they migrated from the winter grasslands in the south to summer farther north. The divide separates the Brazos and Colorado River watersheds, which provided the perfect place for Native Americans to set up camp to process the meat and hides. Once the Comanche mastered the horse, they dominated the divide until the Anglos conquered the region.

Settlers thought the location of Buffalo Gap was a great place to set up camp as well. Buffalo hunters arrived in the 1870s, and the town organized around 1878. Buffalo Gap was the only community in Taylor County and was the first county seat, which was later moved to Abilene after the railroad pulled into that town. Despite never being able to maintain any sizable population, Buffalo Gap continued to host youth camps and hold outdoor events, including the Old Settlers Reunions.

In 1918, the city of Abilene voted to create a reservoir along Elm Creek southwest of Buffalo Gap. The reservoir provided a short-lived supply of water for the growing city; however, it ran dry several times in the 1920s, and the leadership of Abilene began exploring other water options. The lake did provide a place to recreate outdoors.

Tombstone Tale

Cherubs most often represent love or innocence. In cemeteries, the winged cherubs usually signify they have come to escort a loved one home. They are often on the grave markers of children. According to this marker, this family lost all three triplets on the same day.

In 1933, the State of Texas acquired roughly five hundred acres south of the lake with the intent of making it a state park. Not long after the land was set aside, another camp was established in the vicinity of Buffalo Gap. The Civilian Conservation Corps Company #1823 comprised mostly World War I veterans who constructed the buildings and swimming pool at the park, along with the roads and picnic areas. To this day, Abilene State Park remains a great place to camp, hike, bike, picnic, and bird.

Speaking of birds, when you visit Buffalo Gap Cemetery, which is located between the town and the state park, keep an eye out for a jaunty American Robin to greet you as you enter the stone gate. When I visited on a windy May afternoon, I spotted over twenty species that included Lesser Goldfinches, Lark Sparrows, Eastern Bluebirds, and Black-crested Titmice. During the spring and into the summer the habitat supports Summer Tanagers, Painted Buntings, Black-chinned Hummingbirds, Mississippi Kites, and Ash-throated and Scissor-tailed Flycatchers. This is a favorable place to look for vireos during the spring when the Bell's, Yellow-throated, and Red-eyed, and White-eyed Vireos all pass through or nest in the area. The threatened Black-capped Vireo has been sighted multiple times at Abilene State Park, and it would not be out of the question to see or hear one in the scrub brush along the edges of the cemetery.

During the fall and winter, a cadre of sparrows shows back up, including Spotted Towhees; White-throated and White-crowned, Field, and Lincoln's Sparrows; along with Dark-eyed Juncos. Pine Siskins and Brown Creepers are two other smaller birds that return in the fall along with raptors such as American Kestrels and Cooper's and Red-shouldered Hawks.

There is a lot to like about this small, country cemetery. During the spring, the wildflowers and waving grasses fill the landscape, and the dirt roads are shaded by an archway of cedar and live oak trees. Perhaps one of the most interesting features is the stone chapel that sits atop the hill. It is perfectly placed to catch the breeze and offers a quiet place for reflection and remembrance. When I visited in November, I saw a woman filling the bird feeders next to the chapel, where the Northern Cardinals and Carolina Chickadees quickly converged.

As I walked around the tranquil space, I noticed a fair number of twins and even triplets that had been lost in the first days of their lives. Bringing a child into the world in a remote town like Buffalo Gap in the time before modern medicine would have been difficult at best. Bringing twins or triplets into the world was extremely difficult and often ended in sorrow for the families. In early American history, the midwife was the most important person for bringing a child safely into the world. It was not until the mid-nineteenth century that women's health, especially as it related to reproduction, was studied at medical schools. In fact, it was not until 1930 that the American Board of Obstetrics and Gynecology was formed and the field was recognized as an important specialty.

The gravel roads here are not suitable for wheeled mobility devices; however, most of the bird habitat can be observed from a car. Nearby places to bird include Abilene State Park and Lake Abilene, which support over two hundred species throughout the year.

Tombstone Tail: Painted Bunting

The French got it right when they named this colorful songbird Passerin nonpareil, which translates to "without equal." The males are cobalt-blue, scarlet-red, and lime-green; they look like they have been dipped in the boldest colors of an artist's paint selection. The females are a bright green, which camouflages them well in the new foliage of spring. They build their nests in dense underbrush across most parts of Texas, Oklahoma, and Louisiana and winter in Central America and the Caribbean. In the 1840s, James Audubon reported thousands of these birds in cages in New Orleans; sadly, they are still captured for the illegal caged-bird trade.

Merkel: Rose Hill Cemetery

Wilson and North Second Streets

This is a great place to stop if you are making the I-20 run from Fort Worth to Midland. I have stopped here many times to stretch my legs and walk my dogs, long before I was observing birds. The cemetery is pretty large compared to the size of the town. I have no doubt there are a great many people buried here who were on their way to somewhere else.

At the cemetery, you will find large flocks of Rock Pigeons and Eurasian Collared Doves, as well as a number of other birds worth noting. A Greater Roadrunner greeted us near the gate with a lizard in its mouth and seemed intent on hustling back to a nearby nest. On our visit in May, my husband and I watched the Barn Swallows sweep low among the headstones on their black-and-bluish blade-like wings. We also came across Western Kingbirds and Scissor-tailed Flycatchers that looked like they had just arrived on their migration and in their boldest breeding colors. Also reported in April and May are Clay-colored, Lark, and White-crowned Sparrows as well as Northern Bobwhites. With so many slow flyers like Rock Pigeons, Eurasian Collared Doves, and Mourning Doves, it is no wonder that there are also several Red-tailed and Cooper's Hawks that frequent the cemetery. There are also reports of a Great Horned Owl that hangs out in an old cottonwood across the street.

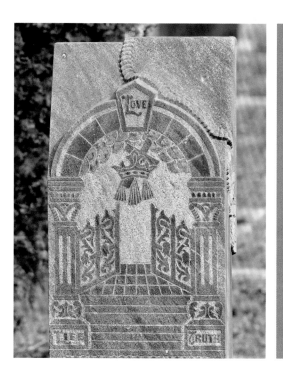

Tombstone Tale

The open gates represent the passage into the kingdom of heaven. The arch is commonly used to convey the passage from one realm to the next, and on this one it includes the motto "Life, Love, Truth.

The flat, graveled roads offer an easy place to walk but might not be suitable for a wheelchair. The term "nearby" is relative in this part of the county, as towns and parks are scattered about the vast, open landscape. The Merkel wastewater treatment plant offers good birding year-round, as do Abilene State Park and Kirby Lake.

Tombstone Tail: Great Horned Owl

This master of camouflage is one of the most common owls that live from Alaska to Central America. The owls' keen yellow eyes are perfectly adapted to see at night. Their sharp hearing is aided by discs on their face that funnel the sound to their ears. Armed with stellar vision and hearing, plus crushing talons, Great Horned Owls can find prey on the darkest of nights and deliver a spine-severing blow. They are capable of taking down an animal larger than themselves and will even harass other raptors. Like all mammal-eating raptors they often die after eating prey that has ingested pesticides, including rat poison. Healthy owls can live over twenty-five years in the wild.

Post: Terrace Cemetery

1250 US Highway 380

The town of Post sits just east of the Caprock and is often referred to as the gateway to the High Plains. The town was founded in 1907 by breakfast-cereal tycoon Charles William Post (1854–1914), who had traveled to Texas some years earlier in hopes of healing his myriad of health issues. The king of Grape-Nuts and Post Toasties purchased two hundred thousand acres in the Panhandle of Texas with the vision of establishing an agrarian/utopian community. He formed the Double U Company to build and manage the town originally known as Post City. The concept was that families could own or rent small farms from the company; in return they could live in a town free from the vices of drinking, gambling, or prostitution. The company laid out the town in an orderly grid design, and between 1907 and 1914, it built an attractive town filled with bungalow houses, tree-lined streets, churches, and businesses.

One of the drawbacks to creating an agrarian utopia on the edge of the High Plains is the lack of rain to maintain crops. Jan Reid describes how Post addressed the lack of water and extreme weather in his March 1987 *Texas Monthly* article "C. W. Post."

Utopia or not, people still needed a final resting place. After the death of Vertie Rogers Conn in Post, the board of directors of the Double U Company wrote to Post to inquire about establishing a cemetery. He responded by letter: "I wish there was no need for any such spot, but we have to conduct our affairs in accordance with the dictation of a power much superior to our own intelligence."

These thoughtful words can be found on the historical marker at the entrance to the cemetery. Post donated the original 19.35 acres of land for the cemetery located

Tombstone Tale

The fern frond is often partnered with ivy and a calla lily on the base of Woodmen of the World markers. The fern symbolizes humility and sincerity.

just east of town on Main Street. The cemetery acreage has been increased over the years and now sprawls over the terraced hillside.

When I visited in late May, I liked the location as soon as I drove through the attractive stone gate. I will note that the gate has one of the worst-placed historical markers that I have ever encountered. Only because I had my binoculars could I read the marker that sits on top of the arched gate. To summarize its information—the round rocks of the gate were collected from local ranches, and the gate was designed by George Samson and built by James Napier. Whoever wrote the text wanted to make sure that everyone understood that Samson and Napier came from Scotland. Both men are buried at the cemetery.

The location has a commanding view of the vast plains. On the evening that I visited, a storm was brewing in the east with magnificent thunderheads boiling up toward the heavens. The mature trees in the older part of the cemetery had nesting Bullock's Orioles, Scissor-tailed Flycatchers, Western Kingbirds, and Northern Cardinals. On the southeastern section of the cemetery there is a small draw with large trees and understory plants. In this section I could hear the Yellow-billed Cuckoo's distinctive call, and I watched a male Painted Bunting perch in the hackberry tree and sing his song. Also, a male Curve-billed Thrasher rambled off his varied warbles. On that visit, I also found Eurasian Collared Doves, Mourning Doves, Lark Sparrows, and Golden-fronted and Ladder-backed Woodpeckers. I listened carefully as a Northern Mockingbird displayed his song. I noticed he often mocked the sound of a Northern Bobwhite, which makes me think there must be some in the area.

In the fall and winter, this would be a great place to watch the flocks of Sandhill Cranes and Canada Geese as they move between the playas and the fields. Also, look to the trees at this location to find Northern Flickers that return in the fall along with Savannah, Song, and White-crowned Sparrows; Brewer's Blackbirds; and both types of meadowlarks.

Before you leave the cemetery, I hope you will take a few minutes to sit quietly at the scenic overlook to listen to the wind ease through the mixed-grass prairie and reflect on the past. Let your mind and body be still for a moment as the peace of nature moves around you. Once you have had your fill of birding (if that's even possible) and are exiting the cemetery, look for the large arrow sculpture just outside the gate. The arrow is one of eighty located throughout the Rolling Plains and High Plains to mark sites along the Quanah Parker Trail. The trail helps tell the story of the nation of people who lived in the Comancheria. There are more than thirty historical markers in Post and Garza Counties that document the natural and cultural history of the unique region.

There is an accessible pavilion that looks out over the fields and portions of the cemetery. The hard-packed dirt roads offer miles of easy walking but might be challenging for people using wheeled mobility devices. For more birding in the area, check out the playa just east of the cemetery near the airport or at the Post City Park off Highway 84. Both locations are good places to see wintering ducks and geese. White River Lake is northwest of the town and has over 292 species of birds recorded in eBird.

Tombstone Tail: Eurasian Collared Dove

This large dove is not native to North America but hales from India and Sri Lanka. According to the Cornell Lab of Ornithology these doves "made their way to North America via the Bahamas, where several birds escaped from a pet shop during a mid-1970s burglary; the shop owner then released the rest of the flock of approximately 50 doves. Others were set free on the island of Guadeloupe when a volcano threatened eruption. From these two sites the birds likely spread to Florida, and now occur over most of North America." Their mournful coo seems appropriate in cemeteries, where they often perch on headstones or mill around looking for insects or seeds.

County Road 24 and Avenue D

I visited this cemetery complex on a windy day in May. The cemetery and the adjacent property on the west side have an exceptional number of trees for the prairies of the Llano Estacado. The mix of trees, prairie, and nearby wetlands is home to over one hundred species of birds that live or pass through on the spring and fall migrations.

During the spring migrations and summer, look for Eastern and Western Meadow-larks, Lark Buntings, Horned Larks, and Lark Sparrows feeding in the grasses or singing from a perch. On my May visit, I watched Bullock's Orioles and Western Kingbirds returning to their nests with insects for their chicks. I was surprised to only see one Killdeer at the complex, as it seemed like good habitat for this species. I also saw one Great Blue Heron pass overhead, which surprised me. When I looked on eBird.com, I noticed that a few Great Blue Herons and Yellow-crowned Night-Herons, Snowy Egrets, and even Belted Kingfishers have all been recorded at this location as they fly

Tombstone Tale

We often think of roses as representing love and passion, but they can also represent a life that was in full bloom.

over to the ponds just west of the cemetery. There were plenty of Eurasian Collared, White-winged, and Mourning Doves, which also makes me think this might be good hunting grounds for hawks and owls.

The sparrows return in the fall, with Chipping, Clay-colored, Cassin's, Field, White-crowned, White-throated, Song, and Lincoln's Sparrows all present at the cemetery and surrounding area. The Red-breasted Nuthatch also returns in the winter and can be found scooting up and down the trunks of the trees. There are also reports of Eastern, Western, and Mountain Bluebirds being spotted at this location from October to April. Fall is the time for the parade of ducks, geese, and Sandhill Cranes to pass by in their great flocks.

The town of Tahoka, the county seat of Lynn County, was founded in 1903 and has a current population of about twenty-six hundred people. The word *tahoka* is reported to be a Comanche word that means "clear spring." Just north of town is the spring-fed Tahoka Lake, where more than 180 species of birds have been recorded.

The Tahoka daisy was first noted near the springs in 1898 by Effie Paralee, wife of Jack Alley, the foreman and later owner of the Tahoka Lake Ranch. The pretty lavender aster was again noted in 1925 by Roberta Neal Myrick, who was driving from Lubbock to visit friends south of the lake. The wife of land developer W. A. Myrick, Roberta, is reported to be the first woman in Lubbock County to own and drive her own car. Roberta was a charter member of the Lubbock Garden Club and transplanted several of the flowers from the lake area to her yard. When the flower seeded out, she sent the seeds to a plant-growing company in Pennsylvania. The species later appeared in the Burpee Seed Catalog. The hardy prairie flower continues to be sold in seed packets and at nurseries around the country. I did not see any of these flowers at the cemetery, but it might be a great place to cultivate a few.

The dirt, unshaded roads are easy to walk when the weather is agreeable but might be too exposed on hot days. The roads, as they are certainly flat, might be suitable for some wheeled mobility devices. Nearby birding can be found at Tahoka Lake or Buffalo Springs Lake outside Lubbock.

Tombstone Tail: Northern Bobwhite

The distinctive call of the Northern Bobwhite is one of my favorites. The bob-white call can carry quite a distance, and odds are, you will hear these well-camouflaged, ground-feeding birds or their covey long before you see them. Bobwhites prefer a mix of agricultural fields, grasslands, and wooded areas where seeds and insects are abundant. Once thought to be monogamous, they can have multiple partners and multiple broods during a season. Despite their ability to produce multiple offspring, their population is in steep decline mostly due to habitat loss and land fragmentation. Females lay their eggs in a nest scratched out on the ground, which makes them easy prey and susceptible to being trampled by livestock or machinery. At night, the covey will roost together in a circle, often with the chicks in the center for safety.

Lubbock: City of Lubbock Cemetery

2011 East Thirty-First

Birds are not the only exciting thing at the Lubbock Cemetery, as this is the final resting place of one of Texas' most legendary musicians, Buddy Holly. He was only twenty-two years old in 1959 when he died in a plane crash along with fellow musicians Richie Valens and J. P. Richardson. His simple gravestone lies flat on the ground in section 44; there is a historical marker and sign to show you the way.

Buddy Holly is not the only artist buried here. Bess Bigham Hubbard was a printmaker and sculptor who made her home in Lubbock along with her husband, Chester A. Hubbard. Initially, her art was simply a much-loved hobby, but by 1925, she turned her attention toward making it something more. Her subjects were often the land and the growing community that surrounded her in Lubbock. In the 1940s, she started sculpting in a modernistic style that won her many awards. You can also see an example of her work at her family plot.

The cemetery has been in operation under various leadership since 1892 and is the final resting place of more than sixty thousand people. Since the population of the newly formed city of Lubbock was just over thirty-five people in 1891, the cemetery

Tombstone Tale

The hand reaching out of the clouds represents the hand of God. This hand is holding a bouquet featuring a morning glory, which symbolizes the dawning of a new day in the afterlife.

did not fill quickly. It was not until water could be extracted from the vast Ogallala Aquifer that the farming industry took off and the population started to grow. By the 1930s, cotton was king of the agricultural products produced in the area and has remained so ever since.

The bonus of this location is that it is flanked by Dunbar Lake and is close to the wastewater treatment plant. The cemetery has an abundance of mature trees, shrubs, and grasses that are attractive to the birds in all seasons. There are several empty lots across the street that have prairie dog towns. Keep an eye out for the mighty Ferruginous Hawk to raid the prairie dog towns during the winter months. Because this is the High Plains and the grasses are good, there have been fourteen species of sparrows recorded at this location. House Finches live in the area year-round; however, Purple and Cassin's Finches return in the fall along with American and Lesser Goldfinches. The birding here is best from October to March, when the wintering birds are in the area. The rows of trees support Red-naped Sapsuckers and White-breasted Nuthatches, while the lake is a draw for Ring-billed Gulls, Gadwalls, American Wigeons, and Northern Shovelers. Spring and summer bring an influx of migrants such as Swainson's Hawks and Mississippi Kites along with Cordilleran, Scissor-tailed, and Ash-throated Flycatchers; Cassin's Kingbirds; and the always lovely Summer Tanagers. With more than two hundred birds recorded at this location, there is always something interesting to see.

Only a portion of the roads here are paved; however, the hard-packed dirt roads might be suitable for sturdier wheeled mobility devices. For additional birding, consider visiting the system of parks along the Yellow House Draw, Clapp Park, or the Lubbock Lake Historic Landmark. Resthaven Memorial Park is also a good place to bird and is a bit more accessible.

Tombstone Tail: Canada Goose

This big, black-necked goose ranges from Texas to the Arctic Circle as it migrates in large V-shaped flocks. The geese are known to mate for life with low "divorce rates" and can live up to thirty years. Young geese will stay with their parents for the first year and do not partner or start breeding until they are approximately four years of age. They are almost as common to see feeding on lawns or agricultural fields as they are dabbling for food in shallow wetlands. Because they are able to eat grasses from lawns and grain from agricultural fields, they have adapted well to living around humans.

Amarillo: Llano Cemetery

2900 South Hayes

This cemetery is almost as big and beautiful as the birds that live here. The tree-filled, park-like cemetery was established in 1891 when the Llano Cemetery Association was formed. However, the site had already been in use since 1888 when twenty-four-year old Lillian Marrow died while traveling west with her family. The history of this cemetery is well preserved on the Llano Cemetery Association website and the historical marker in front of the administration building.

The original twenty-acre cemetery has been expanded several times over the decades and now encompasses over two hundred acres. As sections were added, a variety of trees were planted that create peaceful, shaded groves for birds and people. Early photos of the cemetery show it devoid of trees and simply covered in short grasses or dirt. Today, most of the grounds are covered in mowed grasses to emulate the shortgrass prairie that dominated the Llano Estacado, otherwise known as the Staked Plains. The Llano Estacado is a geographical region that covers thirty-two thousand square miles in Texas and New Mexico. It is the one of the flattest regions in the United States and was the homeland of the Comanche. In this arid landscape,

Tombstone Tale

The art deco style was popular from the 1920s to the late 1930s. Art deco utilized clean, smooth, sweeping lines and stylized rather than realistic features. The style was frequently used in monuments such as the poppy field war memorial at the Llano Cemetery.

water is a gift. Thankfully, the cemetery has a small memorial pond that is attractive to Canada Geese throughout the year and supports a variety of visiting ducks during the winter.

When I said the birds here were big and bold, I meant it. On my visit in March I came across a Great Horned Owl perched in one of the older cottonwood trees, witnessed two Cooper's Hawks drinking from a puddle near the pond, stirred up a Red-tailed Hawk near the Veterans Memorial, and said hello to several groups of Canada Geese who were feeding on the grass and basking in the winter sun. Some of the smaller birds I encountered included White-crowned Sparrows, Cedar Waxwings, Dark-eyed Juncos, and Killdeers. I was really hoping to see Yellow-headed Blackbirds, which winter in the area and are often sighted just down the road at Southeast Park. I would have also liked to have caught a glimpse of the Townsend's Solitaire, which had been seen at this location just a few weeks before my excursion.

This is a favorable place to find American Robins, Western Meadowlarks, and Common and Great-tailed Grackles throughout most of the year. I am interested to learn more about what arrives in the spring to enjoy the watered lawns, ponds, and mature trees that make for quite an oasis in on the Llano Estacado. This location can be hot in the summer and is best enjoyed in the morning or evening in most seasons.

The streets here are paved and excellent for people with limited mobility. Nearby birding can be found at Southeast Park, Wildcat Bluff Nature Center, or Thompson Memorial Park. I also highly recommend a day trip to either Palo Duro Canyon State Park or Buffalo Lake National Wildlife Refuge.

Tombstone Tail: Cooper's Hawk

This medium-sized hawk is found across North America and has adapted well to living in urban areas. These hawks have a bluish-gray backside, rust-and-white chest, a black cap, reddish eye, and a long, banded tail. The long tail helps them skillfully navigate flying through forests at remarkable speeds. Look for them where forested areas meet open spaces. They feed primarily on small birds, especially Rock Pigeons, European Starlings, and

doves. Females are larger than the males and will occasionally feed on the smaller males. A healthy bird can live up to twenty years.

Haskell: Willow Cemetery

Avenue H and South Sixth Street

According to my grandmother, Martha Head Scott (1918–2020), her grandfather, George Ruben Couch, camped in 1881 along the spring-fed creek that runs through what is now the center of Haskell. Just north of him along the creek there was a family of Native Americans camping as well. When he awoke in the early morning to prepare to perform his surveying duties, he noted the Native Americans had slipped away silently in the cover of the night. My grandmother's story has always represented the end of an era in her mind and mine.

Haskell has a delightful library with a history room filled with great stories of yore. The majority of the businesses still center around the large courthouse square, which is a place that holds special meaning to our family. Just out of high school, my grand-

Tombstone Tale

The temple boxes reflect that the departed held fast to his or her faith. This particular style was called the Royal Sarcophagus and was sold by Sears Roebuck for around $234 in the early 1900s. The granite was carved and shipped from Virginia to almost anywhere in the United States.

mother was working at Perkins Department Store when she saw my grandfather, Walter Scott, drive into town in a brand-new car during the height of the Great Depression. He parked the car, got out, and walked into the courthouse dressed in his one and only suit to report for duty as the new county agricultural agent. Martha was smitten and told her coworker, "I'm going to leave town with that man."

She meant what she said. Growing up in Haskell, Rule, and Aspermont during the Spanish flu, Dust Bowl, and the Great Depression was hard on everyone. For my grandmother, it meant that she did not want to be tied to the land or banking (her grandfather owned the banks in Haskell and Knox City). There were several men in the county who expressed their interest in the blue-eyed bombshell, but she did not want to be the wife of a rancher or cotton farmer. She held true to her statement, and in 1938 she married Walter Scott and left Haskell the next day on what she calls "the grand adventure of life."

The Willow Cemetery is full of my ancestors, and for that reason, I feel a special connection with the place. One of my first memories was formed there while attending my great-grandfather's funeral. After the service, I remember catching fireflies in an old Mason jar and playing with distant cousins.

The mature trees and grasses of the cemetery support more birds than might first meet the eye. When I visited with my mother in May, we were excited to find a nesting pair of Bullock's Orioles and several pairs of Western Kingbirds. Spring also brings Lark and Grasshopper Sparrows, Ash-throated and Scissor-tailed Flycatchers, and Painted Buntings. As fall returns, so do the sparrows with Clay-colored, Field, Song, Harris's, White-crowned, and Vesper Sparrows and Dark-eyed Juncos. Keep an eye open for a Lark Bunting to pop up, as this species reported in the area as well.

While visiting the town one winter, I was watching a flock of Canada Geese come in for a landing in an agricultural field. Suddenly, they scattered in a panic as a pair of Bald Eagles drifted into view. That is one cool thing about birding in the Rolling Plains; the wide-open spaces allow you to watch the soaring birds for a long time. The cemetery is a great place to listen to the songbirds, as there are not many competing noises.

The unpaved roads are not accessible for people using a mobility device. Nearby birding can be found at Lake Stamford Park outside Stamford or Aspermont Cemetery.

Tombstone Tail: Bullock's Oriole

The male Bullock's Oriole is flame-orange and black and white, while the female is a more subdued lighter orange and gray. Both sing to each other and are in constant communication during the breeding season. Look for them on larger trees, especially cottonwoods, where they glean insects, or look for their distinct hanging nests. In addition to feeding on grasshoppers and other insects, they eat fruit and sometimes drink nectar from agave and prickly pear cactus. They summer across parts of Mexico, Texas, and the western United States and winter in southern Mexico and Central America.

Mineral Wells: Elmwood Cemetery

Northeast Ninth Avenue

I have always had a special place in my heart for Mineral Wells, as it was the town where my grandparents spent their honeymoon in 1938. They stayed two nights at the Baker Hotel when they moved from Haskell to their new home in College Station. In 2019, the famous Baker Hotel and downtown area were under construction when my husband and I arrived to camp at Lake Mineral Wells State Park on Halloween. I called my 101-year-old grandmother to tell her about the renaissance happening in the town and how pleased I was to see her cherished hotel being given new life.

The healing waters have long since been the draw to this small town set in the Rolling Plains of Palo Pinto County. In 1880, James Lynch and his wife, Arminda, drilled a well on their property to provide water for their growing family and livestock. The water looked and tasted strange, and at first, they were afraid to drink it. After desperation drove them to start consuming the water, something miraculous happened—their

Tombstone Tale

The Woodmen of the World use the tree stump, axe, and hammer on their tombstones to represent the taming of the wilderness and building community. The stumps usually are also emblazoned with the WOW brand.

health improved. In particular it seemed to have improved Arminda's rheumatoid arthritis. They shared the good news, and before long, Mineral Wells was a booming health resort.

Elmwood Cemetery was started in 1883 and is the final resting place for the Lynches in addition to a number of other founding citizens of the community. The Ladies of the Civic League adopted the cemetery in 1913 as one of their beautification projects and planted a number of elm trees throughout the grounds. Around the same time the cemetery's name changed from City Cemetery to Elmwood.

The cemetery is flanked by a small hill that offers a fair amount of brush and tree habitat to the moderate-sized cemetery. As you walk the grounds in October and November, be sure to listen for the honking sounds of Sandhill Cranes or Canada Geese passing overhead. The fall and winter are also a good time to find Spotted Towhees and White-throated, Song, Chipping, Vesper, and Lincoln's Sparrows feeding in the grasses and brush along the fence line. The fence line and brush are also busy during the spring and a good place to look for nesting Painted Buntings, Western Kingbirds, and Scissor-tailed Flycatchers. When I visited in mid-May, I was impressed by the number of Scissor-tailed Flycatcher nests throughout the cemetery. One of the birds I most enjoyed hearing at this location was the Canyon Wren.

The unpaved gravel road is not accessible for people with limited mobility, but most of the habitat can be seen from a vehicle for a little car birding. Nearby birding can be found at Lake Mineral Wells State Park, Clark Gardens, and Possum Kingdom State Park. The Texas Parks and Wildlife Department is developing the Palo Pinto Mountain State Park, which is set to open in 2023 as part of the centennial celebration of the state parks.

Tombstone Tail: Black-chinned Hummingbird

Unlike the Ruby-throated Hummingbird, the Black-chinned Hummingbird travels overland during its migration from southern Mexico to as far north as Montana. These birds are among the most adaptable of the hummingbirds and can be found from the desert to mountain forests and in suburban settings where flowering plants are abundant. When migrating, they typically stay at a location for one day before moving on unless there is extreme weather. They breed and nest in Texas along the Rolling Plains, Edward's Plateau, Trans-Pecos, and South Texas. Some Black-chins no longer migrate and will stay along the Gulf Coast and Rio Grande Valley year-round. Their tiny nests are made of lichen, feathers, and spider's silk that allows the nest to expand as the chicks grow.

American Goldfinch on a cold winter morning

Male Summer Tanager on headstone at Galveston Cemetery

Bibliography

General Information

Adgent, Nancy. *Deep East Texas Grave Markers, Types, Styles, and Motifs.* Nacogdoches: Stephen F. Austin University Press, 2010.

"American Gravestone Evolution, Part 1." Atlas Preservation, 2019. https://atlaspreservation.com/pages/historical1.

Baugher, Sherene, and Richard F. Veit. *The Archaeology of American Cemeteries and Gravemarkers.* Gainesville: University Press of Florida, 2014.

Gwynne, S. C. *Empire of the Summer Moon: Quanah Parker and the Rise and Fall of the Comanches, the Most Powerful Indian Tribe in American History.* New York: Scribner, 2010.

Harvey, Bill. *Texas Cemeteries: The Resting Places of Famous, Infamous, and Just Plain Interesting Texans.* Austin: University of Texas Press, 2003.

Jordan, Terry G. *Texas Graveyards: A Cultural Legacy.* Austin: University of Texas Press, 1982.

Massey, Cynthia Leal. *What Lies beneath Texas Pioneer Cemeteries and Graveyards.* Helena, MT: TwoDot Book, 2021.

Newcomb, W. W., Jr. *The Indians of Texas from Prehistoric to Modern Times.* Austin: University of Texas Press, 1961

Snider, Tui. *Understanding Cemetery Symbols: A Guide for Historic Graveyards.* N.p.: Castle Azle Press, 2017.

Weed, Howard Evarts. *Modern Park Cemeteries.* N.p.: R. J. Haight, 1912.

Tombstone Tales

"All about Birds." Cornell Lab of Ornithology, 2022. https://www.allaboutbirds.org.

Clark, Gary. *Book of Texas Birds.* College Station: Texas A&M University Press, 2016.

Rural Cemetery Movement

Cothran, James R., and Erica Danylchak. *Grave Landscapes: The Nineteenth-Century Rural Cemetery Movement.* Columbia: University of South Carolina Press, 2018.

"Environmental Stewardship." Mount Auburn Cemetery, 2020. https://mountauburn.org/environmental-stewardship/.

Leopold, Aldo. *A Sand County Almanac, and Sketches Here and There.* 1948. Reprint, New York: Oxford University Press, 1987.

Louv, Richard. *Last Child in the Woods: Saving Our Children from Nature Deficit Disorder.* Chapel Hill, NC: Algonquin, 2006.

Cemeteries

Alpine

Casey, Clifford B. "Alpine, TX (Brewster County)." Handbook of Texas Online. Accessed July 28, 2022. https://www.tshaonline.org/handbook/entries/alpine-tx-brewster-county.

"Spannell Trial to Begin Soon: Murder Charge." *Calexico Chronicle*, vol. 13, no. 136, January 17, 1917, 2.

Austin

"Oakwood Cemetery." Save Austin's Cemeteries, 2022. https://www.sachome.org/oakwood-cemetery.

Texas State Preservation Board 2018 Strategic Master Plan. Texas State Cemetery, October 31, 2018. https://drive.google.com/file/d/1t--b7wf4pcP6Rw1ctRKz4ailxM-sGDeo/view.

Bastrop

"Fairview Cemetery." City of Bastrop, 2019. https://www.cityofbastrop.org/page/city.cemetery.

Beaumont

"Our History." Magnolia Cemetery, 2021. https://magnoliacemetery.org/our-history/.

Wilson, Rosine McFaddin. "William McFaddin (1819–1897)." Handbook of Texas Online. Accessed July 28, 2022. https://tshaonline.org/handbook/online/articles/fmc47.

Brownsville

"Old City Cemetery and Old City Cemetery Center." Brownsville Historical Association, 2019. https://www.brownsvillehistory.org/old-city-cemetery-center.html.

Caddo Mounds

"Caddo Mounds History." Texas Historical Commission, 2022. https://www.thc.texas.gov/historic-sites/caddo-mounds/caddo-mounds-history.

Long, Christopher, and Mary M. Sandifer. "Caddo Mounds State Historic Site." Handbook of Texas Online. Accessed July 28, 2022. https://tshaonline.org/handbook/online/articles/ghc01.

Perttula, Timothy K. "Caddo Indians." Handbook of Texas Online. Accessed July 28, 2022. https://tshaonline.org/handbook/online/articles/bmcaj.

Cleburne

"Cleburne Cemeteries." City of Cleburne, 2020. https://www.cleburne.net/96/Cemeteries.

Elam, Richard, and Mildred Padon. "Cleburne, TX." Handbook of Texas Online. Accessed July 28, 2022. https://tshaonline.org/handbook/online/articles/hec02.

Columbus

Kearney, James C., Bill Stein, and James Smallwood. *No Hope for Heaven, No Fear of Hell: The Stafford-Townsend Feud of Colorado County, Texas 1871–1911*. Denton: University of North Texas Press, 2016.

Lynching in Texas Staff. "Lynching of Sam 'Benny' Mitchell." Lynching In Texas. Accessed July 28, 2022. https://lynchingintexas.org/items/show/512.

Corpus Christi

Simpson, Brooks D. *Ulysses S. Grant: Triumph over Adversity, 1822–1865.* Boston: Houghton Mifflin, 2000.

Dallas

"Greenwood Cemetery." Find a Grave, 2021. https://www.findagrave.com/cemetery/3940/greenwood-cemetery.

"Oakland Cemetery." Dallas Genealogical Society, 2019. https://dallasgenealogy.com/dgs/local-records/cemeteries/oakland-cemetery/.

"Oakland Cemetery: Where Dallas' History Lives." Oakland Cemetery, 2022. https://oaklandcemeterydallas.com.

Simek, Peter. "Lost Dallas." *D Magazine*, February 26, 2018. https://www.dmagazine.com/publications/d-magazine/2018/march/lost-dallas-history-secrets/.

"Uptown: Dallas Neighborhood Guide." *D Magazine*, 2020. http://neighborhoods.dmagazine.com/dallas/central-dallas/uptown/.

Wilonsky, Robert. "Why Oakland Cemetery, Where 127 Years of Dallas' History Is Buried, Has Suddenly Been Abandoned." *Dallas Morning News*, August 30, 2019. https://www.dallasnews.com/opinion/commentary/2019/08/30/why-oakland-cemetery-where-127-years-of-dallas-history-is-buried-has-suddenly-been-abandoned/.

Del Rio

"Del Rio Cemeteries Historic District." Texas State Historical Commission, 2019. https://texaspecostrail.com/plan-your-adventure/historic-sites-and-cities/sites/del-rio-cemeteries-historic-district.

Falfurrias

Lasater, Dale. "Falfurrias, TX." *Handbook of Texas Online.* Accessed July 28, 2022. https://www.tshaonline.org/handbook/entries/falfurrias-tx.

"University Teams Exhume Unknown Migrants' Remains in Falfurrias Cemetery, Brooks County." South Texas Human Rights Center, June 14. 2014. https://southtexashumanrights.org/2014/06/14/university-teams-exhume-unknown-migrants-in-falfurrias-cemetery-brooks-county/.

Fort Davis

Kohout, Martin Donell. "Fort Davis, TX." *Handbook of Texas Online.* Accessed July 28, 2022. https://tshaonline/handbook/online/articles/hlf24.

"The Second Fort Davis: 1867–1891." National Parks Service, 2021. https://www.nps.gov/foda/learn/historyculture/historyofthesecondfortdavis.htm.

Fort Parker Memorial Cemetery

"Fort Parker Memorial Park." Limestone County Historical Commission, 2020. http://www.limestonechc.com/cemetery-preservation/fort-parker-memorial-park/.

Texas Brazos Trail Region. Texas Historical Commission, 2022. https://texasbrazostrail.com/plan-your-adventure/historic-sites-and-cities/sites/fort-parker-memorial-cemetery.

Fort Stockton

"Celebrating Nature and History." Sibley Nature Center, 2022. https://sibleynaturecenter.org/
 about.
Sibley, Jane Dunn, and Jim Comer. *Jane's Window: My Spirited Life in West Texas and Austin*.
 College Station: Texas A&M University Press, 2013.

Fort Worth

Bailey, John T. *For Generations to Come: A History of Greenwood and Mount Olivet*. 2020.
 https://www.meaningfulfunerals.net/fh_live/16800/16858/media/mto-history3.pdf.
Selcer, Richard F. *Hell's Half Acre*. Fort Worth: Texas Christian University Press, 1991.

Galveston

"Broadway Cemetery Historic District, Galveston, TX." Historic Houston. Accessed July 28,
 2022. http://historichouston1836.com/galveston-cemetery-historic-district-galveston-tx/.
Cartwright, Gary. *Galveston: A History of the Island*. Fort Worth: Texas Christian University
 Press, 1991.
Casto, Stanley D. "Origin of the Audubon Society in Texas." *Bulletin of the Texas Ornithological
 Society* 18 (1985): 2–5.

Georgetown

"Old Georgetown Cemetery." Texas Historical Markers. Accessed July 28, 2022. https://texas
 historicalmarkers.weebly.com/old-georgetown-cemetery.html.

Glen Rose

Ferrer, Ada. "Glen Rose, TX." *Handbook of Texas Online*. Accessed July 28, 2022. https://tsha
 online.org/handbook/online/articles/hjg03.

Granger

Scarbrough, Clara Stearns. *Land of Good Water: A Williamson County, Texas, History, George
 town, Texas*. Georgetown: Williamson County Sun Publishers, 1973.

Hamilton

"Amilia Ann Whitney." Find a Grave, 2022. https://www.findagrave.com/memorial/19968659/
 amilia-ann-whitney.
"Miss Ann Whitney, the Frontier Heroine." *Frontier Times Magazine*, August 13, 2018. https://
 www.frontiertimesmagazine.com/blog/miss-ann-whitney-the-frontier-heroine.

Haskell

Felker, Rex A. *Haskell County and Its Pioneers*. Mount Pleasant: Published in Cooperation with
 the Haskell Bicentennial Committee, Nortex Press, 1975.
Scott, Martha Head. Interview by the author, 2008.

Hearne

"Colored Graveyard in the Old Town of Hearne." Texas Historical Markers. Accessed July 28,
 2022. https://texashistoricalmarkers.weebly.com/colored-graveyard-in-the-old-town-of-
 hearne.html.

High Island

"High Island." Houston Audubon, 2022. https://houstonaudubon.org/sanctuaries/high-island/se-gast-red-bay.html.

"Texas Ornithological Society Sanctuaries." Texas Ornithological Society, 2022. https://www.texasbirds.org/tosSanctuaries.php.

Wiggins, Melanie. *They Made Their Own Law: Stories of Bolivar Peninsula*. Houston: Rice University Press, 1990.

Houston

"About the Foundation." Glenwood Cemetery, 2021. http://www.glenwoodcemetery.org/about/.

Bailey, Olga. *Mollie Bailey: The Circus Queen of the Southwest*. Dallas: Harben-Spotts, 1943.

Gray, Chris. "Walking through Houston History in 'the River Oaks of the Dead.'" *Houston Chronicle*, March 7, 2019.

Turner, Suzanne, and Joanne Seale Wilson. *Houston's Silent Garden: Glenwood Cemetery, 1871–2009*. College Station: Texas A&M University Press, 2010.

Indianola

King, C. Richard. "Eberly, Angelina Belle Peyton (1798–1860)." *Handbook of Texas Online*. Accessed July 28, 2022. https://tshaonline.org/handbook/online/articles/feb02.

Malsch, Brownson. *Indianola: The Mother of Western Texas*. Austin: Shoal Creek Publishers, 1977.

Kingsville

Neely, Lisa A. *King Ranch and Kingsville: A Match Made in South Texas*. Kingsville: King Ranch, 2011.

Kountz

"Mrs. Bruce Reid, Naturalist, Dies." *Fort Worth Star-Telegram*, April 29, 1962.

Reid, Bessie M., and Florence Stratton. *When the Storm God Rides: Tejas and Other Indian Legends*. New York: Charles Scribner's Sons, 1936.

Laredo

"The City Cemetery's Fraternal Section." City of Laredo Cemeteries. Accessed July 28, 2022. https://www.cityoflaredo.com/Cemetery/html/Fraternal-Section.htm.

Thompson, Jerry. *Tejano Tiger: Jose de los Santos Benavides and the Texas-Mexico Borderlands, 1823–1891*. Fort Worth: Texas Christian University Press, 2013.

Liberty Hill

"History of the Liberty Hill Stagecoach Stop." Accessed July 28, 2022. http://www.forttumbleweed.net/libertyhill_stagestop.html.

Marathon

Willeford, Glenn P., and Gerald G. Raun. *Cemeteries and Funerary Practices in the Big Bend of Texas, 1850 to Present*. Alpine: Johnson's Ranch & Trading Post Press, 2004.

McKinney

"Final Rites for Charlie Bristol Held Wednesday." *Daily Courier-Gazette*, February 26, 1958.

Grave Adventures: A Self-Guided Tour of Historic Cemeteries. McKinney: Colin County Historical Society and Museum, 2022.

"J. S. Forsyth Came to Texas in Year 1886." *McKinney Democrat*, October 28, 1926.

Mercedes

Garza, Alicia A. "Mercedes, TX." *Handbook of Texas Online.* Accessed July 28, 2022. https://www.tshaonline.org/handbook/entries/mercedes-tx.

"Historic Mercedes' Cemeteries." Development Corporation of Mercedes, 2022. https://mercedesedc.com/mercedes-corner/mercedes-historic-cemeteries/.

Mineral Wells

"Lake Mineral Wells State Park & Trailway." Texas Parks and Wildlife Department. Accessed July 28, 2022. https://tpwd.texas.gov/state-parks/lake-mineral-wells/park_history.

"Mineral Wells, Texas." TexasEscapes.com. Accessed July 28, 2022. http://www.texasescapes.com/TexasTowns/Mineral-Wells-Texas.htm.

Nacogdoches

Baker, Karle Wilson. *The Birds of Tanglewood.* 1930. Reprint, College Station: Texas A&M University Press, 2006.

Jackson, Sarah Ragland. *Texas Woman of Letters: Karle Wilson Baker.* College Station: Texas A&M University Press, 2005.

New Braunfels

"Historic Preservation Plan for Municipal Cemeteries." City of New Braunfels, November 2010. https://www.nbtexas.org/DocumentCenter/View/1701/Historic-Cemetery-Master-Plan-New-Braunfels-November-2010-FINAL?bidId=.

Williams, John F. *The Writings of Ferdinand Lindheimer: Texas Botanist, Texas Philosopher.* College Station: Texas A&M University Press, 2020.

Ozona

"Butterfield Overland Mail: Stagecoaching in Texas." *Texas Almanac*, 2021. https://texasalmanac.com/topics/history/stagecoaching-texas.

Harrell, Lucile I. "Ozona, TX." *Handbook of Texas Online.* Accessed July 28, 2022. https://tshaonline.org/handbook/online/articles/hgo02.

Post

Lucko, Paul M. "Post, TX." *Handbook of Texas Online.* Accessed July 28, 2022. https://www.tshaonline.org/handbook/entries/post-tx.

"Quanah Parker Trail." Quanah Parker Trail and Texas Plains Trail Region. Accessed July 28, 2022. https://www.quanahparkertrail.com/Quanah_Parker_Trail/Events/Events.html.

Reid, Jan. "C. W. Post: The Cereal King Made His Fortune with Grape-Nuts, but He Saw His Salvation in Texas." *Texas Monthly*, March 1987, 118.

Rockport

McCracken, Karen Harden. *The Life History of a Texas Bird Watcher*. College Station: Texas A&M University Press, 1986.

San Antonio

"About Mission Park." Mission Park Funeral Chapels and Cemeteries, 2022. https://www.missionparks.com/about-us/about-mission-park.

San Jacinto Battlefield and State Historic Site

"Battle of San Jacinto." History.com, 2022. https://www.history.com/topics/mexico/battle-of-san-jacinto.

Estep, Raymond. "Zavala, Lorenzo de (1788–1836)." *Handbook of Texas Online*. Accessed July 28, 2022. https://tshaonline.org/handbook/online/articles/fza05.

"San Jacinto Battleground State Historic Site." Texas Historical Commission, 2022. https://www.thc.texas.gov/historic-sites/san-jacinto-battleground-state-historic-site.

Sugar Hill

Collins, Christopher. "The Creature of Marin Creek Lake Won't Die." *Texas Observer*, September 23, 2019.

"Martin Creek Lake State Park." Texas Parks and Wildlife Department. Accessed July 28, 2022. https://tpwd.texas.gov/state-parks/martin-creek-lake/park_history.

Terlingua

"Mercury Poisoning Linked to Skin Products." US Food and Drug Administration, November 23, 2021. https://www.fda.gov/consumers/consumer-updates/mercury-poisoning-linked-skin-products.

Ragsdale, Kenneth Baxter. *Quicksilver Terlingua and the Chisos Mining Company*. College Station: Texas A&M University Press, 1976.

Tahoka

Abbe, Donald R. "Tahoka, TX." *Handbook of Texas Online*. Accessed July 28, 2022. https://www.tshaonline.org/handbook/entries/tahoka-tx.

Stephens, Christina. "Texas History: How the Tahoka Daisy Sprang into Existence." *Austin American-Statesman*, February 22, 2021.

Victoria

Roell, Craig H. "De León, Martín (1765–1833)." *Handbook of Texas Online*. Accessed July 28, 2022. https://tshaonline.org/handbook/online/articles/fde08.

Shook, Robert W. "Victoria, TX (Victoria County)." *Handbook of Texas Online*. Accessed July 28, 2022. https://tshaonline.org/handbook/online/articles/hdv01.

Waco

"Our History." Oakwood Cemetery Association, 2020. https://www.oakwoodwaco.com/history/.

Turner, Thomas. E. "Neff, Pat Morris (1871–1952)." *Handbook of Texas Online*. Accessed July 28, 2022. https://tshaonline.org/handbook/online/articles/fne05.

Willis, T. Bradford. *Some Notable Persons in First Street Cemetery of Waco, TX*. Denton: University of North Texas Libraries, 2009.

Weatherford

Blackman, Joseph Andres. "Ikard, Bose (1843–1929)." *Handbook of Texas Online.* Accessed July 28, 2022. https://tshaonline.org/handbook/online/articles/fik03.

"Brief History." City of Weatherford. Accessed July 28, 2022. https://ci.weatherford.tx.us/721/Brief-History.

Weslaco

"Kelley Killed Instead of Couch: Cam Hill Charged." *Brownsville Herald*, October 29, 1933, 1, 12.

Zavala

Wright, Andrea. "Legacy of Land." *Beaumont Enterprise*, May 22, 2002.

Index

Note: Photographs and maps are in **boldface type**.